A SHORT HISTORY OF AIR POWER

A SHORT HISTORY OF
AIR POWER

James L. Stokesbury

William Morrow and Company, Inc.
New York

Grateful acknowledgment is made to Her Majesty's Stationery Office for permission to quote from Sir Charles Webster and Noble Frankland, *The Strategic Air Offensive Against Germany, 1939–1945,* Volume III, Prime Minister Churchill's 28 March 1945 memorandum to the Chief of the Air Staff.

Library of Congress Cataloging-in-Publication Data

Stokesbury, James L.
A short history of air power.

Includes index.
1. Air power—History.   2. Aeronautics, Military—
History.   I. Title.
UG630.S76   1986   358.4'03   85-43431
ISBN 0-688-05061-1

Printed in the United States of America

BOOK DESIGN BY RICHARD ORIOLO

FOR LIZ

ACKNOWLEDGMENTS

As in my earlier works, I wish to thank my colleagues in the Acadia University community for their invariable support over the years. A number of friends, when told I was working on air power, suggested, loaned, or even gave me books I might not otherwise have obtained, and thanks are due to Dr. Robert H. Berlin in Fort Leavenworth, Truman Strobridge in Washington, Wallace Turner of Wolfville, Nova Scotia, and Gerd A. Kloss of Kentville, Nova Scotia. Special thanks also to Ann Elmo and Howard Cady in New York, the former for her support and encouragement, the latter for his books and for being among the world's most tolerant editors. Carolyn Bowlby of Acadia typed the entire manuscript, and I hope she was rewarded by sufficient mention of the Avro Lancaster to satisfy her lifelong love for that great aircraft. In a book of such broad and general nature as this is, I am bound to have missed at least one of everyone's favorite planes, or cherished anecdotes, but the warts, as Cromwell said, are all mine, and none of the above persons are responsible for errors of fact or interpretation.

My final thanks are for my wife. Any man who has been happily married for a quarter of a century to a woman who will tolerate several hundred models of aircraft, ships, and miniature soldiers around the house is fortunate indeed.

CONTENTS

CONTENTS

I

THE PIONEERS

At the turn of the twentieth century, powered flight was an idea whose time had come. Since the earliest days of man's existence he had dreamed of flying, of slipping John Magee's "surly bonds of earth" and soaring aloft to the heavens. When the Wrights got off the ground at Kitty Hawk, North Carolina, on December 17, 1903, they were the first to make a controlled, powered flight, but far from the first to fly. For more than a century men had been going up in balloons, gliders, and other assorted contraptions. The problem was not merely to get aloft—the Montgolfiers had done that in a hot-air balloon back in 1783—but rather to do it when you wanted to and to be able to go where you wanted to. That was the trick the brothers from Dayton, Ohio, managed, and by the time they did it, they were part of a veritable crowd seeking to do the same thing. Predecessors had built kites and gliders and had studied and endlessly tried to emulate the motions of nature; the Wrights themselves were great watchers of birds, especially buzzards.

They were all at work, Otto Lilienthal in Germany; Hiram Maxim in Great Britain; Clement Ader in France, who actually managed to get a steam-powered machine off the ground for more than a hundred feet in 1890; Percy Pilcher in Scotland; Samuel Langley and Octave Chanute in the United States. The invention of the airplane fully conformed to the modern theory of scientific development—that progress is less the "Eureka!" experience than it is the accumulation of many trials, errors, and missteps until someone gets all the factors together in the right proportions. The Wright Brothers did.

The early machines were not capable of a great deal. They were tinkerers' delights, and perhaps rich young men's toys, but they had a long way to go before they would have any practical application. Who, other than a thrill seeker, would be interested in a machine that could carry you up into the air? Still, flight had seemed so desirable for so long that men kept working at it, flying longer and higher, playing with the shape of airfoils, putting marginally improved engines on their contraptions, refining the shape of the paddle-blades or propellers, and trying to work out efficient control mechanisms. Was it better to have movable controls, such as rudders and ailerons, or was it better to warp the wings the way a bird did? All of this had to be worked out, mostly by trial and error, and a lot of men died in the process, including Lieutenant Thomas Selfridge, killed as Orville Wright's passenger when their plane crashed on a demonstration flight before the military authorities in Washington in September 1908. Selfridge fractured his skull when he hit one of the plane's struts, and thus became the United States' first military aircraft casualty.

Three days earlier an enthusiastic Orville had written to Wilbur from the capital that he was getting a warm reception, and "they all think the machine is going to be of great importance in warfare." Other people were beginning to agree. Wilbur was then in France trying to interest the French army in his machines. Glenn Curtiss, the second American to fly, had already sunk a battleship, or at least a simulation of one, on a lake in New York, and had confidently announced that "the battles of the future will be fought in the air." As the most recent war, the Russo-Japanese, had been the best kind of conflict—far away and fought by someone else—this did not seem especially ominous.

The Americans were far from alone in all this—indeed, the Wrights were disappointed in the initial response to their achievement, and American aviation was rapidly outstripped by European enthusiasm. There were experiments throughout the Western world. The first flight in the British Empire was that of the Silver Dart, off Lake Baddeck in Nova Scotia. To British minds, of course, Canada was a long way from the center of things. In 1907 an American, S. F. Cody, piloted a balloon from the Royal Balloon Factory over London, taking great care to circle the War Office, which had refused permission to build a heavier-than-air machine, and the next year, in October, he got off the ground on the first airplane flight ever in Britain. In 1909 the great French aviator Louis Blériot crossed the Channel on July 25. He should not have made it; his engine customarily overheated and seized up after about fifteen miles, but Blériot needed the prize money offered for the feat and headed out over the Channel. Fortune smiled, and halfway across, as his engine began to act up, he ran into a rain shower. The rain cooled the engine enough to get him down in England; the statue of Napoleon, staring out over the cliffs at Boulogne, must have smiled. Some weeks later a young American lieutenant, Henry H. Arnold, en route home from duty in the Philippines, observed Blériot's plane on display in Paris and wondered what it meant for the future.

A year later Eugene Ely took off in a Curtiss biplane from an improvised flight deck on the USS *Birmingham*, and early in 1911 he managed the more important feat of landing back on a ship, this time the *Pennsylvania*; if one chose to make the effort, the airplane could go to sea. Progress was now so rapid that by 1912, when the British government held trials for a military airplane, it could set specifications that would have seemed utterly impossible even two or three years earlier: a plane to carry four and a half hours' fuel, fly three hours, climb to 4,500 feet, cruise at 55 miles per hour, and carry a 350-pound payload. Thirty-two planes entered the contest.

By that time the airplane had already gone to war. Europe in the 1900s was champing for a fight, the effect of not having had one for a considerable period of time. The Continent was already dangerously split into hostile alliance systems, militarism was very much in fashion, uniforms were to be seen everywhere, there was a wild arms race going on, and national prestige was measured in battleships and the number of divisions a state possessed. With the promise of war somewhere soon down the road, countries were quick to look to new ideas that might increase their military power. Not the least of these countries was Italy.

The transformation of the Italian peninsula into a modern state had been a painful and long-delayed process. By the time it was completed, Italy was already far behind in the great imperial race of the later nineteenth century. She lost Tunisia to France, and an attempt in the nineties to take over Ethiopia ended in catastrophe. In 1911 the Italians tried again. This time it was Libya, a poor second choice to Tunisia but better than nothing. Libya was under the rule of the Ottoman, or Turkish, Empire then, and when the Turks resented and then resisted what the Italians called "peaceful penetration," Italy declared war.

It was not much of a war, but it corresponded pretty closely to the accepted standards of colonial wars. The Italians opened with the almost obligatory naval bombardment of ports, and then landed troops to seize the important towns along the seacoast. The Turks, after a desultory resistance, contented themselves with preaching holy war among the Libyan tribesmen. This kept the Italians in their coastal enclaves for six months, and it was not until July 1912 that they began to push into the countryside. But they had already employed airplanes on reconnaissance, to pick up information on the wandering Turkish troops and the tribes of the desert, on whom they even managed to drop a few primitive lightweight bombs. There was no means by which the planes could communicate with their bases, for radio had not progressed that far yet, but the amount of territory planes could cover before returning with information was sufficient to justify their use in war. It was a chancy business; the planes were flimsy and the engines unreliable, and the prospect of being forced down and put to the mercy of the tribesmen was not at all appealing. Nonetheless, the airplane had had its baptism of fire, and unreliable or not had proven its worth as a reconnaissance vehicle.

Such use continued in the next round of little wars, which were not quite as little as the Libyan one. In late 1912 Turkey made peace and ceded Libya, not because she was overpowered by the Italians but rather because trouble was brewing closer to home. This time it was the Balkan Wars of 1912–13, an imbroglio so complex, and with motives so mixed up, that only the Balkans themselves could understand them. In the first phase of these wars the Christian Balkan states combined to take Turkey's European possessions away from her. In the second Balkan War the winners fell to quarreling among themselves and took the fruits of the first war away from the biggest winner, Bulgaria.

Though it was a sordid little business, there was some very substantial fighting in it, at least by pre-World War I standards, and once again the airplane was used as a reconnaissance machine by both sides. The aircraft, even the limited one of 1912, was again useful. Soldiers have always been obsessed with what Napoleon called "the ability to see the other side of the hill," and, to a certain extent, that was exactly what the airplane provided. In some respects it was less useful than the simple tethered observation balloon. That had been around for a long time, and there were techniques by which an observer could signal to the ground the information that he could see. The balloon would remain an important component of army observation until the end of World War I, providing a relatively steady platform and worth its weight in gold and antiaircraft batteries for artillery observation and correction. But the airplane possessed advantages of its own—speed and range—and it could bring back reports the balloon could not match. The balloon would last only until a lightweight and truly reliable radio was developed for use in the airplane itself.

In 1913 the Balkan Wars died down, dampened partly by the fear of the greater states that they would flare up into a general war. By now the powers were sidling up to war as an eager youth might approach the first early swim of the season, anxious and even eager to get into the water but hesitant about the first cold plunge. Bismarck had long ago predicted that the next war would be fought over "some damned fool thing in the Balkans," but in 1913 no one could quite see war on behalf of the minor states. If one of the major powers were to get involved, that would be different.

The airplane had now made a small niche for itself in the armed forces of the world. The French were the leaders in this move; Blériot was far from the only daring French aviator, and his countrymen had taken to the air with a vast enthusiasm. The Voisins had opened a workshop to make aircraft as early as 1906, to be followed two years later by the Antoinette and Farman firms. All three were aircraft manufacturers for many years, but the first French military machine was a Wright Flyer, purchased by the Ministry of War in 1909, fruit of Wilbur Wright's visit to France the year before and public pressure resulting from the new fad. The French officially began training pilots in 1910, and in that same summer they took aircraft on army maneuvers in Picardy. The pilots enjoyed themselves thoroughly, flying in squally and rainy weather, taking photographs and even moving-picture films, carrying messages, and generally impressing everyone. Unfortunately, of the thirteen aircraft employed, seven had serious crashes of one sort or another. Given the fact that these were merely maneuvers, lasting only six days, with no serious opposition, this suggested that the attrition rate of aircraft in a real war might be rather high. Few arms of the service could stand to lose 50 percent of their effective equipment per week in war, but the airplane was new, after all, and some teething troubles were to be expected.

The higher French military authorities were impressed enough that the next month military aircraft became an independent entity with the creation of the Permanent Inspectorate of Aeronautical Services, with its own commander, General Roques, and it was soon on its way to becoming a full-fledged branch of the service. By 1912 the army had three air commands, at Versailles, Rheims, and Lyons, a naval air service was created in 1913, and balloons and military aircraft separated early in 1914. At the declaration of war, the Service Aéronautique possessed 138 aircraft in 25 squadrons.

Whatever France did in a military way, her enemy and archrival Germany inevitably did as well. German aircraft development had been somewhat warped by preoccupation with the rigid airship, the Zeppelin. Its father, Count Ferdinand von Zeppelin, would of course have denied that, insisting rather that the advent of the airplane had sidetracked the true course of aeronautical progress, which was the Zeppelin itself. A veteran of the Franco-Prussian War, he had begun construction of his airships at Friedrichshafen in the 1890s and pursued his dream with considerable success.

In 1910 Germany possessed fourteen military airships, while the entire rest of the world had only twelve. German aircraft construction had some indigenous designers and builders, but the best material they were producing in the immediate prewar years was inspired by the French, and it was those French maneuvers of 1910, repeated in 1911, that turned attention to the airplane. Though one of the most famous of the early World War I aircraft used by Germany was the Taube, a design closely modeled after birds, with warping wings for turning, official German opinion favored slow, heavy, and reliable aircraft, and at one point designers were told the German army absolutely did not want fast aircraft: If the plane flew too fast, the observer would be unable to make accurate reports of what he had seen. The aircraft was to be regarded specifically as a reconnaissance machine, nothing else. It did not at this point occur to the German military mind that if it was desirable to see what the enemy was up to, it was equally desirable to keep him from seeing what you were up to. Though German designers were considering armament even before the war, the authorities were definitely not interested in it.

In an organizational sense the Germans were even more conservative. They set up an Inspector of Aviation Troops, but they subordinated his office to that of the Commander of Railways and Transport. For the operational side of flying, they parceled out their units, usually flights of about six aircraft, among the various army and corps commands. There was to be no overall control of flying units in the field; they were to serve purely as adjuncts to headquarters and the combat arms commands. They did have nearly 100 more aircraft available than the French did, some 232 of them all told, but in every other way they were behind their enemies.

By 1914 everyone else had some form or other of military aviation as well. The Belgians caught the enthusiasm from the French, and in midsummer of 1910 the war minister, General Hellebaut, instructed his military officers to establish a training program for flying. Skeptical, the senior officers set up a committee to study the idea, recognizing that a committee was the safest way to do nothing. They were outsmarted by the eagerness of younger officers, however, who went out and learned to fly privately. By the summer of 1911 the Belgians had a school, a military airfield, an aircraft, generously given by a private citizen to the bemused King Albert, who gratefully passed it on to the army, and they soon had a few dozen trained pilots, with whom the conventional army did not know what to do.

On September 12, 1912, the nascent Belgian air force achieved something of a milestone: They mounted a newly designed Lewis machine gun on the front of a pusher-type Farman aircraft, took off, made a pass over the airfield, and shot to pieces a white sheet staked out on the ground as a target. As a reward, the local quartermaster insisted the pilot and gunner be court-martialed for destruction of military equipment. But here too the airplane was making a place for itself.

By 1913 the Belgian air service was organized in squadrons, each with its own supporting troops, transport, and workshops. When Belgium mobilized to resist the German invasion on August 1, 1914, she had twenty-four airplanes, two squadrons operational and two more on paper and thirty-seven qualified pilots. Eight more civilians came in to volunteer; a couple of them brought their own planes with them.

In eastern European countries there was less to build on. The Austro-Hungarians, looking resolutely backward in this as in most things, had little interest in the earliest stages of aviation. The Imperial and Royal Army had acquired a few of the Famous Taube monoplanes—they were after all designed by an Austrian—but it was not until 1912 that they decided to do something about aviation in a formal way. Colonel Emil Uzelac was appointed to command the Luftfahrtruppen; he did not at the time know how to fly, but a man who held a master mariner's papers in almost landlocked Austria-Hungary ought to be good for something. Besides, he was a noted equestrian and fencer, two talents that opened doors in prewar armies. Actually, Uzelac turned out to be a good choice; he commanded the Austrian air arm throughout the war, which made him an expert at making bricks with little straw. First he learned to fly himself, showing he had a better sense of priorities than many officers who transferred to air forces. He then went on to organize his service, while acting also as Austria's chief test pilot, and at the start of the war, Austria had eighty-six aircraft in service, plus a handful of balloons.

Russian aviation had the presence of one of the big names in aircraft design, Igor Sikorsky, and the benevolent interest of the Tsar, but it did not have much else. The Russians had used balloons to good effect in the siege of Port Arthur during the Russo-Japanese War, and, as one of the few armies with recent extensive combat experience, they should have been in a generally reforming and innovative frame of mind, especially as they had lost the war. The Russian economic and industrial infrastructure, however, was not really advanced enough to spawn the kind of thinking that was going on in the United States and western Europe. For practical purposes, Russia was still in the early throes of the Industrial Revolution. Nevertheless, there were an inspired few who followed aeronautical developments with great interest. A flying school opened in Gatchina, outside St. Petersburg, in 1910, and a second soon followed at Sevastopol. There was a Military Aviation Meet in 1911, and one of the several Grand Dukes, Alexander, became Inspector-General of Aeronautics. In 1913 Tsar Nicolas presented Sikorsky with a gold watch for his services to aviation in Russia.

In spite of Sikorsky, though, most of Russia's aircraft were imported from France, and there were only a few firms in Russia that claimed to make aircraft. The manufacturing of planes was really little more than a cottage industry in most places, but there were surprising advantages to that along with the drawbacks. A man with ideas could actually do something about them, and as early as 1913, a Russian lieutenant named Poplavko was working on some sort of interrupter gear that would permit a machine gun to fire through the whirling propeller of an airplane. When war was declared, Russia had 224 aircraft, though just as in Austria-Hungary, only about half of those carried on strength were thought to be combat-worthy, whatever that might mean by the standards of 1914.

Of the other industrialized states, neither Italy nor the United States entered the war at its outbreak in 1914. Italy was allied with Germany and Austria-Hungary, but the alliance was a defensive one only, and because her partners were technically as well as in fact the aggressors, Italy announced her neutrality. The Italians would not jump off the fence for almost another year. They did, however, have the experience of the Italo-Turkish War behind them, and as well the considerable public enthusiasm, both for armies and for airplanes, that that little war had provided. In 1912, for example, more than three million lire had been raised for aircraft purchases for the army, by public gifts and subscriptions; in 1914 there were fourteen military airfields, two flying schools, and thirteen squadrons. Many of Italy's planes were license-built French models, but the Italians had an advanced if not large industrial base, and firms such as Macchi, Fiat, and Savoia were turning out French designs and experimenting with their own.

Development in the United States, in spite of the Wright Brothers, Glenn Curtiss, and several others, had lagged behind the pace on the Continent. It was indeed disappointment with American response that had led the Wrights to go to Europe to push their accomplishment, and it took several years before there was any considerable enthusiasm for aircraft development at home. Not until 1909 did the U.S. Army buy its first aircraft, a Wright Flyer, and succeed in getting six officers qualified as pilots. All six were taught by the Wrights themselves; one of them was the commander of the Signal Corps' new Aeronautical Division, Captain Charles Chandler, and another was the young officer who had seen the Blériot cross-Channel plane in Paris, Lieutenant Henry Arnold.

The next year, in a Curtiss exhibition on Long Island, an army lieutenant shot several holes in a target, using a Springfield rifle that he fired from a circling airplane. The press was very excited by this, producing visionary stories of airborne hosts, but the army remained determinedly unimpressed. In October 1911 Lieutenant Riley Scott successfully demonstrated the ability of an airplane to drop bombs on a target—a repeat of Curtiss's earlier shows—but again the army insisted it was all a lot of foolishness. Scott eventually resigned his commission and went off to Europe, where the public appeared more interested in the destructive possibilities of airplanes.

In 1912 the army announced it would no longer fund aviation experiments, branding its youthful aeronautical officers as time- and money-wasting dreamers. The dreamers continued working, however, often with their own time and money. They read about what was happening in Europe, they tried their own ideas, and, by constant tinkering and refinement, they made them work. Within its first decade, military aviation had assumed one of its major characteristics: Officialdom was going to be skeptical of its promises and claims, and to overcome that skepticism, aviation's protagonists were going to make more and more far-reaching predictions. They would achieve a great deal of what they promised, but never all of it, and the resulting shortfall would simply further encourage the doubt of officialdom. Aviation was already trapped in a vicious circle, not entirely but at least partly of its own making.

By 1914, Scott and Lewis, inventor of the lightweight machine gun, had taken their ideas off to Europe, and the U.S. Army was still insisting that aircraft might be useful for reconnaissance, and possibly even for artillery observation, but they would never be any good for anything else. The British had made more progress since the days when Samuel Cody, that impertinent American, had flown his dirigible around the pristine air above the War Office. The Air Batallion of the Royal Engineers was formed in February 1911—two companies, one for balloons and one for heavier-than-air craft. Fourteen months later this became the Royal Flying Corps, the great organization that was to fight the war for Britain. It had a naval and military wing and a Central Flying School. The Royal Naval Air Service was officially established a year later, early in 1914.

These new services attracted some odd characters. Most of them were young men with the itch to fly, but there were a few of a different cast. Major Hugh Trenchard was thirty-nine, within a few weeks of being too old for it when he got into the RFC. He had soldiered in India, fought in the South African War, mapped Nigeria; he was rotting on depot service in Londonderry when he got a letter from a friend who was learning to be a pilot: "Come and see men like ants crawling." By the time he had chivied his commanding officer into a recommendation, his friend was dead, killed in one of the all-too-frequent crashes of the day. But Trenchard arrived at the Sopwith school and informed the owner he had to learn to fly in two weeks; otherwise he would be over age for admission to the Central Flying School (in the time-honored British fashion, before one could be admitted to the Central Flying School to learn how to fly, one already had to be a qualified aviator). Thirteen days later Trenchard got his certificate, with one hour and four minutes' flying time. When he reported to Upavon, the site of the school, he was immediately drafted to be the permanent staff's adjutant, as there were providentially few forty-year-old flying candidates around who possessed the rank of major and had Trenchard's experience. He was launched on the career that earned him the oft-quoted title, which he himself hated, of "father of the Royal Air Force."

In 1914 a "Royal Air Force" was four years away. The RFC was a collection of a few hundred pilots and a few more hundred ground staff, fitters, mechanics, and support personnel, and a very unimportant element in the British armed services. At the Admiralty, Winston Churchill, the navy's political master, was planning some role in aerial reconnaissance and coast defense for the Naval Air Service, ideas which in peacetime foundered for lack of money. The army decided that its aerial squadrons, of which it was not sure whether it could muster three or four, would accompany the British Expeditionary Force to France, when and if the long-delayed but often foreseen war should come, and serve as reconnaissance formations for the separate divisions.

They would not be good for much else. The aircraft were unarmed, though the observers might carry personal weapons. A few of the airplanes could carry either observers or their weight in bombs, but not both. There were good airplanes around; the Avro 504 was one of the great planes of history (it was still flying in the thirties, as a trainer and sport aircraft), and Sopwith was designing for racing the forerunners of a great stable of fighters. But unfortunately the RFC chose for quantity production a plane, the B.E. 2c, that was known to its long-suffering pilots as "the Quirk." It was a stable observation plat-form, which was why it was chosen, but that was all it was. It just sat there in midair until the last year of the war, feeding up young Englishmen to German guns; no less than twenty-one of Manfred von Richthofen's eighty victims were B.E. 2c or derivative types.

On June 28, 1914, Gavrilo Princip shot and killed the Archduke Francis Ferdinand, heir to the throne of Austria-Hungary. This was noted with shock in Great Britain, but not too much regarded; the government, press, and armed forces were all preoccupied with a constitutional crisis involving northern Ireland and Home Rule. But through July things on the Continent began to look serious; lights burned late in European chancelleries, and slowly it dawned on peo-ple, civilian and military alike, that this might be the great insur-mountable crisis for which they had all waited so long and so eagerly. The Germans, the French, the Russians all consulted mobilization timetables and unrolled their maps. In Britain the fleet mobilized. The four available squadrons of the Royal Flying Corps were concentrated at Netheravon, ready to go over to France. The war officially began for Great Britain on August 4, when her ultimatum to the German Empire ran out.

What happened to the Royal Flying Corps in those first few days was typical of the tragicomic way in which humanity conducts its great affairs. Trenchard, who was to remain in Britain as commandant of the Military Wing, was with great solemnity given the keys to the confidential war-plan box. The next day he found the box was full of shoes. The active squadrons of the RFC moved to Dover, preceded by their supporting vehicles, hastily requisitioned trucks bearing such warlike slogans as PEAK FREAN BISCUITS and DRINK BOVRIL. Ten days after the war began, the thirty-seven planes of the RFC squadrons crossed the Channel to France. Pilots and observers, loaded down with pistols, water bottles, and odds and ends, climbed into their little frag-ile planes and headed out over the Channel, the first mass flight in history. Some carried automobile inner tubes to use as floats if they had to ditch. In the confusion of those first days, no one knew where the enemy might be or what he might attempt. Someone asked what to do if a Zeppelin were sighted, and the answer was "Ram it." So the world went to war.

II

THE EYES OF ARMIES

Ideas on the basis of which wars are fought are much harder to destroy than the men who are killed while proving them wrong. The commanders who directed World War I had developed their mind-set in the late nineteenth century, and the most recent examples of war they had to go on were the wars of German and Italian unification. These had produced a series of theses about modern war; it would be short, sharp, and decisive. It would employ masses of men and material, and the belligerent who got his masses mobilized and in the field first would enjoy the initiative. By attacking vigorously, he would force the enemy to conform to his moves, thus disrupting the opponent's organization and forcing him into a progressively more difficult situation. He would fall into disarray, and suffer ultimate collapse.

What was important, then, was that a combatant mobilize rapidly and have a well-articulated plan that would permit him to operate immediately and effectively against an enemy. By 1914 all the major powers had such plans, more or less highly developed; the Germans were the most thorough, the British with their minuscule army were the vaguest, and the rest fell somewhere in between. The German plan, known after its originator as the Schlieffen Plan, was designed to solve for Germany her age-old problem of a two-front war. Faced with an alliance of France and Russia, Count Alfred von Schlieffen, Chief of the German General Staff from 1891 to 1906, had worked up a flexible and imaginative answer to how to defeat them. Almost the entire German army would be mobilized for a rapid right-wing hook through neutral Belgium and parts of the Netherlands. This would sweep down on Paris from the north and west, capture the capital, destroy French communications, and roll the still mobilizing French armies up against the Rhine frontier, where they would collapse. Then, utilizing their superior railroad network, the Germans would rapidly transship their armies to the east, to meet the slowly organizing Russians. They would defeat them in some great battle and the war would be over. Six to eight weeks, that was all it should take. The plan was first enunciated in 1895. For nearly twenty years, all the Germans did was play with it. When Schlieffen died in 1913, his last words were, "Keep the right wing strong. . . ."

Ever since 1914, historians and military men have been arguing about whether or not Schlieffen's Plan might have worked. All that can be said for certain is that as put into practice, with possibly but not certainly crippling modifications, it did not work. If it had, World War I would not have been a world war, several million young men might otherwise have lived out their natural life spans, and the airplane and aviation would have developed much differently, and much more slowly, than they did.

Through August, Europe lurched and stumbled into war. The diplomats whose small-minded deals and triumphs had created the impasse folded their papers and stepped off the stage. Cheering crowds sang national anthems over and over again while puppetlike monarchs reviewed their troops and reservists rushed to join their ships and regiments. Guns muttered on the distant horizon, and long columns of horse-drawn wagons, cavalry that still carried lances and sabers, and heavily laden infantrymen wound through the towns and along the highways and country lanes of Europe. The complication was incredible—millions of men, thousands of horses, hundreds of trains, all to be equipped, fed, controlled, moved, timed, commanded, used. The only thing that exceeded the complication was the confusion.

Eventually the opposing columns bumped into each other, and battles, immense by the standards of the last century but a mere prelude of things to come, flared up, along the Sambre and Meuse, those old rivers of war, in the Ardennes, east of the Vosges, in the swamps and marshes of East Prussia. Meeting by surprise, the armies fought, fell back exhausted, moved, met, and fought again. The plans did not work. The Russians moved faster than they were supposed to, were defeated but not destroyed, came on again. The French were defeated too, but the Germans were more confused by victory than the French were hurt by defeat. The great German juggernaut lost momentum, then lost the initiative. In early September, along the Marne River to the east of Paris, the French stood fast and stopped the German advance for good. The kaiser's great armies began to move back, to good defensive positions along the heights. By the time the fall rains came on, there was a solid line running from the Swiss border to the Channel coast. It would not move decisively for three and a half years.

The role of the airplane in this was minor but of considerable interest, and contributed a couple of points of real value. It was all improvisation, of course. When the four Royal Flying Corps squadrons concentrated at Amiens, they were supposed to fly reconnaissance missions for the infantry divisions of the British Expeditionary Corps. In those early days the observer was rather like the conductor of a train: He had little to do with the mechanical business of the enterprise, but he was the commander of the craft. The pilot was simply akin to the engineer, or the chauffeur of a car; all he did was drive. Usually, however, the observers failed to observe. The squadrons had no maps, and could not find any; all the military maps were of course being used by the army, the *real* army, and not available for jaunting about in the air. Eventually the British managed to get one Michelin map, which was better for sightseeing than for military operations, but still better than nothing at all.

French public opinion had greeted the British ecstatically, for fear of the ubiquitous Hun, and there were wild rumors and occasional panics about the immense damage the Zeppelins were doing, always someplace else. But the truth was that the Germans were as ineffectual as the Allies were. On both sides there were numerous reconnaissance missions, but no one was sure of exactly what he was looking for. Since at this time none of the armies had yet thought of camouflage against aerial spying, ammunition dumps or headquarters positions were not hard to spot, except that none of the observers knew what he was looking at from the air. Most of them were volunteer officers from the cavalry or the artillery, often trying to get in and out of a fabric and wire airplane while wearing sword and spurs. They would have done a good job if the aircraft could have flown at the height of a man sitting on a horse, but the somewhat two-dimensional view one got from an aircraft several hundred feet in the air meant nothing at all to them. German observers flew absolutely unmolested over the British concentration area around Amiens for two weeks, yet the German army did not even know the British were across the Channel until they bumped into them on the ground at the battle of Mons.

The French were no more successful. They had the largest and ostensibly best organized and equipped air service at the start of the war, but for reconnaissance purposes it was concentrated at the wrong place. Almost all the French squadrons were on the eastern front, supporting operations toward Alsace and Lorraine. Here the French were attacking, suffering enormous casualties in the process, and the Germans were relatively static. The northernmost of the French squadrons were assigned to cover Luxembourg and the Ardennes sector, and they flew what missions they could, though with only a dozen planes available they were not very thorough. They managed only a few flights over southeastern Belgium and they missed the main German move, so their initial observations led to the incorrect conclusion that the north was safe.

In these early stages, casualties were more from accident than anything else. Even without enemy action, planes still crashed on takeoff or landing, or the wings buckled in midair or shed their fabric, or engines seized up, or they ran out of gas. Everyone had vastly underestimated the wastage that would be incurred with unreliable machines and marginally qualified pilots under war conditions. There was right from the start a constant drain of personnel and machines from noncombat causes, and that went on from the beginning of the war until the very end.

Yet another cause of wastage was unforeseen. Troops on the ground shot at anything that flew. The first French casualty was a dirigible, the *Montgolfier*, which had its gas bag shot full of holes when it flew too low over its own infantry for the purpose of cheering them up. At a very early stage it became necessary to provide some means of identification for aircraft. The Germans and their allies adopted a form of the iron or maltese cross, usually known as a cross pattée. The British countered with the Union Jack painted in assorted sizes. Unfortunately, from the ground, shape is more readily discernible than color, and the Union Jack looked to harassed troops very much like the German cross. Allied troops shot at British planes even more. The French hit on a logical answer, and they responded to the cross with a roundel that was modeled after the national cockade—red, white, and blue rings from the outside in. The British soon followed but reversed the colors, with blue on the outside. The Russians had chosen the same route even earlier, with red, blue, and white. To make it complete, the Belgians used a roundel in their national colors—red, yellow, and black—and the Italians used red, white, and green. Infantry throughout the war still reserved the right to shoot at anyone who appeared less miserable than they were.

In the early weeks of the war, fliers tended to consider themselves figuratively as well as literally above the sordid events happening on the ground, but this was illusion; it was the war that gave meaning to what they were doing, and what they were doing, even in those first uncertain days, was going to change the way men lived—and died.

The airmen's first real intervention in the war came late in August. As the British Expeditionary Force moved into battle, it fell in on the exposed left flank of the French armies being forced back from the Belgian frontier to the south. No one had much idea of what was going on, but the general effect of the developing struggle was to warp the Schlieffen Plan. In the original plan, three German armies were supposed to swing wide through the Low Countries. This was later modified, and they went only through Belgium, leaving the Netherlands neutral. As the French reacted against this, they moved troops up and came into contact with the innermost of these three armies. Ideally, the Germans would have conformed to the movements of the outermost, for it had the farthest to go and was the key to the success of the plan. But instead of that, the Germans responded to the pressure of the French; the outer army, Kluck's First, began to edge to the left instead of swinging wide to the right. This had two effects: immediately it brought Kluck up against the British Expeditionary Force, of whose presence he was totally unaware, and, more important in the long run, it compromised the entire Schlieffen Plan, for it meant the Germans were cutting in east of Paris. Ten days after this shift, the German flank would be open, and Paris would be left as a focal point from which the French could launch a counterattack and then set up the climactic Battle of the Marne.

What may well have saved the British from the avalanche coming down on them was aerial reconnaissance. The BEF's commander, General Sir John French, was not quite as ignorant of the Germans as they were of him: He at least knew they were there. But he did not know what they were doing until August 22, when reconnaissance planes of Nos. 4 and 5 Squadrons reported that the Germans to the north of them were shifting direction. Hitherto they had been moving southwest, but now they were moving due south, right toward the BEF. At the moment he got this news, French was debating an appeal from his ally, General Lanrezac of the French Fifth Army, to attack eastward to relieve the pressure on him. Given this new information, Sir John French refused, threw his troops into a defensive posture around Mons, and fought the BEF's first battle of the Great War. Some historians have argued that without that providential bit of information discovered by the RFC, the British might well have been caught on the move, with an open flank, and virtually destroyed. That may be slightly overstating the case for the aviators, but the episode turned Sir John French into a believer, and in his official dispatch on the opening stages of the campaign, he gave full credit to the Royal Flying Corps for the "incalculable value" of their work.

On August 26 the British claimed their first enemy plane brought down in action. *Brought down* is the operative term, for when Lieutenant H. D. Harvey-Kelly led a three-plane flight of No. 2 Squadron aloft that day, they were all unarmed. Harvey-Kelly spotted a single German plane off in the distance, far below, and dove on him; his two wingmen followed him down. By good luck as much as good management, Harvey-Kelly ended up just above the German, and his followers took station to either side of him. The British then simply flew lower and lower until the German had nowhere to go but into the ground. He landed in a field, left his plane, and ran into a nearby woods, chased by the irrepressible British lieutenant who had landed a bit ahead of him. The German was faster on the ground than in the air, and succeeded in getting away in the trees, whereupon Harvey-Kelly returned to the enemy plane and set it afire. When the British got back to their base, this all seemed like the greatest lark, and soon British pilots throughout the RFC were trying the same trick, a couple of times even succeeding in it.

They had less luck with anything more lethal. Lieutenant Louis Strange had crossed the Channel a day after the RFC's historic flight, delayed by engine trouble. He had put the lost day to good use, strapping a Lewis gun to the struts of his plane. When he caught up with his squadron he could hardly wait to try out his new toy, and finally he got his chance. On August 22, a lone Taube flew over the British airfield. Strange took off in not quite hot pursuit, for his Farman-type plane, with the weight of the Lewis gun and the gunner, could labor up only to 3,500 feet. The Taube, at about 5,000 feet, continued along in blissful ignorance. A chastened Strange returned to the airfield to be told by his commanding officer to get that useless piece of dead weight off his plane; everyone knew machine guns were infantry weapons.

Although airplanes could not carry machine guns, Zeppelins could carry bombs, and the same day that Harvey-Kelley was scoring the RFC's first victory, the Germans were up to something even more portentous. The front was still fluid at the end of August; the German armies were still advancing on Paris. They had in their passage through Belgium pushed the Belgian army away to the northwest, and the Belgians were holding on to Antwerp, invested by a detached German corps. To finish off the affair, the Germans sent over the Zeppelin *Sachsen,* and it opened an aerial bombardment by dropping nearly a ton of small shrapnel bombs on the city. The Germans regarded this as a legitimate military operation, aimed at the fortifications and military defenders of the city. The Belgians insisted that the Germans had hit a hospital, and that twelve civilians had been killed. Thus began another of the controversies that would plague air power throughout its history: Those who bombed would always insist that they were aiming at military targets and hitting what they aimed at; those who were bombed would insist exactly the opposite on both counts.

By September the kaiser's armies were nearing the Marne, and German troops were only twenty or thirty miles off to the east of the capital. Late in the afternoon, several days in succession, a German Taube monoplane came droning in over the city. There were few French aircraft around Paris, and no one thought yet in terms of airplanes shooting down other airplanes anyway, so the arrival of Lieutenant Karl von Hiddessen each day was hailed futilely by the fortress guns of Paris banging off in the general direction of Germany. Von Hiddessen was even less dangerous than they were, and he flew over the Eiffel Tower dropping notes demanding that the city surrender. Cheering Frenchmen watched his progress, the first example in history of an operation that later generations, less impressionable, would call "bed-check Charlie." After a week or so, von Hiddessen must have gotten tired of his leaflets, for a Lieutenant Dressler came along and dropped a batch of handheld four-pounder bombs on the eastern outskirts of Paris. The bombs did no harm, and as the eastern part of the city has always been the working-class and industrial section, the incident was given less attention than it might have received had they been dropped on a fashionable quarter.

Later in the month more immediately fruitful experiments were tried. By now the Marne battle was over and the Germans had fallen back to defensive positions. The French and British were trying unsuccessfully to outflank them, in a series of battles known as "the race to the sea." The British, coming up against enemy positions along the Aisne River, were harassed by artillery fire. Unable to observe the Germans, they sent up two lieutenants in an aircraft equipped with a wireless transmitter. The two fliers, Lieutenants Lewis and James, flew around at low level until they spotted the hidden batteries, and then they signaled back for a British counterbarrage. They hovered over the German position, correcting the fall of shot from their own guns until the latter was on target. The signal was sent by Morse code: HIT. HIT. HIT. The British gunners laid down a barrage, and the two fliers came home. In this undramatic way, the airplane found its most successful, if least publicized, role in the Great War. The largest part of what was done for the next four years would be done just so someone could signal HIT. HIT. HIT.

Perhaps the most enterprising of these early efforts were undertaken by the Royal Naval Air Service. Members of this branch should not, strictly speaking, even have been in France, but they were. Upon the outbreak of the war, naval squadrons took up patrol positions along the British east coast, waiting for the Germans to appear. The naval fliers were soon bored with doing nothing; when the German advance looked as if it might force an evacuation from France of the BEF, and it was suggested that naval squadrons should cross the Channel to cover this possibility, the navy jumped at the chance.

Lieutenant Rumney Samson, commander of the Eastchurch squadron of the RNAS, moved his force over to Dunkirk and began to look for the war. It proved annoyingly hard to find. There was very little aerial activity around his base, the weather was uniformly bad, and Samson was soon close to distraction. As the first Englishman to fly a plane off a ship, and the first to fly a seaplane, he was not likely to sit passively for too long. Finally he teamed up with a retired French infantry officer who knew the district, organized a couple of armored cars, and began forays into the surrounding countryside. Occasionally he met the first tentative German patrols, which he chased back to the east; then, as the weather cleared, he began sending his planes on reconnaissance. When they reported the presence of the enemy, Samson would dash off with his armored cars and shoot them up. It was not quite as exciting as flying, but it was the next best thing. In those first weeks of the war, fighting still seemed the jolly good sport that it was supposed to be.

Samson soon got his opportunity for greater things. He sent a couple of his planes forward to Antwerp, where the Belgians and some British marines were still holding out. From there the British could reach Germany, and in retaliation for the Zeppelin attacks against the city, they tried their hand at bombing. A first effort failed to find anything to bomb; the weather was too bad and the night too dark. But on October 8, just as Antwerp itself was about to fall, one British plane hit the Cologne railroad station, where it killed three civilians, and a second actually hit the Zeppelin shed at Düsseldorf, destroying the newly built Z-9 in a spectacular fire. The British pilot flew his damaged plane back almost to Antwerp, crash-landed, and finished the trip by bicycle.

The small but gratifying success led the British on to greater things. Winston Churchill was the political minister in charge of the navy, the First Lord of the Admiralty, and he proved highly imaginative, often to the despair of both his political colleagues and the more conservative of his senior naval officers. He was now bitten by the Zeppelin bug, and hearing that there were Zeppelins at their home base, Friedrichshafen, he decided to go after them. Unfortunately, Friedrichshafen was on Lake Constance, and that, on the border between Switzerland and Germany, was water difficult for even the Royal Navy to get to. Never daunted by geography, Churchill detailed Commander E. F. Briggs to do the job. Briggs dismantled four Avro 504 biplanes, packed them into unmarked trucks, and drove them to the French border town of Belfort. There the planes were reassembled and made ready for the attack.

Only three of them made it; the engine of the fourth acted up, leaving its swearing pilot to sit out the raid. The other three, each carrying four twenty-pound bombs, took off and made the long flight—it was 250 miles there and back—arriving over Lake Constance without incident. They skimmed the distance of the lake, then climbed to altitude and came in and bombed. The Germans were taken completely by surprise, and though they responded rapidly with whatever guns were available, the raid was a success. The Zeppelin sheds and the nearby gas works burst into flames, as the Avros darted back and forth, doing as much damage as they could. Two of the planes returned safely, but Commander Briggs took a bullet through the fuel line of his plane and was forced to land about fifteen miles from the Zeppelin works. He tried to get away to Switzerland, but he had been hurt in the crash, then manhandled by civilians who finally caught him, and he had to be rescued by German soldiers. These brought him back to Friedrichshafen, where he was immediately accorded the status of hero by the German pilots who regarded him not as an enemy but as a fellow comrade of the air.

The official response was less amused. The Germans accused the British of bombing civilians, which, in this instance at least, was not true, and of violating Swiss neutrality by overflying that country's territory. This was rather a weak argument from the men who had just invaded Belgium, and the Swiss graciously accepted the British disclaimer that if, indeed, they had done so, it was quite unintentional. The British were delighted, thinking they had done grave damage to the enemy; the Germans, especially after they found the raid's results were really quite superficial, let the matter drop.

The Germans were beginning to think of bombing too, and not just with Zeppelins. At the same time the Friedrichshafen raid was mounted, they were forming their first airplane bombing unit. This was officially titled Carrier Pigeon Unit Ostende, which suggested they were not entirely certain of the morality, or perhaps the practicality, of the exercise. They did not become fully operational until the new year. Before then, England itself had been bombed. A German seaplane flew across the Channel to Dover and dropped a bomb on December 21, and on Christmas Day an Albatross seaplane flew up the Thames, looked over London and assorted other spots, and dropped two bombs on the forts along the river. The British tried to intercept it, and sent up planes to shoot at it futilely with rifles and pistols, but the impudent German escaped unharmed. The British were relieved that the intruder was a mere airplane, which could not do much harm, and not a Zeppelin, of which the public had conceived an exaggerated fear.

The British were attempting the same sort of thing as the Germans, and in November they decided to strike with seaplanes at the Zeppelin base on the German coast at Nordholtz, near Cuxhaven. This was much farther than an aircraft could fly at the time, but in the opening weeks of the war the Admiralty had converted three Channel packets to serve as seaplane carriers. These were far from aircraft carriers in the modern sense; they were equipped with cranes and hangar space, and could lift float planes on and off the water, in effect providing movable bases for the short-ranged aircraft of the day.

Planned in November, the raid did not materialize until Christmas. The three seaplane carriers, *Engadine, Empress,* and *Riviera,* left Harwich on Christmas Eve with destroyer and cruiser escorts, and at daybreak on Christmas morning they were fifty miles northwest of Cuxhaven. This was a fairly dangerous place to be, deep in German waters, with the ships required to stop and lie dead in the water while the planes were hoisted over the side. Nine planes were lowered to the water, but only seven were able to be started. It took half an hour for the planes to get off; five minutes after they left, a German Zeppelin appeared and dropped bombs around *Empress* before being chased off by the fire of the escorting destroyers.

For all their trouble, the British did not accomplish much. They got to the general area of the Zeppelin base only to find it completely blanketed by fog, so that they saw nothing. They then flew over the fleet anchorage at Wilhelmshaven, where the air was clear, and they dropped some bombs on a German cruiser. Next they appeared over the Schelling Roads and dropped a few more bombs. The German return fire was heavy, and of the seven planes, only two made it back to their carriers. The others ditched here and there, one alongside a destroyer, one near a Dutch trawler. The most dramatic rescue was of three seaplane crews by the submarine *E-11,* which saved the men but had to abandon the planes when bombed by a Zeppelin.

Air warfare at sea was thus off to a rather unpromising start. Just as with the Friedrichshafen raid, losses were heavy, especially of equipment, and the return was small. On a cost-efficiency accounting, it was hardly worth the effort. But, as with the earlier raid, it was a beginning; there would someday be better airplanes, and better techniques, and greater results.

By the end of 1914, when the war was supposed to be over, it was in fact just settling down. In aviation, an early pattern was developing. The French were the first to recognize it, and had split their service into three types: reconnaissance, which was attached to the army commands and functioned largely as the light cavalry of earlier wars; observation, the mundane business of artillery spotting and correction; and bombing. After only three weeks of war the French had designated three squadrons, or escadrilles, as bombing units. All three of these flew the Voisin 3, an ugly but serviceable biplane that in one variant or another lasted throughout the war. It could carry only about five hundred pounds, including the pilot and the observer, so its effective bombload was necessarily small, but it was a stable flying platform, able to absorb a tremendous amount of damage to its steel and wire frame. Its crews liked it, which is the best testimony to it as an aircraft.

The Voisin also had the distinction of being the first French aircraft to shoot down an enemy plane in combat, for on October 5, Sergeant-Pilot Joseph Franz and an observer-mechanic named Quenault destroyed a German observation plane near Reims. As they succeeded in doing this armed only with the standard cavalry carbine, this hardly inaugurated the era of aerial combat, but it did earn the Voisin its place in history.

Carrying at most two hundred pounds of bombs, the French were soon active on the eastern part of their front, and they flew bombing missions against German munitions factories and steelworks in the industrial Rhine and Ruhr areas. Again they were not very effective, and the most substantial work was still being done by the artillery observers, followed by the reconnaissance machines. But that in itself was valuable enough to give the air service a continued mandate. Even before the war the French had experimented with aerial photography, and by the winter of 1914 they were sufficiently advanced in this that the British sent some people around to find out exactly what the French were up to. The result of this cooperation was an efficient aerial camera designed by Major W. G. H. Salmond and Lieutenant J. T. Moore-Brabazon, which enabled analysts to spot and map enemy positions. Eventually this called into being a whole apparatus, on the one side, of photo interpretation, and on the other, of camouflage and deception. And initially it all depended upon some nineteen- or twenty-year-old boy leaning out over the side of his airplane with a camera strapped to his chest, in bitter cold, with no parachute, and often the target for any antiaircraft gun within reach.

Observation and reconnaissance were so obviously important, so early in the war, that they rapidly generated their own nemesis. Higher commanders who desperately wanted to know what the enemy was doing equally desperately wanted to keep the enemy from seeing what they themselves were up to. Antiaircraft weapons developed rapidly, from machine guns mounted on posts so the gunner could fire upward and field guns with their trails dug into the ground to purpose-built weapons. But ground-based antiaircraft fire was essentially passive; the target had to come to it. A better way to go was to develop an effective means of fighting in the air.

As a weapons system the airplane was like the earliest firearms. No one knew exactly what to do with it, or what its limitations were, so all kinds of weird ideas were tried. The machine gun had in the opening stages proved too heavy and unwieldy for the power of the aircraft, and until that dilemma was resolved there were some pretty far-fetched experiments.

The first pilots, of course, just waved at each other in a friendly fashion, but that did not last very long. War was too nasty a business even for the fraternity of the air, and the man in the other plane soon made the transformation from fellow flier to enemy. How to dispose of him remained the big problem, and various alternatives were tried.

The pistol and the rifle were the obvious weapons to take aloft, but pistols are notoriously inaccurate, and to shoot effectively from one platform moving through three dimensions at another moving through three dimensions is far beyond the skills of most riflemen. Franz's accomplishment was largely a lucky fluke. Some fliers tried throwing hand grenades at the enemy, but that was not very useful; even if the thrower were right above the target, he had to have everything exactly right, and, as far as is known, no one ever did. The same techniques were tried with steel darts, *flechettes,* but with an equal lack of success. A few pilots tried trailing a bomb on the end of a wire, hoping thus to blow up an unsuspecting—and presumably comatose—opponent. A variation on that theme was to trail a hook on a long wire, with the idea of entangling it in the enemy's rigging or even his wing and tearing it off. On the face of it, if one could get close enough to entangle the other plane with a hook, one ought to be able to shoot him down with a rifle anyway, and the novelty of the trailing-wire idea quickly wore out.

Pilots soon ran out of options and discovered the same thing as their more mundane comrades on the ground—aimed fire was insufficient. Massed fire therefore had to be the answer. It had to be the machine gun. And that, of course, meant better aircraft and lighter machine guns.

Almost everyone was reaching the same conclusion about the same time. The persistent Lieutenant Strange had now graduated from Farman biplanes to Avro 504's, and the 504 was a lovely little plane. In mid-October, in spite of being told by his commanding officer to stop his nonsense, Strange had a Lewis machine gun mounted on the top wing of an Avro. The top wing mounting was the only place Strange could find to get forward fire without cutting off his own pro-peller, and this required his observer-gunner to stand up on his own cockpit seat to fire the gun. Strange produced a safety harness and got a fellow enthusiast, Lieutenant Rabagliati, to try it out. They took off after a German reconnaissance plane, caught it, and fired off a whole drum of ammunition without any noticeable effect. However, if they had no adverse effect on the German, they also had no adverse effect on the Avro, which seemed to fly happily along, oblivious of the extra weight, the recoil of the gun, and the gyrations of the gunner.

Meanwhile, the French were not resting on the laurels of Sergeant Franz. Most of the French reconnaissance aircraft were pushers rather than tractors, with the engine in the rear rather than on the nose. They therefore did not have to worry about clearing the propeller arc. Corporal Stribick managed to fit a Hotchkiss machine gun to the front cockpit of his Farman biplane, and with this he actually shot down a German observation plane. But once again this was a fluke; the Far-man was not suited for the type of flying aerial combat would entail, and the Hotchkiss was too bulky, heavy, and generally cumbersome to be useful in the air. Corporal Stribick and his observer, David, were given the Medaille militaire for their feat, but it was still a one-time effort.

The problem was on the verge of solution, and as soon as all the right elements were combined, the entire complexion of war in the air was going to change. Within a short time the air would be con-tributing its share to the slaughter of a generation.

III

THE ADVENT OF
THE ACE

In August 1914 the French government had shut down the munitions factories and called the workers to the colors, on the thesis that the war would be fought with existing stocks and nothing new would have time to reach the fighting troops before it ended; in the same vein, the army had closed down the flying schools for the air service. By Christmas the world had changed in its course, and it was obvious that the early ideas had been incredibly optimistic. No one now knew how long the war would be, but everyone knew it was far from over. The new situation created a demand for things that had not even been imagined six short months ago.

The most significant of these from the airmen's point of view was the fighter. Everything so far had been improvisation, as is only natural in a great war after a long peace, and even more natural in a new service in a new element. But by the spring of 1915, some of the pieces began to come together. This was still a year of groping, right from the highest echelons on down. Useful command and liaison structures had to be worked out, tactics and strategy were in their infancy, and everyone connected with the business of war in the air, from aircraft designers and engine manufacturers to the pilots themselves, was just learning his business. At the sharp end, it took skill, and perhaps even more—luck—to survive long enough to master this strange new world.

Most of the great names of 1915 would eventually fade into the background before the even greater names of 1916 and 1917, but it was men such as these—Hawker, Garros, Immelmann and Boelcke—who set the stage for the battles and aces to come. By later standards, their planes were nothing much and their number of kills small, but as Wright and Curtiss and Blériot were the pioneers of powered flight, they were the pioneers of aerial fighting.

The career of Major Lanoe G. Hawker illustrates the improvisational nature of air fighting in 1915. He was flying with No. 6 Squadron on July 25, 1915, when he won the first Victoria Cross ever awarded for air combat. At that time all the RFC squadrons had mixed equipment; most of their aircraft were two-seaters, for observation work. Each squadron had a couple of single-seaters, but not much was done with them. The problem of flying the plane and firing a gun was still basically unresolved; machine guns were carried on the two-seaters and fired by the observer either above the wing from the front cockpit or over the tail from the rear cockpit. Single-seaters were usually unarmed, and used for fast reconnaissance flights. Hawker, however, believed the single-seater was the plane of the future, and he went up with a cavalry carbine fixed to the side of his plane outside the cockpit, braced so it would fire at an angle clear of the propeller arc. It would be difficult to imagine a more awkward mounting, yet on the evening of August 25, Hawker managed to shoot down three German observation planes, and thus earn his Victoria Cross.

The same day, the first British plane designed to be a fighter arrived in France. This was the Vickers F. B. 5. The British designers had solved the problem of machine gun versus propeller by building a pusher airplane. The engine was at the rear of the fuselage nacelle, surrounded by wires and the twin booms leading back to the tail. The pilot sat just under the forward edge of the top wing, and the gunner sat forward of him, armed with a free-mounted Vickers machine gun with which he was, presumably, lord of all he surveyed. Pushers would be the main type of British fighter for nearly two years, and the Vickers F. B. 5 was followed by the 9, the "Gunbus," the Royal Aircraft

Factory's F. E. 2b, or "Fee," perhaps the most famous of them all, and the De Haviland D. H. 2, which was a single-seater pusher built as a direct response to the German successes of early 1915. Theoretically, the pusher was a good idea, for the engine was right near the center of gravity, and the planes were moderately maneuverable and useful craft; many served, even after they were outclassed as fighters, in other roles until the end of the war. But the pusher was not as clean a design as the tractor, which was soon to outpace it. For one thing, early rotary engines occasionally shed cylinders, even before they were hit by enemy fire, and a broken cylinder flying out through the maze of wires and struts that constituted the pusher airframe was the end of many a promising young career. Indeed, the pusher need never have been developed at all, for plans for synchronizing gear for gun and propeller were gathering dust in London. They had been submitted to the War Office in 1913 by an aspiring inventor and promptly laid aside and forgotten, just as in Germany a similar gear had been patented before the war by Franz Schneider and then completely ignored.

Hawker and his fellows soldiered along in the machines available to them for all of 1915. The first real fighter squadron in the RFC was formed on F. B. 5's in July, but for the most part the fighters were still parceled out as mixed equipment to the all-purpose units. They were not working very well, and this was the period of the "Fokker scourge," when British and French airmen were killed faster than they could learn to fly. Not until early 1916 did the first fighter squadron of single-seat planes, D. H. 2's, arrive in France. This was No. 23 Squadron, with Hawker in command, and this was the squadron that produced the first fully developed ideas of formation flying and offensive patrol tactics for the RFC. Through 1916, Hawker, one of the legendary leaders of his kind, continued to lead his squadron, working out the new ideas and practices of air warfare. He had shot down nine Germans when, on November 23, 1916, he himself was killed in one of the most famous single combats of the war. He became Manfred von Richthofen's eleventh victim.

Hawker's career, which lasted two years, was longer than that of many of the early fliers who became famous, and the British technical and tactical development it illustrated was slower than that of the other combatants. The Frenchman Roland Garros set in train the events that finally brought aerial combat into its own. An almost archetypal aerial daredevil, Garros had been the first man to fly the Mediterranean and had toured with exhibitions before the war. Stranded in Berlin at the outbreak of hostilities, he had escaped by feigning drunkenness, climbing out a bathroom window, and stealing his own plane from amused guards who thought one drunk could not start a plane by himself, let alone fly it at night. Back in France and posted to Escadrille M. S. 23—French squadrons were named after the type of plane they flew, and Garros was flying Morane Saulniers—he became obsessed with the possibilities of shooting down Germans. He tried pistols, but that did not work, and eventually he decided that the only way to get a clear shot was with a head-on approach; the collision course was the only angle from which the enemy presented a stable target. That brought up the propeller-blade problem again, as the French were flying tractor planes, but Garros was determined; finally he decided simply to shoot through his own propeller. He reasoned that there was more space than blade in the propeller arc, and some bullets, enough to shoot down an opponent, were bound to get through. The mathematics of the proposition dictated that he would inevitably shoot off his own propeller in the process, but with a Gallic shrug he insisted that such things happened, and if prepared for it, he could glide to a landing behind his own lines anyway.

The more he thought of it, the more feasible it seemed. He went to the ordnance shop and demanded a Hotchkiss gun to mount on his plane. Then he got a boost from an armorer who had been involved with similar experiments before the war: If he fitted steel deflector plates at an angle to the back of his propeller blade where the bullets would strike, those bullets that *did* hit the blade would mostly be shunted aside. Apparently this had already been tried by another French aviator, Eugene Gilbert, but Garros seems not to have known of this and is usually credited with the idea. There would be a lot of wear, and he might be forced down once in a while, but it ought to work.

It did. On the morning of April 1, 1915, Garros came up in his Morane Saulnier, flew into a flight of four German observation planes, and, before they realized what on earth he was doing, shot two of them down. The other two fled for home with news of this strange new departure.

Garros then went on a very short-lived rampage, sowing death, destruction, and above all terror among the German airmen in his area. No one could figure out how he did it; committees were formed to study the problem, and nonflying officers compared the German air service to a girls' school in the grip of hysteria. Then, on April 19, Garros gave the game away. He shot down his sixth German, and then, his engine failing, was forced to land behind German lines. Before he could set his plane on fire he was captured with it intact, and there was the magic weapon for all the world to see. Garros went off to prison, where he stayed until January 1918, when he escaped, returned to France and to active service, and was shot down and killed a month before the Armistice. The plane went to Berlin, and the German authorities invited a young Dutch designer and aircraft manufacturer named Anthony Fokker to have a look at it. Fokker was building a single-wing plane much like the Morane; perhaps he could duplicate the deflector mechanism as well.

Fokker was one of the great characters of the period, and his name became almost synonymous with some of the finest aircraft of both the Great War and the twenties. Indeed, his designs influenced the classic American biplane fighters produced by Curtiss for the U.S. Army Air Corps in the interwar period. In 1915, however, he owed his success more to the war than to any as yet proven merit; he had been playing with airplanes and their designs for nearly a decade, and about all he had so far managed to do was to run through several thousand dollars' worth of grants-in-aid provided by his long-suffering but providentially wealthy father. By 1914, Fokker had an aircraft factory at Schwerin, up on the German Baltic coast; he was selling planes to the German army and navy, and insisting to his father that with a little more money he would be on his way to fame and fortune. This time he was right.

When he was called to have a look at Garros's captured innovation, Fokker was busy building an airplane known as the E. 1, for *Eindekker,* or monoplane. This was a simple little thing, with a square-section fuselage, a large single wing with a whole tangle of external bracing, and completely movable tail surfaces. Its chief virtue was that it was fast, with a top speed of about eighty miles per hour. This was the plane to which Fokker was asked to fit Garros's plates.

As soon as he got back to Schwerin, he began to play with the idea. Surely there must be a better way to make this work, because it was obviously sheer luck that had kept the foolish Frenchman from killing himself. Fokker had a good team in his plant, the best of them being Reinhold Platz, who started out as a welder and became the real brains of many of the Fokker designs. They took apart a Parabellum machine gun—the name came from the old Latin tag, *Si vis pacem, para bellum:* if you want peace, prepare for war—and within forty-eight hours they had reinvented the mechanism that had been so casually discarded and forgotten by military authority before the war. The interrupter gear was a simple series of cams and rods, acting in such a way that the firing pin of the machine gun was prevented from striking when the propeller blade was in a position where it could be hit by a bullet. This was not a synchronizer (that came later), but it was perfectly adequate for the needs of the moment.

Fokker then mounted the whole rig, gun and interrupter gear, on the front of his E. 1 and went back to Berlin to show off. Authority was unimpressed; having asked for deflector plates, that was what they wanted. Fokker fired his gun from a sitting plane, a short burst at a time; they said it must be a trick of the short bursts. He fired off a whole belt of ammunition; they said it must be because the plane was on the ground. He took off and sprayed a target laid out near the observers, forcing them to scatter in panic from the ricochets; they said now that it would not work in combat. Finally they demanded that he take his invention to the front and shoot someone down; then they would believe him.

Fokker agreed to do it, and he spent a week at the front, searching in vain for a target. Finally he found a French Farman. The Frenchmen watched curiously as he closed in on them, then at the last moment he decided he could not go through with it. Later he wrote, "I was flying merely to prove that a certain mechanism I had invented would work. . . . Let them do their own killing!" So he turned for home and, indeed, let them do their own killing. When a later generation perfected strategic bombing, they would decide that the man who made the killing machine was as legitimate a target as the man who used it to kill. But Fokker was still able to clothe himself in the comfortably ambiguous argument that he was only a businessman producing a product that a customer found useful.

Having returned to his airbase after this sudden and unusual attack of conscience, Fokker willingly agreed to teach a handful of German pilots how to use his plane so they could do their own killing. The first of them was Oswald Boelcke, and the second was Max Immelmann.

THE ADVENT OF THE ACE

* * *

Oswald Boelcke was the first great German ace, and therefore a popular hero. By the middle of 1915, the war had assumed the grinding quality of a battle of attrition between huge, dull-colored masses of nameless men. The public at home, desperate for some of the glamour and glory they had been taught to expect—the heroic exploits that would keep them interested in, and supportive of, the war effort—soon fastened on the names of pilots that began to appear in the reports of the fighting. If thirty infantrymen were blown to pieces in an artillery barrage in some unidentifiable mudhole, that was not news. But if some daring flier shot down two or three equally daring enemy fliers, that was news.

The idea of the "ace" was a newspaper rather than a military one, and it was first used by the French. To become one a pilot had to shoot down a certain number of opponents, though the number varied from country to country and time to time, being variously quoted as twenty, ten, six, or five. Though military authorities refused to acknowledge the concept officially, government was quick to recognize the psychological value of aerial stories and air heroes. French and German aces became household names, and were given medals and assorted perquisites, such as special planes, special squadrons, and preferential treatment. They were, in fact, remarkably like the sports heroes and musical stars of a later age. The British resisted this as much as possible. Where Manfred von Richthofen flew in a brightly decorated red airplane, and Charles Nungesser adorned his plane with French tricolor stripes, the British remained determinedly dull-colored, staying with khaki and olive-drab, and reprimanding any pilot who tried to appear distinctive. Yet British names, such as Ball and Bishop, Mannock and McCudden, became as famous as their counterparts in other countries. In a ghastly world of death and maiming, lice and dysentery, poison gas and jagged iron, the "knights of the air" appeared to offer some redeeming quality. In faded photographs they still stand before their jaunty little airplanes, wrapped in leather flying coats and silk scarves and emanating youth and confidence.

It was all a trick, of course. The only difference between the infantryman dying in the mud and slime and the pilot burning in his airplane as he plummeted to earth was that the latter was a little cleaner when he died. Until the end of the war, authority would not let fliers wear parachutes, to ensure that they would not abandon government property and let it be destroyed prematurely, and many a young pilot or observer carried a pistol not so he could shoot the enemy but so he could shoot himself when his plane caught fire. The redemptive quality of aerial heroism was in the minds of journalists who had never pulled a charred corpse out of the wreckage. The fliers died often enough. If the poor quality of their flying, or the undependability of their aircraft, or the antiaircraft fire, did not kill them, then the aces did.

Boelcke was the German equivalent of Major Hawker—not only an ace but an organizer as well, a serious student and tactician, an adored leader of his men. He had already shot down one French plane when he met Fokker, a feat at that time so unusual for a German that he had been given the Iron Cross First Class for it. Until midsummer of 1915, the German air service had confined itself almost exclusively to observation and nuisance missions, and was remarkably unoffensive.

Boelcke's meeting with Fokker changed that, and by the time Fokker got back to Schwerin, he was met with the news that the German flier had flown three patrols and had succeeded in shooting down a French plane. From that time on, his score mounted rapidly. He spent a good deal of his time over the next fifteen months or so away from operations. For one thing, he had a good technical mind, so he was often working with Fokker himself. The E. 1 was somewhat underpowered for the weight of its gun, so Fokker, aided by Boelcke's active experience and his advice, gradually upgraded the little monoplane. The best of the series, the E. III, had an uprated engine that could push it to nearly ninety miles an hour. This was the airplane of the deadly Fokker scourge period, in late 1915. German scores mounted rapidly, and Allied pilots bitterly referred to themselves as "Fokker fodder."

During his relatively short career, Boelcke shot down forty planes, mostly on the French sector of the western front. But he also toured all the war areas, including Turkey, and, like Hawker, he organized fighting units and produced rules for aerial formations and combat. It was he who suggested the formation of fighting squadrons, the Jagdstaffeln, literally "hunting squadrons," and he became commander of Jasta 2, later named Jasta Boelcke in his honor. It was also Boelcke who began the process of recruiting promising young airmen into his unit, to make it an elite force. Some of Germany's most famous pilots passed through Boelcke's hands and all of them benefited from his ideas and his training.

For Boelcke it all came to an end on October 28, 1916. In company with several members of his squadron, he was flying after a British single-seater scout. A second British plane, chased by von Richthofen, came clawing up in front of him. Boelcke suddenly turned, and his wing hit the undercarriage of the plane alongside him; the port side of the wing carried away, the plane spun down, and Germany's first great ace was killed. Von Richthofen carried his medals in the funeral procession, and a plane from the RFC flew over and dropped a wreath.

Eighty-four German pilots downed more planes than Max Immelmann, yet he was one of the most famous, and one of the earliest, of German air heros. For a while he was Boelcke's understudy, taking over older planes as Boelcke received new ones to try out. He received his first Iron Cross simply for getting his unarmed observation plane safely back to base after an encounter with a Frenchman who shot him up. From that he worked his way up to fighters, and got his own first victory on August 1, 1915, when he shot down a British plane raiding his aerodrome. That got him the Iron Cross First Class and made him a full-fledged fighter pilot. When most of the German squadrons were drawn off to prepare for the great offensive at Verdun that opened early in 1916, Immelmann was one of the few left facing the British front, and it was there that he earned his nickname, "the eagle of Lille."

Unlike Boelcke, who soon went on to the first Albatross biplane fighters, Immelmann stayed with the Fokker Eindekker, and he became the great exponent of that type of airplane. He was also famous for a maneuver named after him, the Immelmann turn. Immelmann was a withdrawn and introverted type, who wrote almost every day to his mother and whose only close friend was his dog, but he was an absolute perfectionist in the air. He studied the planes available to the enemy and eventually reasoned out the best ways to attack them. Given the Fokker's superiority, Immelmann would dive on an enemy from behind, firing as he came. Then he would zoom up in front of him, as if to go into a loop and attack from the rear again. Instead of looping, he would do a half-roll and come down again from the front, building up speed yet again and firing as he came. This zoom and half-roll became the Immelmann turn, and it was good enough to account for more than half the planes Immelmann shot down.

Idolized by the press, he was for a time even more famous than

Boelcke; he received Germany's highest award, the Pour le Mérite, and was as respected and feared by the British as he was respected and admired by his own side. But, like so many of his colleagues, his career was short. He died on June 28, 1916, and no one is sure how. The British say he was killed while attacking an F. E. 2; the gunner, Corporal John Waller, hit him. The Germans say his aircraft failed; he had been having trouble with the interrupter gear, and a few days before his death he had shot off his own propeller but managed to land safely. This second time, they say, he shot off one blade, and the resulting shudder tore the engine loose from the plane before he could shut off the engine. Fokker rejected that idea and, after examining the wreck, pronounced that Immelmann had been hit by antiaircraft fire, probably German. At the time, Fokker's monoplanes had been developed about as far as they could go and were under official scrutiny for structural deficiencies, so he was not likely to conclude that it had been the plane's fault, though on balance, the mechanical failure seems the most probable of the three possible explanations.

By 1916 and the death of Immelmann, and later Boelcke, the days of the Fokker scourge were coming to an end. For a year the German secret device had driven the British and French to distraction, and they had produced all kinds of bizarre aircraft of their own in an attempt to counter it. Of the British pushers, the Fee and the D. H. 2 could meet the Eindekker on more or less equal terms, but they did not come into squadron service until early 1916, and they reached the front in significant numbers only by spring of that year.

The French were pressed to even more desperate alternatives in their attempts to counter the threat, and to that end they produced what was arguably one of the most vicious airplanes of the war. This was the infamous Spad A2. The A2 was in most respects a conventional tractor airplane, except that it had the rotary engine set right at the forward edge of the two wings; forward of that again, in a nacelle or a sort of pulpit, stood a gunner with a machine gun. This nacelle, which hinged downward for access to the engine, was attached to the main frame of the aircraft by the kind of rig that surrounds an electric fan. The gunner's back was protected, in theory, by a metal screen. This contraption was not entirely satisfactory, especially from the gunner's point of view. The nacelle kept the propeller from functioning very efficiently, the pilot could not see much ahead of him, the gun was mounted in such a way that it had a remarkably restricted field of fire, given the effort that went into getting it out in front, and, worst of all, the whole affair was so heavy that the plane tended to nose over on the ground on the slightest provocation, with almost invariably fatal results for the poor gunner. The French built about a hundred of these, and shipped slightly more than half of them to the Russians, who were so desperate for aircraft that they would fly anything. The concept was not peculiar to the French; the British tried the same thing with the B.E. 9, but, fortunately for everyone concerned, it never got into production status.

The French did find a much better answer than the Spad A2, however, and in 1915 they introduced one of the great airplanes of the era. The Nieuport firm had been making planes since before the war, and in 1915, their Nieuport 10's and 12's came into service. These were two-seaters, but they were fast and maneuverable. They were sesquiplanes; that is, they looked like biplanes, but the lower wing was of a much narrower chord than the upper, so actually they were halfway between the monoplane and the biplane. The configuration gave them both strength and handiness. To meet the Fokkers, many of the Nieuports were converted; the forward cockpit was covered over, a gun was mounted above the top wing to clear the propeller, and away they went.

The Nieuport designer, Gustave Delage, thought he could do much better than that. He had already made a smaller version of the 10 for prewar races, but it had been set aside by the pressure of war and the need for observation planes; now he resurrected it, and as it was smaller than its predecessors, he called the Nieuport 11 "the Baby." The Baby was the first of a great line of fighters, and it was followed by the 16, 17, 24, and 27, all progressive upgradings of the sesquiplane idea. The line finally tapered out with the 28; it was a regular biplane, quite elegant-looking but frail. It had a nasty reputation for shedding its wings, and the panels that covered the front of the fuselage were reputed to be made of cardboard. The French passed it over to the Americans, who were in the war by the time it arrived, and they, not knowing anything better, used it to some effect to the end of the war.

But the sesquiplanes, or "Vee-strutters" as they were often called, allowed the Allies to regain at least parity in the air. Everyone liked them, and they were used, and in some cases license-built, by the French themselves, the British, the Italians, the Belgians, and the

Russians. Perhaps the greatest tribute to them is that the enemy liked them too, and the German firm of Siemens-Schuckert built copies of them.

This was in fact thought to be not quite fair. The Fokker scourge had caused so many fatalities among British airmen that it had led to questions in the House of Commons and a suggestion that perhaps Fokker's patent might be acquired for use by the British. As Fokker was both a neutral, a Dutchman, and a businessman, as evidenced by his ideas when stalking Frenchmen, he himself probably would have been willing. However, in his contract he had accorded Imperial Germany the exclusive right to the use of his interrupter gear, and when the War Office let this be known in Parliament, the matter was quickly shelved. Europeans might kill each other with great verve, but they did not steal each other's patents.

With the advent of the Nieuport, they did not have to, and the Fokker scourge was met and mastered at last. By early 1916 there was some sort of technological equilibrium approaching on the western front. In that year both sides could play, on equal terms, for what were becoming very high stakes indeed.

As early as 1914, in the opening days of the war, the Japanese had employed planes for bombing. Japan was allied with Great Britain, and she immediately declared war on Germany, though in fact the British would have preferred that she remain neutral. Japan had her eye on German possessions in the north Pacific, which she rapidly took over in the first months of the war. One of these was a German naval station and concession on the coast of China, at Tsingtao. Before the station fell to Japanese besiegers on November 7, the attackers had launched the first bombing raids in the Far East.

Russian military aviation remained sparse. In eastern Europe, the front was so long and the conditions so marginal that progress there was much slower than in the west. The one great exception to this was Igor Sikorsky, the recipient of the Tsar's gold watch before the war. The ambitious young Russian thought big, literally, and even before the war he was designing and producing, at the Russo-Baltic Railway Factory, huge multiengined biplanes to carry large payloads and fly long distances. These early experiments resulted in a series of large bombers, known generally as the Ilya Mourometz, after a historic Russian hero. These planes would have astounded westerners who thought they knew everything about aircraft. The Ilya Mourometz V had a wingspan of very close to one hundred feet, could climb to ten thousand feet, and, most important of all, could carry a crew of several men and half a ton of bombs. By the end of 1914, the Russians had established bombing squadrons which attacked East Prussia, and they continued this until the Revolution in 1917.

The year 1915 was an experimental one for the naval air services as well as the army, and was marked by a couple of small successes and a couple of larger failures. Just as on land, the problems concerned equipment and technique, because everything had to be worked out for the first time.

The raid against Cuxhaven touched off German retaliation, and in the new year the kaiser authorized the opening of Zeppelin attacks on England, carefully specifying, of course, that these were to be carried out only against military targets. As the Royal Naval Air Service was responsible for coastal defense, it fell to them to intercept the monsters and stop them. This proved very difficult to do; the Zeppelins were not fast but they flew high, and the weaponry and planes available to the RNAS were no better than those of the RFC.

The first successful raid, if it could be called that, was made on January 19, 1915. Two Zeppelins got to England; the first bombed Great Yarmouth, a small fishing town, and the second, after flying over the royal estate at Sandringham, dropped several bombs on the town of King's Lynn. There was no blackout in England, so the Germans were able to navigate without too much difficulty. In this first raid they managed to kill five civilians, including a young boy, wound several others, and demolish a row of cottages.

It took the navy six months to catch one of the dirigibles, and then they did so largely by luck. They were in fact up against tremendous odds. Their fighters were poorly armed, the Zeppelins had a higher ceiling than the airplanes, and by dropping ballast they could climb roughly three times as fast. The pilots had no navigational instruments, indeed hardly any instruments at all, and when a Zeppelin was reported they had to take off blindly and hope to spot the enemy somehow against the night sky.

Eventually they decided that the only way to stop the raids was to hit the Zeppelin bases. On the night of June 7, aircraft of No. 1 Squadron, based at Dunkirk, set out to bomb Zeppelin sheds near Brussels. Unknown to them, there was a raid scheduled for the same night, but the three army Zeppelins involved all had engine trouble and had to turn back to base. Thus, over Ostende, Sublieutenant R. A. Warneford, flying a Morane-Saulnier parasol monoplane and carrying his maximum load of six twenty-pound bombs, sighted LZ37 heading east. The Morane was barely limping along, and with the extra weight of the bombs it could hardly climb at all. Nonetheless, Warneford started stalking the Zeppelin, hoping it would not spot him and immediately climb above him.

The Germans, limping for home, were too busy listening to their unhealthy engines to bother about much else. Gradually they lost height as they moved east over the Belgian countryside. Swooping down from above and behind, Warneford made his first pass; he was spotted by gunners at machine-gun positions on top of the Zeppelin—where the view was matched only by the cold—and driven off. The ship began running for home, but Warneford kept his height. He came back for another try, took the Morane straight over the top of the Zeppelin, one hundred fifty feet above it, and pulled the toggle switch to release all six of his bombs. Five missed, one hit, there was a blinding flash as several thousand cubic feet of hydrogen ignited, the little plane was flipped over on its back, and Warneford, hanging upside down by his seat strap, watched the flaming mass plunge to the ground. Tragically, it landed on a convent and orphanage outside Ghent.

Warneford was an immediate hero, and received an instant Victoria Cross from the King himself. Ten days later he was dead; he had taken a passenger in a flight over Paris, the plane flipped over in a tight turn, neither man was strapped in, and both fell to their deaths. The Zeppelin raids continued.

Meanwhile, a strange and long-playing drama was taking place in Africa. In early October 1914 the Royal Navy had chased the German light cruiser *Konigsberg* into the mouth of the Rufiji River in German East Africa, and, having bottled her up there in the midst of uncounted and unknown channels, could neither get at her nor dared leave her alone. The British decided on aerial reconnaissance, and they comandeered a leaky Curtiss flying boat and its pilot in Durban. The plane was in very poor repair, but its pilot, H. D. Cutler, not entirely enjoying his new status as a temporary officer of His Majesty's Navy, agreed to look for the Germans, and his plane was taken by steamer up the coast. On his first flight Cutler could not find the river and was forced down on a deserted island, where he was providentially found by British searchers. On his second flight he not only found the river, he found the *Konigsberg* as well, but when he reported that she was anchored twelve miles upstream, the British would not believe him; they insisted the river was too shallow and the ship too big to get that far up.

Finally the flying boat was sufficiently repaired to be able to carry an observer. A third flight with a naval officer aboard confirmed that, yes indeed, the ship *was* twelve miles upriver, just as Cutler had said. Then bad weather set in; when it cleared, the navy wanted to be sure its bird was still in the nest. Cutler went out for a fourth time, had engine trouble, and was forced down and captured by the Germans. A British rescue party succeeded only in burning the abandoned airplane.

Ten weeks later the Admiralty managed, by straining every resource, to get two Sopwith seaplanes out to East Africa. These were uncrated and assembled; one immediately crashed and the second proved totally unreliable in the tropical conditions. Another two months passed. It was now April 1915, and the British got three more aircraft out, Short seaplanes this time. These were good enough to fly, and the British once again found the *Konigsberg* and took pictures of her. The Shorts were not strong enough, however, to carry any bombs, and finally, in June, after they had captured a nearby island, the British sent out some monitors and some landplanes equipped with radios. At last they were ready for business. Or almost ready for business; of the four airplanes, two were useless. By the time they were uncrated, the tropics had so warped and unglued them that they were total write-offs. The other two were patched together, and after the monitors were in position, on July 5, the operation got underway. The *Konigsberg* had now been up the river for ten months.

It took two days of intense bombardment before the Germans finally gave up. The British enjoyed the services of their two aircraft, spotting from the air and correcting the fall of shot, but the Germans had observers along the banks of the river, so their fire was for some time even more accurate than that of the British. On the second day they also succeeded in shooting down one of the aircraft, whose observer kept on correcting fall of shot even as the plane was gliding down to ditch as close to the British as possible. Both of the crew were rescued, and subsequently given Distinguished Service Orders. The other airplane finished the spotting, but then crashed on landing and had to be written off. But at last, so was the *Konigsberg*.

This was really a minor overseas operation, important less for what it actually accomplished than for illustrating the immense difficulties of distant campaigns with marginal material. Every one of the planes involved in it, most of them brought all the way from England, were destroyed, largely by the adverse conditions they faced rather than by the enemy.

A much more important and far less successful operation in 1915 was the ill-starred Dardanelles campaign. Conceived as a way of bringing aid to Russia and then knocking Turkey out of the war, this was a huge improvisation in which almost nothing was planned and everything went wrong. At first it was to be solely a naval show, forcing the straits of the Dardanelles; when that failed the army was committed to a landing on the Gallipoli peninsula, where they bogged down and stuck for several months until finally evacuated at the turn of the year. The contribution of aircraft to this was meager but of interest, for again it marked a new departure.

The navy sent out a seaplane carrier, the *Ark Royal,* and a contingent of six seaplanes, to spot for the naval bombardment. However, as the *Ark Royal* was a converted tramp steamer with a top speed of ten knots, she could never work up sufficient way to permit the underpowered seaplanes to fly off her short launching deck. And as the sea was rough during the bombardment stage, she could not lift the seaplanes over the side to fly off the water. It was largely an exercise in futility.

During the later land campaign, the RNAS set up an airfield on the island of Tenedos, a few miles off from Gallipoli, and from here the ubiquitous Commander Samson, last seen chasing around Belgium in his armored car, undertook bombing raids against the Turks. By his own admission he never hit anything, "but it was good practice." The British then sent out another seaplane carrier, HMS *Ben-My-Chree,* and a new batch of seaplanes, Short 225s. In August they scored another first. Flight Commander C. H. Edmonds managed, by dint of flying alone and with only forty-five minutes' fuel, to get one of these into the air with an eight-hundred-pound torpedo hanging between its floats. The Short was a good aircraft, in spite of a rather ungainly appearance, and it actually made the reputation of its manufacturers. Edmonds could get his plane up to only eight hundred feet with its immense load, but he headed for Gallipoli, and off Injeh Burnu he sighted and torpedoed a stationary Turkish supply ship, the first ever aerial torpedoing of a vessel.

The accomplishment was slightly marred by the fact that the ship had already been sunk, as it were, hit earlier by the British sub E14; she was stationary because she had been beached in shallow water and abandoned. Nonetheless, it was a feat just to have carried and launched a torpedo, and the same day another pilot, Lieutenant Dacre, succeeded in torpedoing a Turkish tugboat, so this one day saw the only two effective torpedo plane attacks of the war.

The navy, like the armies, was having its troubles. Seaplanes were just too underpowered to be of much use, and too dependent upon the state of the weather, which at sea is usually not good. Flight decks were too short; ships could not work up sufficient speed for flying off planes. One experiment featured land planes flying off a barge towed at thirty knots behind a destroyer; once the plane was up, the pilot had to hope he could complete his mission and make it to land. Otherwise he was in for a ditching, a loss of his airplane, and quite possibly drowning. It was all very frustrating.

IV

FIGHTING
FOR THE SKY

By the middle years of the war, the fliers and the men who directed them were caught in the "build a better mousetrap" syndrome that has typified western industrial society. The machines, the organization, the tactics, and the techniques they possessed at any given time enabled them to perform at a certain level. Performance at that level solved some problems but created other ones; each solution called forth its own antithesis. Each time they responded to one problem, they were met with a new one. The new problems demanded new machines, new organizations, new tactics, and new techniques. The spiral of development and demand thus begun has continued until the present, and has never been, and indeed perhaps should never be, escaped. In the course of one lifetime it has taken man from Kitty Hawk to the moon, from the steam age to the space age. Paradoxically, it has along the way created the weapons that may take him back to the stone age. With every advance there is the danger of equal regression.

By the end of 1915, with the Eindekker, the Fee, and the Nieuport

Baby, real war in the air was possible. It was a hazardous, groping kind of war, ill-directed and loosely connected with the great struggle going on below it. Nonetheless, leaders could now glimpse, however dimly, some coherence to aerial fighting. Most important, they could now observe the enemy and figure out what he was up to. The other side of the hill was no longer hidden. With the new techniques of aerial photography and interpretation, the enemy's secrets were there for all to read. The Great War was an all-consuming monster, and it devoured huge masses of both men and material. If an army was planning an attack, the preparations were so enormous that they were almost impossible to hide. Gun and tank parks, cavalry lines, ammunition dumps, supply bases, all these told their stories to the high-flying spies.

The passive answers to this were camouflage, moving at night, and dispersal by day. But these were difficult to achieve, and passive answers were not enough. The active answer was to destroy the enemy's reconnaissance aircraft and keep him from entering the area of activity. This was of course difficult to do; there was a great deal of airspace out there, and no matter how good the interceptor aircraft were, they still depended upon the pilot to be in the right place at the right time and to be able to spot and kill his victim. It was a very chancy business, but by 1916 it had become well worth the effort, and that in itself was a measure of how far the airmen had progressed in a little more than a year.

Both the Allies and the Germans were planning massive, war-winning offensives on the western front for early 1916. The Chief of the German General Staff, General Erich von Falkenhayn, had concluded that the war was now one of attrition, and to win it he proposed to attack the French in a spot they would be compelled by their honor and pride to defend. He believed that he could thus draw them into a killing machine in which he could inflict more losses on France than she could afford. In his own words, he intended "to bleed France white," and as his chosen ground he picked the great fortress of Verdun.

In the past, German preparations for offensives had always been telegraphed to the Allies; this time, they took great pains to ensure secrecy. Some of these were the standard deception plans of any war—elaborate preparations for attacks that did not come, spoiling feeler attacks in various sectors of the line, the spreading of confusing rumors. But there were also new procedures related specifically to, or because of, the new factor of air war. A German artist named Franz Marc was hired to design and paint camouflage nets to hang over hidden gun positions; immense strips of painted canvas were draped over whole roads so that traffic could proceed under cover. The twelve hundred guns used for the bombardment were brought up at night, hastily dug in and camouflaged, and not allowed even to register on their targets until the battle began. Most important of all, great underground galleries were burrowed out, and the assaulting troops occupied them by night, where they remained without, the Germans thought, giving the game away to the French. All these precautions testified to the growing importance of aircraft.

That was all passive. But when Oswald Boelcke and Jasta 2 were transferred from the British front down to Verdun, that was more active. For the first time in war, the Germans were organizing an aerial fleet to attempt command of the air. They were still feeling their way, and they went about it in a fashion that many would consider incorrect, but it was still a significant innovation. The Germans concentrated more than one hundred fifty aircraft around Verdun, as well as tethered observation balloons. They then set up a patrol line over the front, the aerial equivalent of the artillery's box barrage, in effect attempting to prevent any penetration by the French of the airspace over the sector. The French took tremendous losses trying to get past the German lines to see what was going on, and German scores mounted rapidly as, day after day, the all but defenceless Farmans and Voisins came up to be shot down by the Fokkers and the newer Halberstadts. Meanwhile, German reconnaissance of the French lines reported that the enemy was making no preparations at all to receive a major attack; the patrols were working and the French were being halted in the air.

This was in fact not correct. In spite of their heavy losses, French planes were getting through the German screen and bringing back reports of heavy concentrations and preattack buildup. The sad thing for them was that their information, achieved at such tragic cost, was disbelieved by the French authorities. Everyone knew that Verdun was a quiet sector of little military value; everyone knew that the Germans would not launch a great attack when it was still winter; everyone—except the fliers who were dying to get it—knew that the material brought back from aerial reconnaissance was worthless. This was the real reason why the Germans thought their new patrols were so successful.

Then, in February, the attack opened; the Germans achieved their surprise, made impressive gains, and were stopped only by the utter and incredibly costly determination of the French that "they shall not pass." General Henri Pétain, a defensive specialist, was sent to organize and command the Verdun sector, and under his phlegmatic but inspiring leadership, the French held on to their last lines around the town. Supplies and men proceeded endlessly up "the sacred way," and the battle, lasting ten months, not only bled France white, as von Falkenhayn had intended, it bled Germany white too, which was not at all what he had in mind.

The German air force contributed less to the attack than it had to its preparation, for the French air service, once its morale had recovered from the losses and the disbelief of the early stages, came back strongly. Way back in 1915, the air service had been again reorganized; to observation, bombing, and reconnaissance had been added a fourth section, *chasse,* hunting or fighting, but no one had done a great deal about it. Now the leader of the service, Commandant Jean du Peuty, organized for the first time separate *escadrilles de chasse,* or all-fighter squadrons, and he threw these into the battle against the Germans. The idea was not his but that of the British, and especially of Hugh Trenchard, now a major general instead of just a major, and commander since August 1915 of the Royal Flying Corps in France. Determinedly aggressive and offensive-minded, Trenchard had insisted that the battle must be carried to the enemy. If the Allied equipment was habitually inferior, if the wind constantly favored the Germans, none of that mattered; the British must fly offensively, replacements must appear immediately, and there must be no empty seats in the squadron messes at breakfast.

The hardest task of a commander is to accept the fact that some of his own men must be killed to carry out a given order, and Trenchard, who was by no means an unfeeling man, accepted it with a forthrightness that often appeared brutal. He also convinced du Peuty that it was the only way to fight. Reluctantly at first, the French grouped their fighters together, left their observation planes to take care of themselves, and went looking for trouble. By late summer their Nieuport 11's and the even better 17's were joined by another of the war's great fighters, the Spad VII, a true classic that was a far cry from the notorious A2, and the days of the Fokker scourge were long over. German soldiers around Verdun were cursing their own air service and shooting at any planes they saw, because they were almost certain to be French rather than German.

Meanwhile, 125 miles northwest of Verdun, Trenchard got a chance to put his ideas into practice for himself. On July 1, 1916, the Allies launched their own offensive on the Somme River.

The Battle of the Somme, which raged from July to November 1916, was conceived as the great Allied blow for the year. The Somme itself is a small, sluggish stream halfway between Paris and the Belgian border. It was of absolutely no military significance whatsoever, and was chosen as a battle site because it happened to be where the French and British sectors of the front joined. In that sense it was much like Verdun: as good a place to kill the enemy as any. Between the conception and execution of the battle the Germans opened their own drive on Verdun, and therefore as the spring wore on, the forthcoming Somme offensive became increasingly British in tone. When the battle was actually fought it was about three-quarters British, with French support on the right flank.

By observing and arguing with the French, the British had learned a good deal from Verdun. Trenchard and du Peuty were actually good friends, and shared knowledge and ideas more openly than was often the case among the Allies. Trenchard immediately liked the idea of dominating the battlefield—the South African War had taught him all the benefits of taking the high ground—but as he had repeatedly insisted to the French, he thought that both they and the Germans had gone about it mistakenly. The way to dominate the air space over the battle was not to patrol lines, but to go after the enemy and knock him out of the sky. Trenchard was often wrong, in his policies and even in his attitudes, but this time he was right, however much it might cost. It was a lesson still being learned in 1944.

In the spring of 1916 it was more the British than the Germans who were being knocked out of the sky. The RFC lost a plane a day from January through June, and usually lost the crew along with it. The steady drain from accidents and enemy action continued unceasingly. But the RFC was growing at the same time, and by July its strength was double what it had been a year earlier. There were 26 squadrons in France; most of them were still observation squadrons, with mixed types of aircraft. Trenchard wanted bigger squadrons as well as more of them, and he gradually built up to 18 planes per squadron. By the time the Somme began, each of Field Marshal Sir Douglas Haig's four armies in the BEF had an RFC brigade attached, and each brigade had a wing of fighters and a wing of observation planes. The number of squadrons, planes in squadrons, and types of planes still varied considerably. The Fourth British Army, which bore the main brunt of the attack, had 105 planes in support of it.

To fight the Germans, Trenchard used his planes unsparingly. In the week before the great attack began, he sent them after the German artillery observation balloons and pretty much cleared them out of the sky. On July 1, the day the attack jumped off, the planes were up, bombing as best they could, observing for the artillery, signaling the progress of the advance, and looking for trouble. The Germans appeared reluctant to join battle in the air.

On the ground it was different, and the first day on the Somme has gone down in history as one of the worst blows British arms ever experienced. The attack was an utter shambles, and in the first eight hours of it the British suffered 57,470 casualties, of which nearly 20,000 were killed. Confusion was so great, and communications so poor, that they actually believed they had had a substantial victory, and cherishing that delusion, Haig kept on with the battle for the next four and a half months. By the time it burned down for lack of fuel, the British had used up more than 400,000 men, the French another 250,000 and the Germans better than 500,000 stopping both of them.

The battle, designed to be a substantial breakthrough, thus degenerated into yet another of the endless series of battles of attrition that characterized this worst of modern wars. Far from altering this dismal prospect, the airplane simply joined in with it, for Trenchard was an absolutely loyal believer in Douglas Haig, and just as the infantry kept banging their heads against the wall, so did the RFC. Day after day the planes flew, and when the Germans did finally come up to fight, there were bitter losses on both sides. The Fees and D. H. 2's were equal to the Fokker, and soon evened scores with that particular beast, but the B. E. 2c, which was all the RFC had for bombing, was as bad as ever. To carry bombs at all, the pilots had to fly alone, lacking even the pitiful protection that their gunners had provided, and they took frightful casualties. The pilots and observers were flying six and eight hours a day, day after day in the good summer weather, and the turnover rate was appalling. In the course of the battle the RFC had more than five hundred casualties among their aircrew, well over 100 percent of their strength in June.

Trenchard rigidly adhered to his policy that the planes fly all the time, that losses be immediately replaced, and that there be no flagging. No more than any officer on the ground did he recognize the cumulative effects of stress, fatigue, and fear. The Great War simply did not acknowledge these factors; a man must either "show blood" or he was fit to fight. Some of his men thought he should be nicknamed "Butcher" rather than "Boom," and called him that among themselves. In August, one of his squadron commanders, Hugh Dowding, "Stuffy" to his friends, went to see Trenchard and told him the aircrew simply had to have some relief; he suggested rotating the squadrons in and out of the line, as Pétain had done with his infantry at Verdun. Trenchard was skeptical, but he could not avoid the simple arithmetic of the matter and eventually agreed.

Twenty-four years later, Dowding commanded RAF Fighter Command during the Battle of Britain, but Trenchard, after their interview in 1916, characterized him as a "dismal Jimmy," and it took the younger man ten years to get back in his chief's good graces. There was to be no pessimism in the RFC. Trenchard knew his policy was correct, and knowing that, he refused to acknowledge that he might destroy his force because it lacked the strength and equipment to realize the policy.

Both sides were exhausted by the fall of 1916, after the horrors of Verdun and the Somme. Equilibrium had been regained. The Nieuports, D. H. 2's, and Spads had mastered the Fokker Eindekker, and, in the air as on the ground, they were back where they had started. There had been significant innovations, of material, tactics, and organization, but as both sides had made them, they canceled out. They were now, with much more sophistication than they had possessed a year ago, still fighting for mastery of the air. By the end of 1916, as the new German Albatross fighters appeared, they were ready for another round all over again. Late 1915 and early 1916 had brought the Fokker scourge; early 1917 brought Manfred von Richthofen to the peak of his fame—it brought "Bloody April."

In 1917, air fighting and the aces reached their zenith. That was the year when the largest number of good fighters were introduced.

The British brought out the Sopwith Triplane and Camel, and then the Royal Aircraft Factory's S. E. 5. The French upgraded both the Nieuport and especially the Spad, and the Germans introduced the Albatross D. III and the Fokker Triplane, more or less a copy of the Sopwith "Tripe." Any one of these was a great airplane, and some were greater than others. The Camel, for example, shot down more enemy planes than any other single British type during the war.

It was a fairly conventional little airplane, but its performance showed how far aircraft development had progressed in a few short months. It had a ceiling of 24,000 feet, a maximum speed of 118 miles per hour, a good rate of climb, and two synchronized machine guns. The guns were mounted in a small humped fairing above the engine and ahead of the pilot, and the hump was responsible for the official name of Camel. It was a deadly fighter and was indeed very hard to handle, being a veteran's delight and a novice's nightmare, having a sharp turn and a potentially vicious spin. Some writers say it was the most maneuverable airplane ever built, and those who hated it on the first flight, if they lived through it, blessed it in combat. But the Camel did not appear until July 1917; for the months before that the skies belonged to the Germans.

Just as the name of Boelcke was synonymous with the early stages of the German air service, so the name of von Richthofen came to symbolize that force's greatest period. Indeed, he became a symbol of Germany as a whole to the extent that, a half century later, his is perhaps the one name from the Great War that has instant public recognition.

A somewhat contradictory character, von Richthofen has been described as a ruthless killer, a glory-hungry souvenir hunter, an inspiring leader, a devoted son, and, occasionally, a warm human being. He may or may not have been all or any of these things. What mattered was that he was, at least by his score, the best fighter pilot of World War I. He was officially credited with shooting down eighty Allied planes, though there is still argument among aviation buffs as to whether this represents a correct score. Some authorities reject one claim but advance another, and so on and so forth.

His aerial career began slowly. Born in Silesia in 1892, he was destined for the army from childhood, and entered a cadet school at the age of eleven. When the war came, he was a lieutenant of lancers. In those hazy prewar days, the prestige of a unit was often indicated by the length of its name; von Richthofen's was *Ulanen-Regiment Konig Alexander III von Russland (West Preussisches) No. 1.* As a good horseman and a prodigious hunter, he was in his element. The uhlans took part in the invasion of France, but as soon as the front stabilized, cavalrymen became a glut on the market. Reduced to the indignities of acting as a supply officer, von Richthofen requested a transfer to the air service as an observer. He got his wish in the spring of 1915 and went to the eastern front, where he flew on constant reconnaissance sorties; he was not a pilot, for at this stage pilots were still considered rather an inferior lot. Later in the year he was back on the western front, flying in the ungainly and ineffective bombers attached to the Carrier Pigeon Group at Ostende. In October, quite by chance, he met Oswald Boelcke, and was fascinated to learn that his new acquaintance had already shot down four enemy aircraft. Von Richthofen decided that flying a single-seater was the thing for him. He went off to a training unit, and made his final qualifying flight on Christmas Day, 1915, a studious and careful, but not a natural, pilot.

Von Richthofen returned to the western front in March 1916, near Verdun, and began flying two-seater Albatross biplanes. This machine was still far from a fighter, but the young enthusiast mounted a second machine gun above his wing so that he and his observer could both fire. On April 26 he shot down a French Nieuport, though as it fell in French territory he did not receive credit for it.

Von Richthofen was back on the eastern front later in the year, bombing and strafing Russians with no particular effect. But while he was there, Boelcke was in the process of convincing the higher command of the air service that it should organize the first fighting squadrons. On a tour of the Russian front, Boelcke met and remembered von Richthofen, and in September 1916 the latter was one of the first pilots posted to the newly formed Jasta 2.

The autumn of that year marked the revitalization of the German air effort: new men, new formations, and new planes as well. The jastas were soon equipped with the Albatross fighters, the D. I. and then the D. II, biplanes with in-line engines, not as agile as the Fokkers, but faster, stronger, better platforms for their two machine guns. Boelcke, the instigator of most of this, also introduced the new tactics to go with it—the swarm of fighters, the careful stalk for position, the approach from the sun, all drummed in with the aphorisms that pilots have been learning ever since.

Dividends soon began to come in. Commanding Jasta 2, Boelcke took his pupils out on September 17. Over the railroad yards at Marcoing they jumped a flight of British bombers and fighter escorts, and shot down an incredible eight planes. It was a disaster for the British and a glorious vindication of the Germans for their new ideas. Von Richthofen got his first official kill; and he nearly wrecked his own plane while landing by his victim to claim proof of his victory. From that day through October he averaged one a week.

Von Richthofen was now hot on the trail of Germany's highest decoration, the Pour le Mérite. Immelmann and Boelcke had both received it after eight kills, but the newer pilots were up against grade inflation: So many enemy planes were now being shot down that the Germans decided to double the ante to sixteen kills. Nonetheless, in January 1917, in spite of generally poor flying weather, he got both his medal and command of Jasta 11 at Douai. By now too, he had started painting his plane scarlet, as a personal advertisement; the "Red Baron" had come into his own, commander of men and national hero.

In the later winter of 1916–1917, the Germans added yet another wrinkle to the increasingly sophisticated business of air fighting. They established the *Flugmeldedienst*, an aircraft warning system—observer posts all along the front, connected with a central control. They not only warned of incoming enemy formations, they also recorded and identified downed aircraft. This had effects both before and after the battles: It enabled the Germans to concentrate against Allied attacks and also let the pilots record their own and their unit scores more effectively. As there was great competition between the different jastas, they were soon all adopting variations on the identifying color that von Richthofen had introduced. His jasta used scarlet, Jasta 10 used yellow, Jasta 3 had black and white checks on the fuselages, the members of Jasta 4 adopted a snake motif. The British, in their dull machines, with contempt and perhaps a bit of envy, were soon referring to the German "circuses."

With spring, activity picked up. This was the spring when the Germans were at their height; all along the line they were outclassing the Allies in material and technique. April was the month of the great Canadian victory at Vimy Ridge, but it was also the month when the French army, led once too often to the slaughter, mutinied and refused to advance. It was the month when von Richthofen surpassed the dead Boelcke to become Germany's leading ace; for British aircrew, it was Bloody April.

The wonder is that the British stood to it as well as they did, for in this spring, before the arrival of the Camel and other new types, they were hopelessly outclassed. On April 13 von Richthofen hit three aircraft, and his squadron had thirteen victories for the day. In the morning they had caught a flight of six R. E. 8's, reconnaissance planes from No. 59 Squadron, and shot down all six of them in six minutes. The Red Baron was credited with twenty-one planes that month. Twenty-five of the thirty-eight men in them were killed; most of the others, who were all taken as prisoners, were wounded. At the end of April, von Richthofen had fifty-two victims to his credit. Two months later the Germans took another step forward. They grouped selected jastas into the first Jagdgeschwader, in effect a self-contained fighter wing, with the express purpose of gaining air supremacy over any given area of the front. Von Richthofen was named to command Jagdgeschwader No. 1.

Through the summer the air battles increased in numbers and intensity, but slowly the Allies began to pull even again. The Sopwith Pup appeared, of all world war airplanes perhaps the most delightful to fly; one of its pilots boasted it could turn twice where an Albatross could only turn once. It was followed by the Sopwith Triplane, a new departure. The advantage of the biplane was that it could be stronger than a monoplane, because of the possibilities for bracing between wings, and it did not need as long a wingspan, so it could also be more maneuverable.

Sopwith's designer, Herbert Smith, thought that if the biplane had advantages over the monoplane, then perhaps a triplane would have equal advantages over a biplane. He was right, and his new machine was tested in 1916. At the time, the Royal Flying Corps was getting Spad VII's, and liked them, but the Royal Naval Air Service loved the Tripe, and offered to swap all its Spads for all the RFC's Triplanes. Authority regarded this sort of picking and choosing as rather unorthodox, but finally agreed, and the RNAS went on to make the lovely little triplane peculiarly its own. Its most famous exponents were Naval 8 and Naval 10 Squadrons, and the latter had a "Black flight," the nose of its machines painted black, led by Raymond Collishaw, which knocked down eighty-seven Germans in eight months. With their planes bearing such names as *Black Maria, Black Prince, Black Roger, Black Sheep,* and, most ominous of all, *Black Death,* the flight of five, all Canadians, were perfectly capable of meeting the Germans at their own game.

The Triplane was actually a bit of a fluke, and only about 150 were produced before the advent of the Camel. Nonetheless, they had such an impact that designers went scuttling around trying to imitate or better them. If three wings were better than two, why not four instead of three? Quadraplanes did not work, however, and were soon given up. But no less than fourteen German and Austrian firms tried to produce triplanes of their own, usually simply by sticking a third wing between the two of some already existing biplane. None of these did much, but Fokker's idea worked. He saw the British plane in April 1917, and told his designer, Reinhold Platz, to produce something similar; Platz never saw the Sopwith, and did not care for the idea, but he produced a chunky little fighter with three wings. It was a design marvel. The lower wing was on the bottom of the fuselage, the middle one on the top, and the upper wing was on struts above the fuselage; those were all the struts it had—no interplane struts, no bracing, nothing. When Fokker showed it to the authorities, it scared them silly. They ordered him to put struts on it and make it look respectable. It was slower than the Albatrosses, but more maneuverable. The great German ace Werner Voss flew it and shot down twenty planes in twenty-four days before he himself was shot down and killed. It became von Richthofen's favorite airplane, but, like the Sopwith Triplane, its service life was fairly short. Defective workmanship caused it to shed its wing covering, and few triplanes lasted into 1918. Von Richthofen's was one of them.

With the advent of new Allied aircraft, German dominance began to fade somewhat. Even the great aces were mortal, and accident or the enemy got them somehow. Eighty-one German airmen received the Pour le Mérite during the war, but thirty of them died before it was over, a large number of them in the closing months, as the Allies increasingly achieved supremacy in the air as well as on the ground. But in the summer of 1917 it all still hung in the balance; no one at that point could yet predict how the war was going to end, let alone when.

Von Richthofen's career continued, seemingly unabated. He met the kaiser, he spent time showing an airplane to the empress, and on his occasional leaves he hunted game unceasingly. This sort of leisure activity has led writers to speculate that he was really nothing more than a killing machine, which rather ignores the fact that slaughtering game was simply one of the things that gentlemen of the privileged classes did in those days. All unadmitted, the war and the tension were taking their toll.

In July, von Richthofen was actually shot down, A lucky shot from three hundred yards hit him in the head. He lost consciousness, fell to five hundred feet before recovering, and barely managed to get his plane, an Albatross D. V, down before he passed out again. He spent some time in the hospital, but was back with his *geschwader* by August. From that time on, however, he had occasional but recurrent bouts of nausea and headaches; periodically he was in the hospital, and some who knew him claimed he was never as good after his injury as he had been before it. By the end of the month he was flying his new Fokker triplane.

Whether or not he was now impaired, the score kept mounting. Occasionally members of his jasta would grumble that he was glory-hungry, that he took easy pickings, or that he claimed for himself victories that should have been shared by the squadron. Once he speculated that Boelcke, if he had lived, might have shot down a hundred enemy planes, and said that he would like to do that himself. When Germany opened her last desperate drives for victory, the spring offensives of 1918, it looked as if he might make it. His sixty-third victory had been in November 1917; he got nothing more until March of the new year, but he got eleven in that month, and nine of the eleven were formidable British types, mostly Camels. By April 20 his score had reached eighty. The next day he led his squadron out on a sweep and failed to return. A brief British news release on April 22 reported that he had been shot down and buried with full military honors. Germany was plunged into grief at his death, and there was a great deal of press comment worldwide, almost all of it magnanimous in tone.

Ever since, there has been argument about who actually killed the Red Baron. A Canadian, Captain A. R. Brown of No. 209 Squadron, flying a Sopwith Camel, was officially credited with the victory, but gunners from some Australian units in the area where he crashed insisted that they had hit him from the ground. The most authoritative book on von Richthofen still remains inconclusive on the matter.

Von Richthofen typified the rise and fall of the German air service probably more than any other ace did for his own country. But each of the belligerents had similar figures, whose scores were avidly kept by the public at home and whose accomplishments were recounted by the newspapers. Their color and their daring appeared among the few redemptive features of the unceasingly grim war. This was certainly true of the French, whose attitude was poles apart from that of the British. Where the latter only very reluctantly joined in the game of publicizing individuals, the French pilots were individualism personified. Their three leading aces, Nungesser, Guynemer, and Fonck, were a study in contrasts.

Charles Nungesser was the archetypal daredevil/bad boy. He learned to fly while trying to find an uncle in South America. In 1914 he joined a cavalry regiment but transferred to the air service, a reward for killing some German staff officers and capturing their car. Eventually, at the end of 1915, he ended up flying Nieuports, which he invariably decorated with his own personal emblem—coffin, skull and crossbones, and two candles, all in a black heart. From then until the rest of the war he alternated between air fighting and hospitals, for perhaps fewer men have been hurt or wounded more often in the course of their careers. At one point he could no longer even walk, and had to be carried to and from his plane for his daily patrols. When the war ended he had forty-five confirmed victories; he was the third-highest scoring French ace. He had survived almost everything, but he found it very difficult to survive peace. He toured the United States, barnstorming and giving mock dogfight displays. In 1927 he and a companion attempted a transatlantic flight from France to New York. Their flying boat disappeared and no trace of it was ever found.

Like the Germans, the French adopted the practice of grouping their best pilots together in elite units, in their case the Storks, or *Cigognes;* there were several different squadrons of them in the group, but all bore one or another form of stylized stork on their planes. Georges Guynemer, France's second-highest scoring ace, was probably the most famous of them all. Guynemer was a sickly and frail youth, doted on by his mother and sisters, and he was twice turned down for military service when he tried to volunteer. Eventually he got into the flying service by the mechanics' door, then became a pilot, and in mid-1915 he embarked on his phenomenal career. Shot down seven times, he received twenty-six citations and was a captain at age twenty-two. He had fifty-four German planes to his credit when it was discovered that he was missing. The Germans said he had been brought down by a Lieutenant Wissemann, himself later a victim of René Fonck, but neither his body nor the wreck of his plane were ever found. Exactly what happened to him remains a mystery, and French schoolchildren used to believe the story that he had simply flown so high he never came down. He passed into legend.

The greatest of the French aces, indeed the greatest of the Allied aces, with seventy-five official victories, was René Fonck. Like Guynemer, he was a Stork; like von Richthofen, he was a hunter, More than anyone, he was a marksman, and he used to say that he placed each bullet as if by hand. In his most famous demonstration of his skill, he once shot down three Germans in ten seconds, using no more than half a dozen bullets in one short burst for each.

Fonck's career was much like that of his contemporaries: an early interest in aviation, followed by frustration with war as it was waged in 1914. He spent his first few months of military service as an engineer, building bridges and digging trenches. Finally he wangled a transfer to the air service. By late 1915 he was flying observation missions, and it was not until the middle of the next year that he flew fighters, or what passed for them in the French service at that point; in his case it was a two-seat, twin-engine, Caudron G. 4 biplane, which looked much like a bathtub suspended in the middle of a flying bird-cage. Eventually his skill with this unlikely machine won him transfer to a single-seater outfit, and he joined the Stork group in the spring of 1917.

From then on there was no stopping him. The Storks were transferred here and there along the front, much as the German circuses were on the other side. Fonck's score mounted regularly as he practiced one of his favorite tricks: getting high up well inside the enemy lines, then come screaming down on a flight of unwary Germans, catch one on the first pass and break up their formation, and then systematically go to work on the rest. He repeatedly made multiple scores, and on two particular days, May 9 and September 26 of 1918, he shot down six planes in one day.

Unlike so many of his comrades, Fonck lived through the war, and even managed to adjust to peace. He got involved in the transatlantic flight race, and was on the verge of an attempt when Lindbergh beat him to it. Later he was Inspector General of Fighter Aviation for the French air force, after which he lived in Paris until his death in 1953.

The French government saw the utility of making heroes of its aces; the British aces became heroes in spite of their government. The British armed services took the view summed up in Nelson's famous signal at Trafalgar: England expects every man will do his duty. Not only that, they expected that every man would do his duty in the station

71

in life to which he had been called. This was a laudable sentiment, as it meant that the poorest miserable private suffering in the mud was making his contribution just as much as the admiral on his battleship or the pilot in his S. E. 5. But it was not very exciting for a civilian public that had been brought up on tales of the thin red line, fighting the Fuzzy-Wuzzy, and The Last Eleven at Maiwand. Journalists wanted color, the public wanted heroes, and so, with greater reluctance and less flamboyance than their French allies or German enemies, British aces too became well-known names.

The sixty-five men of the Royal Flying Corps, Royal Naval Air Service, or later Royal Air Force, who shot down twenty or more enemy planes during the war were a cosmopolitan group. There was a South African and four Australians, two were American, nine were Canadians, and the rest were from Britain itself.

The highest scoring of them all, Major Edward "Mick" Mannock, was officially listed with seventy-three victories. This was almost certainly undercounted, for, unlike von Richthofen, he regularly gave credit to his squadron for their work, and often allowed newer pilots to gain experience by administering a coup de grâce and receiving credit for a victory. His career was relatively short. He was not in good health, he had a bad eye, surprising for a fighter pilot, and he did not even get to France to fly until Bloody April, which as a new boy he was lucky to survive. But he was a fierce, intense man who fought his war with a personal hatred of the enemy, perhaps because he had been temporarily interned in Turkey at the start of it, and he was constantly out for blood. He was essentially a team man, and has been called the best patrol leader of the war as well as "the King of The Air Fighters" (also the title of his biography), but the team's job was to kill what Mannock called the "German vermin." Inevitably, the fighting told on his nerves, as it did on everyone's, and he became obsessed with the fear of being burned alive. Tragically, that may well be what happened to him. On July 26, 1918, in an episode that is still somewhat obscure, his S. E. 5 was apparently hit in the gas tank by a bullet from the ground while he was flying low over the trenches. Flames licked out of the engine, Mannock was seen to slump in the cockpit, and the plane crashed into the ground and exploded. Mannock was too low to have done anything to escape, although he may have had time to shoot himself with the revolver he was always careful to carry with him. For the remaining four months of the war, British pilots diligently sought, and largely achieved, a personal vendetta against the Germans on his behalf.

The greatest surviving British ace was the Canadian, Billy Bishop. He transferred to the RFC from the Canadian Mounted Rifles in July 1915, but it was March 1917 before he actually got to fly in a fighter. He shot down seventy German aircraft, and he may well have been the greatest pilot and dogfighter in the war, for he did it in a remarkably short space of time. He had only about ten months in actual fighter combat, but during those ten months he flew as much as seven or eight hours a day. He was basically a loner, and though promoted to command a squadron in 1918, he preferred to be on his own. His was the solitary stalk, the sudden attack. In one twelve-day period he brought down twenty-five aircraft. Between flying tours the government used him to foster recruiting in Canada, and King George V told him that he was the only man on whom he had pinned the Victoria Cross, the Distinguished Service Order, and the Military Cross at the same time. Bishop survived the war, took up commercial aircraft in Canada between wars, and was an air marshal in World War II. He died in 1956.

The men who lived to be aces, by the very nature of their talents, lasted longer than a lot of young airmen. One of the shortest careers on record is of a new German pilot who arrived at his first posting while an air raid was in progress; he climbed into a plane, tried to take off, and was shot down and killed just as his wheels lifted off the runway, a career lasting perhaps ten minutes. In aerial as in land combat, the first days were the most dangerous.

But even those who became veterans were hardly old men; they just looked old. Mannock was an ancient man of thirty-one when he died, von Richthofen was twenty-six, Immelmann and Boelcke were both twenty-five, McCudden was twenty-three, Guynemer was twenty-two, the American Frank Luke was twenty-one, and Albert Ball, England's first popular hero, died three months after his twenty-first birthday. They were like Rupert Brooke, who in 1914 had written, "Now, God be thanked, Who has matched us with His hour," and was dead at the Dardanelles nine months later.

What these young men had done, however, besides leaving their names and stories inextricably linked with the new element, was to alter the uses and needs of air warfare, and air power, for the perceptible future. A decade earlier, indeed a few short months before the first of them launched their careers, no one had conceived of really fighting in the air itself. The air was a medium, and airplanes were a vehicle for navigating through that medium. By so doing, one could achieve certain things, and from the beginning of flight these things had been foreseen by prescient fliers. The airplane was useful for reconnaissance and observation, for communications purposes, and it might have been of some use in carrying bombs, small and inaccurate though they necessarily were. But that was all. No one had yet realized that the airplane must inevitably create its own nemesis in the form of other airplanes designed to destroy it.

The new system was so successful that it bred its own reaction. Few of the poeple who flew these planes, and even few of those who organized and ran the air services, saw the issue in these Hegelian terms. They were problem solvers rather than philosophers, and their problem in this instance was how to prevent the enemy's reconnaissance and observation aircraft from seeing what they themselves were doing, or, conversely, how they themselves could see what the enemy was doing. So they "invented" the fighter, and while they did so, they also developed the doctrine of how to use it.

In doing that they automatically thought, as all men do, in terms with which they were already familiar. The German patrol system over Verdun was the airborne equivalent of the artillery's box barrage, and the British drive for command of the air over the Somme was a fairly conscious parallel with the time-honored British idea of command of the sea. Many of air warfare's early ideas, and its terminology, were borrowed from the sailors, for just as sailors went about their business in a foreign element, so did fliers. From the earliest ballooning days, fliers referred to themselves as aeronauts, and airplanes did not have left and right sides, but rather port and starboard sides. Just as command of the sea was defined as keeping it clear for your own purposes and denying it to the enemy for his purposes, so was command of the air. When Trenchard sent his planes intruding over German territory, trying to dominate the Somme valley by dominating the space over German airfields, he was practicing exactly what the Royal Navy had always done during the close blockade in the days of sail. To command the sea, a navy began at the enemy's shoreline. To command the air, an airforce began at the enemy's airbases. It was a costly policy in the short run, but, if successfully pursued, it was a rewarding one in the long run.

The fighters of World War I were up against incredible technological limitations. Even the best of their aircraft were inadequate for any fully developed theory of command of the air; all they could hope for was temporary dominance over a small tactical area, and even that was extraordinarily costly. It would take another generation of men, and a couple of generations of machines, before it was possible to achieve thorough command of the air. But these newly invented fighters, and the men who flew them, were a means by which that end might someday be attained.

V

LEARNING ABOUT BOMBING

Oswald Boelcke, at the height of his fame, had produced a humorous set of answers to questions often asked by newsmen; passing a sheet around at the start of an interview saved him a lot of bother. Two of the answers concerned bombing: "Yes, we have dropped bombs," and "Yes, an old woman was supposed to have been injured, and we scared some transport columns." However devastating aerial bombing might be, and its protagonists would proclaim its value in glowing terms, a man such as Boelcke was not very impressed with it. Even before the war, futuristic writers had had a sure market for stories predicting death and destruction from the sky. The reading public thrilled with horror at the thought of armadas of invulnerable Zeppelins sailing serenely overhead, dropping tons of bombs on their innocent victims. When war actually came, and the Zeppelins came along with it, they did not do a great deal of damage, but they did have an inordinate effect on people who had habitually regarded war as something visited upon someone else.

Ideas of war were, as they always are, ill defined and even remarkably confused. Ever since the establishment of professional armies in the seventeenth century, the tendency had been to attempt to confine war's effects to its actual participants, and to separate the soldier from the civilian. Frederick the Great said that a good war was one the civilian population was totally unaware of, one that was fought solely by the military forces without interfering with the productive classes of the state.

Such an ideal was inevitably more often proclaimed than achieved, but the eighteenth and early nineteenth centuries did their best to adhere to it. By the later nineteenth century, the trend began to move back the other way. In the American Civil War and the Franco-Prussian War there were the first real glimmerings of war not solely against the political entity of the enemy but against his whole society. Sherman's march to the sea in Georgia, Sheridan's ravaging of the Shenandoah Valley of Virginia, the Prussians' siege of Paris and its large civilian population—these presaged a new type of war. After all, if civilians insisted on acting as if they were at war, which under the influence of nationalism they did, they must expect to pay the consequences. At the turn of the century there was an attempt to stop this growth, and a series of conventions produced rules for the conduct of war. Among others, the sinking of merchant ships without warning or proper provision for crews and passengers was outlawed, and the bombardment of unfortified places was strictly prohibited.

Society's attempts to impose rational limits on the irrationality of violence quickly went into the discard pile. Submarines were soon sinking merchantmen, and long-range artillery began bombarding unfortified places the minute military men perceived the necessity of doing so. In this latter situation, aerial craft were simply delivery systems; indeed, the first bombs dropped by Zeppelins were not bombs at all: They were artillery shells. In the fashion of the tail on the kite, the Germans tied army blankets on the butt end of the shells in the hope that this would make them fall straighter.

During the course of the war, the Germans dropped some 9,000 bombs on England, totaling about 280 tons. In just over 100 raids, they killed about 1,400 people and wounded 3,400 more, and they did £3 million of damage in four years. The historian Robin Higham has pointed out that this was not a great deal when compared with the fact that rats in Britain did an estimated £70 million of damage each year. The effect of the German effort then, as indeed of the entire bombing campaign of all the belligerents, was far more psychological than it was physical. But to a generation unused to war firsthand, that psychological shock was a great one indeed. An indication of public attitudes was the near-hysterical relief that greeted Lieutenant Warneford's bombing of the first Zeppelin to be destroyed.

In fact, though the Germans achieved little in material terms by the Zeppelin attacks, they did have a disproportionate influence in Britain. They caused the British to keep planes and men home from France and from other theaters, and eventually, after the Zeppelin campaign had given way to bombing by aircraft, the government took the defense of Britain away from the Royal Navy and gave it to the War Office and the army. That was really only an expression of frustration, for the army was no more successful in stopping the intruders than the Royal Navy had been.

By the fall of 1915, the Germans were regularly attempting Zeppelin raids over England, and the German army and navy were engaged in a somewhat unseemly rivalry to see which could do more damage and garner more publicity. They got more of the latter than they did of the former. They could rarely reach London and often they could not find it. They hit several small towns along the east coast, and in at least one case a naval Zeppelin commander bombed Dover under the impression that it was Harwich, sixty miles to the north. The winds that habitually favored German fighters on the western front were at the same time constantly against the airships, and the huge machines were far less easy to maneuver than a gullible public thought. Another factor against the Zeppelins was that the British began to install antiaircraft guns. Though they were not very effective, this meant yet another hazard to contend with, and there was no question but that British defenses did gradually get better.

This was essentially the work of Admiral Sir Percy Scott, the Royal Navy's greatest gunnery expert. He was also something of a political adept, and had been around long enough to know whom to touch to get what he wanted, especially when it was a matter of the government's being seen to protect its citizens. New gun batteries were installed around London, new searchlights appeared, and Scott even mounted several French-designed cannons on truckbeds, their crews roaring about the London area, banging off at Zeppelins during the fall nights of 1915. Scott was no conservative, and even though he was a gunnery specialist he also wanted more aircraft, and got them, though they were still at the time too underpowered and too ill-armed to be of much use against the Germans.

Both sides were ready for a major test in October 1915. The Germans sent over five airships. Two never found London, two managed to hit the outer suburbs, and one flew directly over the city. Dropping its bombs right on the Admiralty, it hit the theater district in the Strand, a half-mile away. The British shot back with everything they had, and sent up their available airplanes—four B. E. 2's. None of the aircraft saw anything, though a truck-mounted gun did get close enough with its shots to drive one of the Zeppelins off over the suburbs.

In the new year the Germans began ranging a little more widely, hitting targets in the Midlands as well as along the east coast, and continuing to strike at London, where the Lord Mayor offered a prize for the first one brought down. The German navy's Zeppelin commander, Captain Peter Strasser, kept demanding more and better airships, just as his opposite numbers in Britain were demanding more and better equipment to stop him. Both were doomed to frustration, and neither ever got all he asked for. The German Zeppelin campaign peaked that year, with more bombs dropped by airship, about 3,400, than in all the other years of the war put together.

Finally, on September 2, 1916, the British scored back. Lieutenant W. Leefe Robinson, of No. 39 Squadron, flying one of the cumbersome B. E. 2's, caught up with dirigible SL-11. He put three drums of ammunition in it, in his excitement shooting off a good part of his own top wing, and the airship burst into flame and sank to earth in the village of Cuffley. For several days sightseers went out to look at the charred remains of Germans trapped in the melted wreckage while the locals peddled soft drinks and grisly souvenirs.

That was not quite the end of the Zeppelin menace, but strangely enough that one loss, which sent England rejoicing, seemed to take the heart out of the Germans. Earlier airships had been lost to ground fire, and several went down at sea, but SL-11's death appeared particularly horrible, and it had been witnessed by other airship crews. Though Captain Strasser kept on with his campaign, and even speculated about the possibility of bombing New York after the Americans joined the war, the thrill of flying in a flammable bag over England now began to wane.

The Zeppelin raids really represented something of an aberration in the development of aerial warfare. Bombing with airplanes, as opposed to airships, proceeded perfectly logically and in line with the general escalation of wartime attitudes. As soon as the equipment was available to do so, bombing became a natural way to carry the war to the enemy. The Royal Naval Air Service's raids against the Zeppelin bases, the very earliest French bombing attacks on German marshaling and manufacturing areas—these conformed perfectly to the accepted military doctrine of the day: Seize the initiative, hit the enemy wherever possible; the more you disrupt him, the less he will be able to disrupt you.

It is difficult to distinguish in any firm way between the three levels of bombing activity—tactical, strategic, and psychological. Tactical bombing, strictly speaking, would be that carried out directly in support of operations—isolating the battlefield, attacking headquarters and dumps immediately behind the front, or harassing enemy airfields, for instance. Strategic bombing would involve strikes at purely military targets, including ports, factories producing war material, railroad yards—all those elements of the economy directly involved in the war effort. Psychological bombing might be against targets that strictly speaking were not military, but the intent of such attacks was to impede the enemy population's support for the war effort, either by destroying its morale or by making life so miserable that the war could no longer be sustained.

These three different types of bombing all mingled together interchangeably, however, because in practice it was nearly impossible to differentiate between them. The first two were fairly easy to separate, and one might even draw an imaginary line a given number of miles behind the trenches and arbitrarily declare that everything forward of that line was tactical, everything behind it was strategic. On the western front, for example, the main German railroad supply lines ran from Strasbourg–Metz–Sedan–Mézières–Aulnoye to Lille, anywhere from twenty to fifty miles behind the actual front line. So attacks on these centers and forward of them could be regarded as tactical, and anything on the German side as strategic. The demarcation between a strategic and a psychological target was much harder to draw. Throughout both world wars, air forces were extremely reluctant to admit that they were attacking anything other than strategic targets, that is to say, strictly military objectives. But the problems of aerial navigation, of target selection, and of bombing accuracy meant that even if the targets were purely military, the difficulty of hitting them was such that the effect was more often psychological than it was strategic.

The matter was one of both technology and humanity. The shortcomings of technology prevented the airmen from doing accurately what they wanted to do, but their attitudes, as men who believed in their missions, made it almost impossible for them to admit that they were engaged in something different from what they said they were doing. Though the problem became most acute in World War II, with its greater capacity for destruction, it arose, as did most others, in World War I.

Other than the British units aimed at the Zeppelin bases, the French were the first to officially organize bomber squadrons as such. In the early 1915 reorganization, bombing gained recognition as one of the then triad of tasks of the French air service. Their problem, however, like everyone else's, was equipment. Their earliest bombing attacks had been carried out using whatever planes were available. In 1915 they produced the first purpose–built bombers, but they were very marginal. Voisin, Farman, and Caudron all built series of aircraft; the former were not very good, though the Voisin 5 enjoyed some vogue as a ground-attack plane. The Caudron G. 4, however, was a good general-purpose plane, and was used for observation and even, in the hands of a man like Fonck, for air fighting. In British and Italian as well as French service, the Caudrons soldiered on until 1917.

The British needed foreign aircraft, for they were using the ubiquitous—or iniquitous—B. E. 2 as a bomber. The bombing variant was no better than the observation one, but the British had committed themselves to quantity production of it, and though it was inadequate when introduced late in 1914, it continued in squadron service until 1917. The Germans too recognized the need for a bombing aircraft in the opening months of the war, and their first real bomber was an odd looking creature known as the Siemens-Schuckert R. 1. This was a biplane with three engines buried in the fuselage, driving two propellers out between the wings. Its strangest feature, however, was that the tall fuselage was covered in an odd V-shaped pattern back to the tail, so that the airplane looked rather like a winged clothespin. Only seven were built, but this was a large airplane with a respectable performance and payload, in spite of its strange appearance, and it was the forerunner of even bigger and better aircraft.

Bombing was a more prosaic, day-to-day sort of operation than that carried out by the fighters, and the bomber aircrew have never appeared as romantic to writers on the war. It was the knights of the air in their single-seaters who got the headlines and the public acclaim. Bombing was certainly no less dangerous than dogfighting, indeed it may have been more so, but it lacked the panache of the fighters.

By the middle of 1915 the British were regularly bombing behind German lines, and especially trying to hit such crucial targets as the Zeppelin bases and airfields in Belgium. The French began bombing as far as Karlsruhe in the Rhineland, 150 miles inside German-occupied territory. In November they even bombed Munich, 250 miles away, though they got only one plane to fly that far.

The ability to carry out long-distance raids and drop heavy loads of bombs often depended upon nothing more or less than the imagination of aircraft designers, and while the British, French, and Germans were struggling along with the evolutionary process, both the Russians and Italians had made great leaps. Sikorsky's Ilya Mourometz bombers were hard at work on the eastern front; indeed, only one of them was shot down in the whole war. And in Italy a similarly audacious designer, Count Caproni, produced some of the biggest planes of the war.

Originally allied with Germany and Austria-Hungary, Italy announced its neutrality at the start of the war. Then, after enormous public argument, the government joined on the side of the Allies in May 1915. As most of the things Italy might hope to gain from war were held by Austria, the Allies offered her a better share of the spoils to be won. There was no special virtue in Italy's choice, unless the idea of sacred ego could be elevated into a moral principle. When war began, the Italians possessed a very respectable air force, as a result of their earlier experiences and enthusiasm, and they were soon operating up around the head of the Adriatic Sea and along the frontier with Austria, where most of Italy's fighting was concentrated.

This proved to be a particularly difficult area in which to wage a war, as the Italians were forced to fight both the Austrians and the mountains. Their inability to take ground, and their perseverance in trying to do so, is shown by the fact that between June 1915 and September 1917 they fought eleven battles of the Isonzo River without ever gaining any substantial advantage. But the area did prove to be one where long-distance air power could be used to some effect, as the Austrians were tied to supply routes constricted by the mountain gaps, and in the Caproni bombers the Italians possessed the means to attack them.

Even before the war, in 1913, Count Caproni was working on the possibility of large aircraft for heavy loads. He eventually produced a series of such planes, known by the military designations of Ca. 3, 4, and 5, and with more complex factory numbers. These were all of similar configuration—a central nacelle, usually with a pusher engine, flanked by twin boom fuselages, with tractor engines on the front of them. In the earlier design all the engines were in the center nacelle, with the two outboard propellers turned by extended drive shafts, but this idea was not too successful. Most of the planes were more conventional. The most impressive in appearance, if not in performance, were the Ca. 4 series, for these were triplanes, where the others were biplanes. These were truly enormous aircraft, and must have been incredible sights in the air. The Ca. 42 triplane had a wingspan of ninety-eight feet, just four or five feet shorter than the American Flying Fortress or British Lancaster of World War II; it weighed seven tons and could fly for seven hours, and was capable of carrying a ton and a half of bombs. They were heavily armed, and some even featured a machine-gun position in the biplane tail at the rear of the plane, a very lonely spot in which to fly over the Alps.

Armed with such monsters, the Italians soon began attacking the Austrian bases and lines of communications. In fact, for the first part of the war they put nearly all their effort into bombing. By October 1915 the Italian air service was almost exclusively made up of bomber squadrons, and though the numbers of units fluctuated until the end of the war, the bomber enjoyed a predominance in Italy that it did not attain elsewhere. This was at least in part because the Austrian fighter opposition was relatively meager, but the fact was to have profound influence on theories of air warfare between the world wars.

In August 1915 the Italians began raiding Austrian targets. Gradually the scope of their operations increased. The results were difficult to ascertain, and the Austrians insisted that they shot down many of the Italian bombers, but by 1916, under the pressure particularly of Gabriele D'Annunzio, the Italians began thinking in bigger terms. D'Annunzio was one of the truly rare birds of his day; just in his fifties when the war began, he was famous as Italy's greatest—or at least most flamboyant—poet. He was a fervent apostle of war, but unlike many such aging advocates, he was anxious to fight it himself. He constantly prodded the air service for spectacular attacks.

The Capronis could not reach Vienna, 250 miles inside Austria. In spite of their seven-hour endurance, they could fly only about 75 miles an hour, so there was just not enough margin to hit the Austrian capital and get back home. But they could strike at nearer targets, especially the city of Trieste, which the Italians always insisted was theirs anyway, and the major Austrian naval base at Pola. These were only about 100 miles across the head of the Adriatic. These places were repeatedly bombed, by formations of Capronis, and then, as the Austrian defenses improved, by Capronis with Nieuport fighter escorts. The most substantial Italian raid was in October 1917, when nearly 150 Capronis, plus several Italian flying boats, all struck the naval base at Pola. With one notable exception, however, that was the last Italian spectacular of the war, for just after it, in the great battle of Caporetto, they were severely defeated and driven back toward Venice; from then until the end of the war their aircraft were badly needed for immediate tactical support of their ground troops.

An odd element of the air war in Italy was the presence of a substantial number of Americans, who were initially sent to be trained in camps of instruction around Foggia. The most flamboyant of them was Fiorello LaGuardia, who was not only an officer in the Air Service but a serving congressman as well. He never hesitated to use either his rank or his office, and at one point, on his own initiative, he canceled a contract for bombers being built by an Italian factory; the bombers were totally unfit for combat, perhaps even for flight, and the Italian manufacturers had been delighted to palm them off on the innocent Americans. LaGuardia simply could not be kept down; he not only insisted on flying combat missions, he undertook intelligence operations, he smuggled steel to Italy from Spain, and he stumped the country making inspiring speeches. His wartime career in Italy typified an American ebullience that Italian officialdom found infuriating and the Italian people found incredibly refreshing at the end of a long, hard, and so far unsuccessful war.

On the western front, the French, British, and Germans were all still searching for a big bomber that could actually do things. The war was rushing the pace of development, and manufacturers, with good contracts or at least the hope of getting them, were constantly attempting to improve their products. Engine horsepower was increased, strength-to-weight ratios got better, steel-tube welding replaced wood for airframes, designers were encouraged to push to the limits of safety—and often beyond them. Some terribly bad choices were made, but slowly some useful aircraft began to show up in the squadrons.

The French had a peculiar itch in 1915: They wanted to bomb Essen. Essen was the home of many of Germany's most important war industries, and to attack it the French needed a plane capable of carrying a useful bombload, and of flying five hundred miles. They put their money on an outdated single-engine pusher design, the Breguet Br. M. 5. When finally produced, it turned out to have a real range of only 450 miles, and it was slow, awkward to handle, and poorly armed for defensive work. In fact, there was little reason to recommend it, and after several disastrous attempts to use it for daylight raids, the French relegated it to nighttime work, where it was equally unsuccessful, largely because the pilot was so poorly located, he could not see where he was flying in the dark.

For most of 1916 the British made do with revamped and ostensibly upgraded types, none of which were wholly satisfactory. The B. E. 12 was as dreadful as its predecessor, the B. E. 2, had been. But they did have one successful interim type. The Short seaplane had been so useful to the Royal Navy that more than two hundred of them had been built. Short Brothers now decided that they could very easily modify the plane for land service. After all, seaplanes, were generally inferior in performance to landplanes, so if all the floats and extra wires and struts were replaced with simple wheels, a good landplane should be the result. That was not always the case, but this time the idea worked. Short built more than eighty bombers, which did good service through the worst of 1916.

Even better things were ahead, however. Sir Frederick Handley-Page was the British equivalent of Sikorsky or Caproni, a believer in the large aircraft. When the Royal Naval Air Service was basking in the glow of the fires at the Friedrichshafen Zeppelin works, its leader, Captain Murray Sueter, issued a call for a large and effective heavy bomber, with two engines and capable of carrying "real" bombs, not just the little twenty-pounders of the day. Handley-Page offered such a design, but it took a while for it to get going. While he was working on it, the RNAS made do with single-engine types of one kind or another such as the Shorts. A year after Sueter's request, Handley-Page rolled out the 0/100. The Admiralty took one look and said, "We want it!" Working out the bugs and getting it into production took nearly another year, but in November 1916 Handley-Page's bomber, now called the 0/400, went into squadron service.

The monster had a 100-foot wingspan, which could actually be folded so it could get into a hangar. It could fly nearly 100 miles an hour, with a range of about 650 miles, it could carry three quarters of a ton of bombs, and it was the biggest and best British heavy bomber of the war. Early in 1917 the naval fliers began patrols over the North Sea, but they soon turned to bombing German targets; Sueter, after all, had told the designer what he wanted—"a bloody paralyzer."

Big as it was, the 0/400 was still not the limit of technical ingenuity for the period. Just as the Allies were improving their bomber capability, so were the Germans. In February 1917 the Friedrichshafen G. III began night bombing raids. A contemporary, the Gotha G. V., similar in general appearance and performance, came out that summer. With these the Germans formed a High Command Bomber Group, *Kampfgeschwader der Obersten Heeresleitung,* in effect a semiindependent bombing element, and they first began attacking the British bases around Dunkirk, and then opened a new phase of their campaign against Britain itself.

Due to their position occupying Belgium and northern France, the Germans were far better placed to attack the Allies than the Allies were to hit them. From their bases around Ghent, it was a mere 170 miles to London. In June 1917 a formation of 14 Gothas flew over the British capital at 18,000 feet and dropped 7 tons of bombs, killing or wounding nearly 600 people. The British defenses, now under the army and the Royal Flying Corps, were as ineffective as the navy had been against the Zeppelins. Of the 60 fighters scrambled to meet the enemy, only 5 actually made contact, and these did no harm at all. Flying in diamond-shaped formation, each protected by a fellow, the Germans flew serenely on and came home in triumph. In one raid they had inflicted more damage than all the Zeppelin attacks so far.

A howl of outrage greeted this new German "atrocity," and even though both sides were doing as much as possible to hurt the enemy any way they could, civilians were still shocked and outraged at their new vulnerability. The British government, now under that archetypal wily politician, David Lloyd George, called Trenchard home from France for consultation. His response to the situation was a splash of cold water. In essence, he told the ministers, air power was both ubiquitous and indivisible, and it was going to be very difficult to stop the Germans from doing this kind of thing. He recommended the re-capture of Belgium, which was not much help, as the ground forces had been futilely attempting to do that since 1914. Second, he wanted an increased effort against the German bases behind the front line, on the thesis that this would force them to concentrate for their own defense; this was a repetition of his basic idea of dominating the air beginning with the enemy airspace.

The government, however, would find it tricky to convince panicky civilians that planes in France were doing much to stop Germans over London; like all politicians everywhere, they not only wanted to do something, they wanted it known they were doing it. Trenchard re-plied to that by saying that no matter how many squadrons were dis-posed for home defense, they would not stop the Germans; all they would do was waste fuel, men, and machines flying aimlessly about over London, waiting for an enemy to arrive. On this point, however, the government insisted and several squadrons were withdrawn from France, to the detriment of the air effort there.

Finally the government took up the matter of "reprisals." This was a thorny and convoluted question; getting to the bottom of who did what to whom first in war is rather like peeling an onion, and about as profitable. A more appropriate consideration was what to do. Would reprisal raids work? How far could they be carried? Trenchard was against them, on the philosophical ground that they were repugnant, and on the practical ground that he had no planes that could reach German territory from British bases in Flanders. At Lloyd George's insistence, however, he agreed to start negotiations with the French to lease bases in the eastern part of the country, behind their section of the front lines, from which his big bombers could hit Germany. He thus planted the first seeds of the 1918 strategic bombing campaign.

Trenchard went back to France, the government brought home the fighter squadrons, which certainly needed the rest, and the Germans had a field day over northern France, hitting the ground troops as they prepared for their next round of slaughter, the Third Battle of Ypres. Things got so bad in Flanders that the home-defense fighters were sent back across the Channel, whereupon the Germans hit London again, almost as if they were in cahoots with Trenchard to prove the validity of his ideas about the necessity for an offensive attitude. On July 7 twenty-two Gothas flew over London, lazily bombed the city, and were amazed and delighted at the weakness of the defense. London was now in the grip of severe panic, and the newspapers were crying for German or political blood, it hardly mattered which. Back came the fighter squadrons from France again. Eventually the German bombers, never more than fifty in number, were tying down as many as eight hundred British fighter planes. Trenchard fumed at the dispersion of his strength, but the public was still not satisfied; antiaircraft defenses were increased, and still the newspapers howled. The Germans reaped benefits all out of proportion to their efforts, and some writers have gone so far as to claim that the dispersion of British air strength cost them substantial victory in the Third Ypres battle, otherwise known as Passchendaele, though that seems very farfetched given the kind of unremitting heavy rain in which much of that grisly battle was fought.

The Germans did not press their advantage; indeed, they did not really realize they had it. The actual damage done appeared relatively small, though there was some diminution of war production as a result of the raids. This was more psychological than strategic, in the sense that the falling off came from worker absenteeism rather than damage to facilities. The Germans failed to assess properly the difficulties they were causing the British, and they therefore regarded the raids more as a diversion than as a potentially major disruption. For their part, the British, once the initial panic both among the people and among the government died down, responded to the bombers as they had to the Zeppelins. They ringed London with newer and better antiaircraft guns, they improved their observer communications, and slowly they began shooting down the raiders. The Germans went to less effective night bombing, and by late 1917, equilibrium was approaching once again.

The Gotha campaign was pregnant for the future. The Germans introduced even larger bombers for 1918, and the British set up a committee under General Jan Christian Smuts to sort out the mess in the air.

While strategic bombing was in its gestation period, tactical support of troops made real progress. The Germans used their light and medium aircraft with great effect in Macedonia, against Allied forces that had landed in Greece, and also on the Italian front, where they went to the aid of the reeling Austrians and in the great offensive at Caporetto nearly knocked Italy out altogether. Perhaps the earliest imaginative use of tactical air power, however, was in an out-of-the-way corner of the war, down in Palestine.

Ever since 1914 the British and the Turks had been engaged in a desultory sort of war. There was not only the tragic failure of the Dardanelles campaign, but the British had mounted an unsuccessful expedition up the Tigris-Euphrates Valley aimed at Baghdad; finally, there was a time- and man-consuming, but until 1917 unprofitable, effort out of Egypt and up the Levant coast. In 1917 Lloyd George, who hated Sir Douglas Haig but was not honest enough or powerful enough to fire him, sent General Sir Edmund Allenby out to Palestine to conquer Jerusalem by Christmas. Lloyd George promised Allenby all he needed to do the job, in effect all the troops and equipment he did not want to send to France to Haig.

Allenby was nicknamed "the Bull," which suggested far less finesse than he actually possessed. In midsummer of 1917 he began to whip his formations into shape, and in the fall he launched an attack against the Turks around Gaza. He levered them out of their positions and drove north to Jerusalem, which he entered early in December. In the spring he went on to break the Turkish-German line north of the Holy City, and when asked by a subordinate where to halt and dig in, he replied, "Aleppo." That was three hundred miles north of Jerusalem, but the British and Imperial troops never stopped until they reached it.

Air power was used here the way it was supposed to be used. When Allenby appeared in the theater, the Germans dominated the air even with the few machines they possessed. But Allenby got five squadrons, flying S. E. 5's and the newer reconnaissance types as well as some Bristol fighters, and he soon controlled the air. From then on the British aircraft spotted for their artillery and picked up Turkish troop movements and dispositions; they strafed columns of enemy troops, and bombed and machine-gunned their communications centers and headquarters. They were especially useful in ferreting out the Turkish lines before the big battle of Megiddo in the spring of 1918, and they then harried the retreating Turks all the way to Aleppo. Allenby's campaign has been regarded as one of the few classics of World War I, and the imaginative use of air power was a major element in it.

The year 1917 also saw the U-boat menace at its height, and of the several measures the Royal Navy employed to meet this most dan-

gerous of all German threats, the airplane was one of the most innovative, though by no means the most successful. The British had
gradually improved the capability of their aircraft and their means of
launching them by ship. The seaplane carriers had made no contribution at all to the one great sea battle of the war, at Jutland, but
after that larger ships had been fitted with launching platforms, better planes were available, and the Grand Fleet at the end of the war
carried as many as 150 aircraft among its different units.

The navy also employed dirigibles against the U-boats, and when
they finally began convoying merchant ships, which they did in the
middle of 1917, they often escorted them with airships, which could
spot the submarines and had a good endurance—some of them could
stay up for two days. Even more frequently the British used seaplanes and flying boats.

There were advantages to each. The seaplanes, lowered from their
tenders, could accompany and escort convoys far out at sea; alterna-
tively they could sneak into the North Sea for attacks against German
bases. The flying boats operated from coastal bases, and as their performance improved, they flew long-range maritime patrols. Almost
everyone built flying boats of one type or another, and some of the
early ones were very elegant, made by Lohner in Austria, Macchi in
Italy, or Hansa-Brandenburg in Germany. Their fuselages or hulls were
usually built by specialist craftsmen who had worked on high-speed
racing boats before the war, and their streamlined shapes and var-
nished hulls were a delight to the eye.

The British used several types of boats, including, in the middle years
of the war, many designed and built by the American Curtiss factory
of New York. In 1915 they employed the Curtiss Small America flying
boat, followed almost inevitably by the Large America. Their biggest
type, which set the pattern for flying boats for the next twenty years,
was the Felixstowe F series. These were almost as big as the Handley-
Page bombers, and were impressive performers. The British flying boats
got their first submarine in May 1917, when the UC-36 was sunk by
a bomb, and they also managed to get two Zeppelins over the North
Sea. Seaplane fighters from German coastal bases, and British seaplanes and flying boats, often sparred with each other over the con-
tested waters, a deadly place to fight a little-known aspect of the war.

By the end of 1917, then, the airplane was out of its infancy. If it
had not reached maturity, it had at least attained a useful adoles-
cence. Aircraft were gainfully employed in coastal patrol and mari-

time reconnaissance; they had demonstrated their value as a tactical adjunct to ground operations. The control of the sky must now be pursued, or defended by modern fighter aircraft, and the first hesitant steps toward strategic operations had begun. The period was far more satisfactory for the growth and development of air power than for the war generally, for on all sides the year ended on a note of near despair. Austria and Italy were reeling, and the French were all but done, ruined by the slaughters and the mutinies of the year. The U-boat had failed, but so had Douglas Haig's great offensive at Passchendaele. The Americans were in but the Russians were out, sliding down into the toils of revolution and civil war. On all sides men and women steeled themselves for one last great effort. No one could see the war ending immediately, but no one could go on much longer. The new year must inevitably bring a climactic battle, and in this the new aerial weapon would play a significant role.

VI

AN INDEPENDENT AIR ARM

The winter of 1917–18 brought universal distress with it. There was hardly a home in Europe that had not suffered some loss, and the weariness of the population was exceeded only by the grim determination to see the war through to a successful conclusion. On the Allied side, leaders hoped to survive the attacks that they knew must be coming; if they could do that, then with the added strength and resources of the United States they could eventually win the war. For the Central Powers, it was a case of hurrying to win the war before they inevitably lost it. Time was not on their side. The collapse of Russia gave them men and material hitherto absorbed by the war in the east, but they knew as well as their enemies did that they had only a limited amount of time to take advantage of their superiority. If they did not knock the British and French out before the Americans were fully mobilized and committed to the war, they would not be able to do it at all. Germany's allies, Austria, Turkey, and Bulgaria, were in worse shape than her enemies, and she alone had the force and the will to carry the burden. The war *must* be won in the spring of 1918. General Erich Ludendorf, First Quartermaster-General of the German army, and the de facto ruler of the entire war effort, started planning his battle, pulling the troops, guns, and planes in from Russia. For three years the Germans had stood the rest of the world at bay. Who could doubt that they would triumph in this final perilous hour?

The Allies were hard put to prepare for the impending blow. The French were weary and worn down by the war, racked by internal dissension often fostered by German money, which until 1918 supported defeatist French newspapers with immunity. Their army commander, General Pétain, had made little secret of his formula for fighting the war: Wait for the Americans. That was hardly inspiring, but it was a fair assessment of what the once magnificent and now deathly tired French army was capable of doing. The British were torn by the antagonism between the prime minister, Lloyd George, and the commander of the British Expeditionary Force, Sir Douglas Haig. As Haig's battered infantry prepared for the greatest trial of their history, Lloyd George and his cabinet were juggling figures and actually forcing the army to reduce both the number of battalions in France and the rifle strength within those formations. It was legerdemain of the most despicable sort, playing politics with men's lives.

Out of this unhappy background, when the Germans had already launched the first of their great offensives, and when the western front was reeling and wide open as it had not been since 1914, the Royal Air Force was born. Cynics found it suitable that the new arm of service came into being on April Fools' Day. Both the Royal Flying Corps and the Royal Naval Air Service had performed magnificently, neither saw the need for amalgamation, and the new air force, like the disappearing infantry battalions, had some elements of political hucksterism behind it.

The scheme had its origins in the German bomber campaign of 1917, and the unremitting pressure that the newspapers put on the government because of it. Neither the navy nor the army had been effective in stopping the enemy's Zeppelins and bombers. Smuts, who was newly arrived in England, was asked for two reports, one on the defense of London, and the second, and more far-reaching, on the most effective employment of air power generally. He managed to complete the two short papers within a couple of months, and presented them to the cabinet in the fall of 1917. Always something of a visionary, Smuts was vastly impressed with the possibilities of aerial warfare, and, like most British leaders at the time, he was depressed by what was going on in Flanders as he was producing his reports. What was going on there was the Third Battle of Ypres, and it looked from London as if Haig were pigheadedly sacrificing British soldiers for nothing. To be a little more fair to Haig, it must be said that much of the rationale behind Third Ypres lay in the fact that the French were still virtually useless after their mutinies earlier in the year, a fact of which the London leaders were kept deliberately ignorant by both the French and by Haig. So Smuts's reports were conceived against a bitter backdrop. Not only that, they were based on a misconception as to the immediate future as well. Smuts was led to believe by the people he consulted that in 1918 the British would have a surplus of aircraft; indeed, that some three thousand planes would be available for independent use. He was also well aware of the competition for resources and aircraft types between the army and the navy, and putting all these things together, he came up with a series of apparently logical conclusions. The air services should be amalgamated into one Royal Air Force, and this force would then be able to operate independently as an equal with the other services. Using all those extra planes, it would be able to bring the war to a satisfactory conclusion. If a few German bombers had wreaked havoc on British morale in just one or two raids, think what the fleet of British aircraft that would be ready next year would be able to do to the Germans! In fact, extending this into the future, Smuts believed that he had found the answer to modern war. No more slaughter in the trenches, no more endless battle of attrition. Air forces, clean, surgical, ubiquitous, would take care of everything.

People who were rather more knowledgeable than Smuts were not enthusiastic. Naval aviators, who had a comfortable and effective little empire going, if at some cost of the Royal Flying Corps, were horrified. They saw themselves, quite accurately, subordinated to the larger service to the navy's ultimate cost. But the Royal Flying Corps did not like the idea any more than the sailors did. Trenchard, commanding the corps in France, and fiercely loyal to Haig, saw the scheme as one to diminish both Haig's powers and the air support available to him; most of the senior officers of the corps agreed with him. The only real exception was General Sir David Henderson, Trenchard's superior at home on the War Council, and his support of Smuts was prompted largely by his frustration, rather than by anything more positive. Leaders were convinced the government was killing the bird in the hand for the—to them spurious—expectation of two in the bush. Among the politicians, no one was too keen on expanding the existing Air Board into a full-fledged ministry, so the matter was allowed to lie fallow for a couple of months.

Yet the service chiefs of both the army and the navy gave the plan their guarded approval, and Lloyd George, and Churchill, now back in the cabinet as minister of munitions, were for it. The government announced the formation of a full-fledged Air Ministry, and Lloyd George offered the position of Secretary of State for Air to his most vocal and bitter press critic, Lord Northcliffe. The state of British political matters was shown by the fact that Northcliffe not only declined, which he did with contempt and vituperation, but he did so publicly, in the pages of his own paper, the *London Times*. Swallowing the insult, Lloyd George then turned the trick by offering the job to Lord Rothermere, and as he was Northcliffe's younger brother, there was not too much the press lord could say about it. At the same time, Trenchard was brought home from France and appointed as Chief of the Air Staff, a position he accepted with fully justified misgivings. The new service was officially born on April 1, 1918.

Significant as the birth of the Royal Air Force might have been for the future, it meant very little in the immediate context. Ten days before, the Germans had launched their first great spring offensive, designed to split the British and French and ultimately destroy them. Ludendorf had decided that if he broke the French, the British would fight on, but if he broke the British, the French would quit anyway. On March 21 he struck along the Somme, where the already weakened British formations had extended their line and taken over trench systems from their allies, and where they were totally unprepared for what hit them. The Germans employed new tactics and techniques that they had learned initially from the Russians and perfected at Riga and Caporetto. In forty-eight hours they broke through the British Fifth Army and were in open country. Within five days they had advanced to a depth of thirty miles along a sixty-mile stretch of front, and the war had opened up for the first time since 1914. The British were fighting hard but steadily being pushed back; the French on their right were retreating to cover Paris. Under this pressure the Allies finally agreed to the appointment of a supreme commander—"a French general who will fight," said Haig—and General Ferdinand Foch took up the job. By April 4 the line was stabilized at last.

German tactics were based upon the innovative and audacious use of infantry. They had few tanks, having left development of them to their enemies, but they did rely to a considerable extent upon the support of aircraft, strafing retreating troops, and attacking and assisting the infantry to overcome pockets of resistance left behind in the general advance. The Royal Flying Corps performed yeoman service in the crisis. The British fliers, outnumbered in the immediate battle area, were instructed to use their machines as attack planes too; never mind the German fighters, attack their infantry and, at all costs, slow them down! Foggy and misty weather added to the pilots' difficulties, but the squadrons threw themselves desperately, and sacrificially, into the battle on the ground, flying low over the rolling Somme country, giving the height to the German Fokkers and Albatrosses, and going after the ground troops. One German regiment reported an officer casualty as "run over by an S. E. 5."

Giving the altitude to the Germans meant the RFC had to offer battle at a disadvantage, and losses were heavy, but by the time the front stabilized at the end of the month, the British were winning the battle. Hampered by the loss of airfields and supply dumps, and improvising as they went along, they nonetheless met the best the Germans had to offer, including von Richthofen and his circus, filled the gap, and took the heart out of the German drive. In the midst of the great battle, men were too busy even to note, let alone care, that they were now in the Royal Air Force rather than the Royal Flying Corps.

While Ludendorf was counting the gains and measuring the losses of his first great offensive, and preparing for his second one, the British were up to tricks of their own. The Gotha raids of 1917 had not only triggered the eventual separate air force but they had also brought to the fore the question of a British bombing of Germany, and in the fall of 1917, Trenchard undertook a tour of the French front, negotiating for suitable bases from which bombers might hit targets in the German industrial areas. The idea had not quite languished, though the British had not been able to allocate more than four squadrons to it. There were various reasons for the meager effort. For one thing, Trenchard, though he agreed to it and did much of the preliminary work, did not really believe in it, and he remained firmly wedded to the work being done in direct support of the BEF. Even more important, the British simply did not have the planes, in the numbers needed, and those they did have available were not designed for long-distance work. Even after Trenchard's appointment as chief of the Air Staff, he was calling for more aircraft for use in France rather than for attacking Germany. And in March 1918, two weeks before the German drive began, Trenchard's frustration with Lord Rothermere became so great that he offered his resignation. A month later, when the act rebounded to Trenchard's discredit in the midst of crisis, the government announced its acceptance. They could not get rid of Haig, but they were happy to be rid of his supporter.

That was not the end, however, of either Trenchard or the concept of bombing Germany. He was too important to leave sitting on a park bench. Rothermere too went out of office, and his successor, Sir William Weir, offered Trenchard command of the bombing effort, to be known as the Independent Air Force. Little as he thought of it, it was better than doing nothing, and Trenchard accepted and went off to France to see what might be accomplished.

The Independent Air Force looms far larger in posterity than it did in the minds of the busy and harassed leaders who were trying to cope with the demands of continued German attacks. It was "independent" largely because it was not much of an air force. The French quipped, "Independent of whom? Of God?"; the answer was, independent of the normal British organization, for the force was centered near Nancy, far from any of its countrymen, and isolated in a sea of French lack of interest. It had four squadrons when Trenchard arrived, and eventually worked up to nine, but that was hardly an overwhelming force with which to take on industrial Germany.

Nevertheless, Trenchard set to work, with his invaluable aide Maurice Baring charming the French out of needed supplies, which was a full-time job, and both of them doing their best to keep clear of the claims to command of Foch and other French generals. The Americans, still learning about the war, proved far more tractable allies, and Trenchard looked forward to the day, sometime in 1919, when he would work up an inter-Allied bombing force consisting of squadrons from all three nations. He had a large ground establishment, for he was building an organization capable of handling sixty squadrons in the IAF.

But through the summer of 1918 they made do with what they had, squadrons of Handley-Pages for night bombing, and for daytime work some squadrons of De Haviland 9's, not especially good airplanes because of their exceedingly unreliable engines. About half the strength of the force concentrated on suppression of enemy airfields in their immediate vicinity, and the other half was used for long-distance raids. The airfield suppression work was vital to the success of the effort, and underlined the idea of control of the air. This aspect of the campaign, unfortunately, was usually discounted years later by writers who looked at the distant bombing and blithely agreed, in Stanley Baldwin's phrase, that "the bomber will always get through," without reckoning what it might actually cost to do so.

There were something over a hundred of the Handley-Pages available, and these were used for both day and night operations against German targets. They struck at Trier and at cities along the Rhine from Mannheim down to Cologne. In six months of operations they dropped about six hundred tons of bombs, mostly high explosives and some incendiaries. Trenchard knew he was not doing a great deal of physical damage, so he deliberately kept scattering his raids about, trying to hit as many places as possible rather than to destroy one concentrated target. It was really more a psychological campaign than a strategic one, although that was admitted only in a backhanded way. In September Sir William Weir wrote, "The German is susceptible to bloodiness, and I would not mind a few accidents due to inaccuracy," and Trenchard answered, "I do not think you need be anxious. . . . The accuracy is not great at present. . . ."

It was a very costly operation. Losses, especially on the D. H. 9 squadrons, were brutally heavy, both from wear and tear and from the enemy, as the Germans tried to increase their defenses to meet the new threat. One day, for example, No. 99 Squadron took off with all its planes to bomb Mainz. They were forced by German fighters to settle for Saarbrücken instead. They dropped their bombs, then faced a long running fight all the way home, in which the Germans repeatedly broke up their ragged formation. Only two planes got home ("the bomber will always get through"). In their five months of operations, the Independent Air Force lost well over 100 percent of aircrew, and some squadrons were wiped out twice over. But German morale did suffer, and worker absenteeism did rise. Added to the insidious and increasing effects of the naval blockade—there was serious malnutrition already in Germany—the bombing was a terrible threat of what more years of war might mean. People did not realize how inured to this sort of pressure they could become.

Both sides were planning bigger and better—or worse—things for the future. The British introduced the Blackburn Kangaroo, a land-plane derivative of a successful seaplane, but although it was used for antisubmarine operations, it never reached the bomber squadrons. The Vickers Vimy bomber was also too late; a twin-engined biplane of fairly conventional design, it was made for the express purpose of bombing Berlin. Only three Vimys reached the IAF before the Armistice, and it had its greatest days after the war. Biggest of all, however, was Britain's first four-engined bomber, the Handley-Page V/1,500. This was an engorged 0/400 and, like the Vimy, was meant to be able to reach Berlin from bases in England. It was a great secret, built in northern Ireland by Harland and Wolff, the Belfast shipbuilders, and the monster first flew in May 1918. By November 1918 only three of the great bombers were ready for service, and they never did bomb Germany. But it was the true ancestor of the Allied heavy bombers of World War II; indeed, it was actually bigger than they were, in terms of wingspan, and it could carry three tons of bombs for 1,200 miles.

The Germans had already introduced their own four-engined bomber, and it became operational as early as the end of 1917. This was the Zeppelin Staaken R. VI, built by the protagonists of gigantism. It lacked the performance of the Handley-Pages, carrying less than they did for shorter distances, but it was still a marvel for its day. With a wingspan of 138 feet, it was the largest aircraft of the war, and with it and the Gothas the Germans continued to bomb England during the winter of 1917–18. Fortunately for the British, only eighteen of the R-planes were built; one of them, in a raid on February 16, 1918, dropped the first real blockbuster, a 2,200-pound bomb. It landed on the Royal Hospital in Chelsea, causing a large number of casualties.

The German offensives bore on. The first one on the Somme had taken a lot of territory but had not broken the Allies apart. Ludendorf's second drive was up on the Lys River, near Ypres, designed to rock the British yet again. This opened on April 10, actually succeeded in breaking the line, and forced Haig to appeal to his men in a famous "backs to the wall" order before it was contained by the end of the month.

Ludendorf then reasoned that it was French reinforcements that had saved the British, so he now turned on Pétain, to keep him in his place. The third offensive, intended merely as a pinning attack, struck weak French and British formations along the Aisne River—the latter, tragically, were sent down to this area for a rest—and absolutely shattered them. Opening on May 27, the attack made ten miles the first day, and finally reached the Marne, forty miles away, before it halted. Ominously for the Germans, this battle saw the first intervention of American troops in substantial numbers; time was running out fast. This was in fact the last big German threat. Their fourth and fifth drives, in June and July, were designed to enlarge salients and improve their positions. But they were too little and too late, and the Allies went over to the offensive as midsummer arrived.

Too little too late was the story for the German air service as well. Von Richthofen was killed over the Somme on April 21, and the Germans became increasingly conscious that they were fighting a losing battle. Even their victories were illusory; as the hungry German soldiers advanced, they discovered how well fed and well supplied their enemies were. In Corporal Adolf Hitler's unit they had eaten cats during the winter; morale plunged when they realized how strong their enemies were.

In the air the Allied planes were more and more in the ascendant. The Germans in 1918 brought out the Fokker D. VII, arguably the best fighter of the war. The pilots were at first skeptical of it, for somehow it had acquired a bad advance reputation, due, Fokker claimed, to Allied spies. It went first to von Richthofen's unit, and then gradually spread throughout the lesser jastas. By November 11, there were about eight hundred D. VII's in service, and the Allies were sufficiently wary of them to demand their specific surrender as one of the terms of an armistice.

Beyond the D. VII, Fokker produced the D. VIII, a little parasol monoplane which Allied pilots nicknamed "the flying razor blade" because of its small frontal section. Ironically, the German authorities were its worst enemy; they mistrusted the design and demanded that its wing spars be strengthened. This upset the balance of forces, leading to a number of structural failures, and those in turn caused the plane to be grounded. By the time corrections were made and full-scale production was resumed, it was too late. Fewer than forty of the little planes saw squadron service. The D. VIII was a cheap, efficient, easily built and maintained machine that used a lot of otherwise surplus material. In short, it had everything to recommend it, but it was killed by mistaken direction. The Germans would make that error again.

What the French called "the last quarter hour" had come. Ludendorf had given his best and his soldiers had responded magnificently, but their great effort had not been quite good enough. The battered British Expeditionary Force, its ranks now full of eighteen-year-olds whom the government had promised not to send to the front, stood firm. The French clung tenaciously to the hills of Champagne and rallied on the Marne, helped by the first real American fighting around Château-Thierry. By the evening of July 17, the German assaults had run down. At first light the next morning, Foch launched a limited counteroffensive. It was only a small affair, designed to narrow the German bulge below Soissons, but it marked the beginning of the end. From July 18 to November 11, the Germans never advanced again.

The attack at Soissons, which then became the opening of the Aisne-Marne offensive, was notable for something else as well: It marked the first large-scale commitment of American troops in the war. Over the next three weeks, eight American divisions, each the size of two French or British divisions, were blooded in action. Fresh, ignorant of battle but actually eager to learn, the Americans provided their tired allies with a psychological boost all out of proportion to their actual numbers. The French and British welcomed them with open arms, for they had taken a perilously long time getting there.

It was not America's war, President Woodrow Wilson had insisted in 1914, and he had admonished Americans to be "neutral in thought as well as deed." But as the war went its endless way, that watch-word had become more and more difficult to follow. American vessels were sunk, American civilians were killed on Allied ships, American businesses profited immensely from Allied war orders—and thereby became more and more interested in Allied victory. There was a steady seepage of young Americans across the border and into the Canadian forces. Finally, in April 1917, after being reelected on the slogan "He kept us out of war," Wilson succumbed to the centripetal pull of the great maelstrom and the United States declared war on the German Empire.

Declaring war was one thing, fighting it was another. General John J. Pershing went to France to build up and command the American Expeditionary Force, but a country that had no conscription and only a small standing army was slow to mobilize. There was great enthusiasm at home, but a year after the American declaration of war, the very first combat units had yet to see their very first combat, and most Americans in France were still doing close-order drill.

American military aviation was in as immature a state as the army generally. Most of what had been happening in Europe during the war years had passed the United States by. The vast excitement over the war had not been translated into action, and the American government had remained determinedly uninterested in warlike postures. Even the "preparedness" movement that began around 1916 had been forced on the government rather than initiated by it. In 1914 Congress had established an Aviation Section of the Signal Corps of the U.S. Army, but with an authorized strength of 60 officers and 260 enlisted men, this was not a very important element in the overall picture. In the summer of 1916 the army had engaged in a rough little campaign on the Mexican border, against the famous bandit Pancho Villa. The aerial contingent in this operation, one squadron, was useless. It lost all its planes to winds, dust storms, and Mexican conditions, and it achieved nothing.

This fiasco was concurrent with Verdun and the Somme, and it finally prompted the American government to do something about aviation. Congress voted 13 million dollars for expansion, and eight months later, when the country went to war, the Aviation Section had 131 officers, 1,087 enlisted men, and about 250 airplanes, not one of which was combat-worthy by European standards. At this point the British and the French, who up till now had refused to release any useful information to the Americans, sent over high-powered aviation missions to get things moving. The French came up with, and the Americans accepted, a plan to build 22,000 aircraft, plus 80 percent spare parts and 44,000 aircraft engines. Congress promptly voted another 640 million dollars, without batting an eyelash over it. This was creating a bull out of a frog with a vengeance, and of course the infant American aircraft industry, though it expanded rapidly, never came near these stratospheric figures. The air service itself, one squadron strong in 1916, was to expand to 345 combat squadrons, 263 of them to be in France by June 1918. This was successively watered down; at the Armistice there were actually 45 American squadrons in the order of battle, or in other words, about one eighth of projected strength.

The Americans had the same difficulty with design as they had with production. In spite of the fact that most armed services spend all their peacetime years practicing for war, only combat teaches combat's lessons. Within two months of the declaration of war, the Americans realized they were not going to produce a combat-worthy airplane of indigenous design. They concentrated instead on trainers, including the famous Curtiss "Jenny," and lesser known types such as the Thomas Morse S. 4c and the Standard E-1, both of which aspired to be fighters but were used only as advanced trainers. After enormous argument, quantity production was settled on an American-built version of Britain's medium day-bomber, the De Haviland 4. Although its crews called it "the flaming coffin," this was considered the best plane of its type. The actual manufacturing was preempted by the American automobile industry, which argued that it was prepared for assembly-line mass production while the fledgling aviation industry was still in the "backyard garage" stage. Very close to five thousand of the planes were built in the United States, most of them by Dayton-Wright or the Fisher Auto Body division of General Motors, both in Ohio. By the time American Liberty engines had been put in them, and all the European metric measurements and screw threads changed to American standards, the plane was already obsolete. It still remained the only American-built plane to see combat in France; in innumerable modifications and conversions, it soldiered on with the U.S. Army until 1932.

Aside from that, Americans had to be content with combat planes bought from Europe. Most of these were purchased from the French, the United States supplying the raw materials and the French aircraft industry turning out the finished product. American pilots flew Spad and Nieuport fighters, and the Breguet and Salmson medium bombers. The Breguet was a tough, boxy, all-metal two-seater; the Salmson was a slightly more streamlined affair, with a marginal performance. Both were about on a par with, or slightly below, the D. H. 4, and their chief claim to fame lay simply in their use by the Americans. By the end of the war, the Americans had taken delivery of 4,881 French, 258 British, and a handful of Italian planes.

The 1st Aero Squadron arrived in France on September 3, 1917, and was the first American aviation unit there. But there had been individual American fliers in the war long before that. Some had joined the Royal Flying Corps, either via the Canadian route or through service in the British army itself. The most famous group of all, however, was the Lafayette Escadrille of the French air service, a small gathering of young men whose impact on public opinion and on aviation legend far outweighed its actual physical importance in the Great War.

Americans had long had a friendly feeling toward the France of the Third Republic—it was Jefferson who had said, "Every man has two countries, his own and France"—and when war broke out there were numerous Americans who genuinely wanted to help. The Rockwell brothers, Kiffin and Paul, sailed for France on August 7, 1914, Norman Prince from Massachusetts offered his services, and a wealthy young Yale man, William Thaw, already an aviator and in Paris when war came, tried to volunteer as a pilot. French law forbade the enlistment of foreigners in the regular services. They ended up instead in the Foreign Legion, where they found Bert Hall, a wanderer from Missouri, and Victor Chapman, a Harvard graduate who had been studying architecture in the École des Beaux-Arts.

Many of these men were already fliers, and life in the Legion soon convinced others that they ought to be. However, the French government had no need for foreign fliers; it had plenty of volunteers among its own young men, and it was a long time before the authorities realized the propaganda value of having an American squadron. Eventually they did, prodded by the Franco-American Committee, made up of prominent members of the American community in Paris; on April 17, 1916, Escadrille N. 124, flying Nieuport scouts, was officially formed. After a short training period the squadron was fed into the horror of Verdun. Victor Chapman was the first killed, and Kiffin Rockwell wrote of him, "He died the most glorious death. . . . I have never once regretted it for him. . . ." Three months later Rockwell was dead too.

The squadron soon became formally known as the Escadrille americaine, which finally led the Germans to launch a diplomatic protest to the United States government. The French realized this was causing difficulty and changed the name again, to Escadrille des volontaires. The Americans found that a bit uninspiring, and finally hit upon the name Escadrille Lafayette, thus anticipating the famous "Lafayette, we are here!" During the next two years forty-eight Americans went through the squadron (about one quarter of all the Americans who flew for France), and the survivors then went on to utilize their experience with the new American air service. Most of them eventually gravitated to the 103rd Pursuit Squadron, while the old French Squadron 124, reformed with French personnel, became Escadrille Jeanne d'Arc.

The Lafayette Escadrille was the stuff of which romance is made, but General Pershing was a determinedly unromantic figure, and he was interested only in forming an independent American contingent capable of fighting the war. The Americans throughout the war would remain weak in armor and artillery units, as they had concentrated on getting infantry over to France. But Pershing appointed Colonel William Mitchell as Commander of the Air Service of the AEF, and Mitchell set out to get things done in a hurry.

The stormy petrel of the early days of American air power, Mitchell was one of the first Americans in France. In fact, he was already there as an observer when the United States declared war. He was a flamboyant personality who encouraged strong reactions, either positive or negative, and he was a firm believer in war in the air. One day in 1918 he showed up at Trenchard's headquarters near Nancy, cornered the British commander himself, and started asking questions. He wanted to know "everything," and he thought it would take him about two days to find it out. When the potentially explosive Trenchard asked if Mitchell thought he had two days to show visiting Americans around, Mitchell, unabashed, replied, "Sure. It looks like you've got a good organization going here. If you have, it won't miss you for a couple of days." Trenchard's aides waited with delight for the volcano to erupt, but instead he chuckled and took two days off to guide Mitchell through the command.

It took more than the enthusiasm of Billy Mitchell and his subordinates to get the American air service off the ground in a hurry. Everything had to be done from the start, and it proved extraordinarily difficult to build a service and fight a war at the same time. This, and the American insistence upon independence rather than just using their men as reinforcements, which was what the other Allies would have liked, accounted for the delay in getting American units into the fighting. By August Mitchell's group was building airfields, and by November 1917 there were several Aviation Instruction Centers in operation, with aspiring young pilots driving "Penguins"—airplanes with no wings, used for getting the ground feel of a plane—around the bases. As with the American aircraft industry at home, and as with Trenchard's Independent Air Force, the base facilities were grossly oversize, for everyone was expecting to build immensely bigger forces than were actually in operation by the time the war ended.

The 1st Aero Squadron, the first one to reach France, was retrained on French aircraft and went into operation in mid-April 1918.

Gradually the Americans built up a sector of their own in the quiet area of the front around Toul, southeast of Verdun and not far from Trenchard's base around Nancy. The fighter squadrons grew to groups and then wings; in May the 1st Corps Observation Group was formed, and in June the first day-bombardment squadron was operational. Mitchell organized the 1st Air Brigade that month, which he commanded in combat over and around Château-Thierry, where the Americans got some hard knocks from the numerically superior Germans, who were far more experienced than they were.

The final Allied offensive against the staggering German forces began on August 8, with Haig's attack up in front of Amiens. Behind a rolling barrage and supported by masses of new tanks, Canadian and Australian infantry swept toward and over the enemy trenches. As the Germans broke and fled to the rear, or surrendered in large numbers, the BEF drove steadily on; Ludendorf noted in his diary that this was "the black day" of the German army. All he could do from this time on was try to hold a front together and give the political authorities long enough to negotiate a peace settlement. All along the line the triumphant Allies took up the fight. Foch answered all questions with "Attack, attack!" Suddenly it dawned on men that this might well be the end, that the war need not drag on until 1919 or 1920, that Germany was indeed almost finished.

Two days after Haig's advance began, the First United States Army was officially activated, and three weeks later the Americans took over a sector below Verdun that included the St.-Mihiel salient, a bulge in the front line that had been there ever since 1914. Clearing this salient was to be the first all-American action, and on September 12 Pershing launched his drive against it. For Mitchell, this was his big chance to prove what properly handled aircraft could do. He had almost 1,500 aircraft available, most of them American, but he also had British, French, and even a couple of Italian squadrons under command. He worked up a comprehensive plan of attack and support of the ground forces, designed both to gain air superiority and then to exploit this by bombing, strafing, and harassing the enemy as opportunity presented.

The whole attack proved a small model of an intelligent operation, helped in large part by the fact that the Germans knew they could not hold the salient anyway, given all the other pressures they were subjected to, and were abandoning it when the Americans hit. The

American aircraft completely dominated the sky over the salient on the first day, and it was only a couple of days later that the Germans reacted very vigorously, redisposing their aircraft to challenge the Allies with substantial numbers. Mitchell was highly elated at his success, which Pershing graciously acknowledged, and the Americans would have liked to keep on going, right across the frontier and into Germany, to the Saar and Moselle valleys.

Foch, however, had other plans, and the Americans moved, in a miraculous logistics operation directed by Colonel George C. Marshall, to the northeast, to operate in the great Meuse-Argonne offensive. This was the bottom prong of a pincer; the top was provided by Haig and the BEF, and the aim of the whole was to destroy the German army in France. These operations, begun in late September, were the final blow, and they continued unremittingly until the Armistice came into effect on November 11.

On other fronts too the war was winding down, the Central Powers suddenly collapsing. The Ottoman and Hapsburg Empires slid into history's dustheap. Allied troops broke out of Salonika and advanced up the Vardar Valley into Bulgaria. The Italians advanced to the Piave and then crushed the faltering Austrians in the battle of Vittorio Veneto. In August the poet D'Annunzio led a flight of Ansaldo biplanes over Vienna itself; they dropped only leaflets, but Austrian reports commented ruefully on the combat aggressiveness of enemy pilots and the paralyzing effect of his air control.

Back in France the Germans held hard for about three weeks, and the Americans and French in the Meuse-Argonne especially had hard fighting in very bad country. By mid-October, though, the Germans broke in front of the British, and the fighting began to open up. The RAF made a particularly innovative contribution to this. Once the front was no longer static, the aircraft could roam at will seeking targets of opportunity. In July, after an attack at Le Hamel, the fliers dropped 100,000 rounds of ammunition to advancing Australian machine-gunners, the world's first aerial resupply mission. The experiment had proven so successful that it became standard practice. Early in October, French and Belgian troops on the British front ran out of supplies; rain had left their support trains bogged in the mud in the rear areas. Eighty Allied aircraft took off, each carrying sacks of earth with five or ten rations packed in the dirt. These were dropped from three hundred feet above the advancing infantry. The rations were cushioned by the dirt, and the soldiers on the ground were presumably hungry enough to risk being hit by the sacks. The planes dropped thirteen tons of supplies, which was a fair amount by the standards of the time, and yet another portent of future uses of air power.

Finally the Allies were through the main German defense positions. Sullenly the enemy retreated. The Germans still did heavy demolition work, and held up the advance with machine-gun nests wherever possible. Haig and Foch both wanted to use their horsed cavalry, and Major-General John Salmond, now commanding the RAF in France, said he could offer three hundred planes in support at any place at any time. But the horses, as they had for almost the entire war, proved unable to do much. The British tried a couple of charges—most of their senior officers were cavalrymen, after all—and did with heavy losses what infantry and tanks could have done far more cheaply. The fact was that the airplane, and now the tank, were replacing the horse soldier for reconnaissance and shock action.

By mid-October, with German air bases lost and their supply situation collapsing, Allied planes ruled the sky unimpeded. The fleeing German columns were perfect targets for the RAF, the French, and the Americans, and the only thing that saved the Germans from utter rout was the weather. It turned bad on October 17, raining heavily and unceasingly, and leaving the D. H. 4's, Spads, and Camels sitting disconsolately in seas of mud. Perhaps mercifully, the airplane was deprived this last chance to show what it could do to a broken army. The Armistice was signed on November 11, and it would be another twenty-two years before the roads of northern France and the Low Countries were again choked with defenseless targets.

VII

VISIONS IN THE DOLDRUMS

The end of the Great War brought black despair to the losers, rejoicing tinged with an air of hysteria to the victors. In London, Paris, and New York, men and women danced in the streets and popped champagne corks; in Berlin mobs surged to and fro and rifle fire punctuated the desperate hours. For most, there was immense relief, and young men now knew that they would live to be old men. But aside from that overriding fact, there was a sense of loss, of insecurity, and of indirection. The war had gone on too long; it had taken on a life of its own, and had in fact become a way of life. Society was like an invalid who, having adjusted his entire activity to the fact of his incapacity, suddenly discovers he is cured and therefore does not know what to do with his newfound freedom.

The United States, late to the fray, was not as deeply touched by the immensity of the war as Europe was. But over there, those who lived through it thought of themsleves ever after as "the survivors," the lesser remnants of some great natural catastrophe. People who experience some huge upheaval always think it is the most profound, or the worst, event that has ever happened, but World War I was in all truth bad enough, even without this selectivity of vision. The toll in lives was enormous, and when the entire bill was added up, the findings were astonishing. The Central Powers had mobilized nearly 23 million men and suffered 15.4 million casualties, including killed or died, wounded, prisoners, and missing, a rate of 67 percent. The Allies had even more losses winning than the Central Powers had losing; they had mobilized 42 million men and suffered 22 million casualties, or 52 percent. The now defunct Austro-Hungarian Empire led the dismal parade with 90 percent losses, and for the Allies, Russia lost 76 percent and France 73 percent. The British Empire lost only 35 percent, and the Americans 8 percent. In addition to the 37.5 million direct war losses, authorities estimated that another 12.6 million civilians had died from side effects, mostly starvation, disease, or accident. The influenza epidemic at the end of the war, for example, took a tremendous toll partly because Europeans were so run down as a result of the wartime shortages of food. In Germany, half the babies born in 1916 died before the signing of the peace treaty and the consequent lifting of the British blockade.

The numbers of casualties in the air are difficult to arrive at, but the generally available one is that 55,000 aircrew died, about 30,000 of them British. If nothing else, that is some measure of the British policy of the *offensive à outrance* in the air, which they pursued at all costs and often with obsolete equipment. Numbers of aircraft produced—and lost in combat—are some indication of the utility of the new weapon and the place it made for itself. The major producers by far were Germany, Britain, and France. The Germans built 48,537 planes, and 27,637 of them were destroyed; the British turned out 58,144 and lost 35,973. The French were the most prolific of all; they built 67,987, of which 52,640 were written off. Ranging from 77 percent for the French to 56 percent for the Germans, these figures would tend to suggest, though by no means definitively prove, that the losses in the air war were very roughly proportional to the losses on the ground. On Germany's black day, August 8, 1918, the British lost 45 aircraft in fighting and 52 were wrecked by bad flying. At home in Britain, with no Germans around to intervene, there was still an aircraft wastage that ran as high as 66 percent per month at peak times. The French wastage leveled out at about 50 percent per month. Though much smaller in total than the losses from the ground fighting, in actual percentage terms air warfare seems to have been just about as deadly to its participants as ground warfare was.

Nonetheless, the airplane as an instrument of war had come to stay. As later, more deadly weapons, it was not going to be uninvented, and its usefulness in what was admittedly still an auxiliary role was undeniable. No one knew for certain what armed forces of the future would be like; only a few believed that they would be totally unnecessary, and those few were not soldiers or sailors. Whatever they would be, they would have to have an air component to them. Observation, reconnaissance, attack aircraft, fighters for tactical air control, and even possibly strategic bombers of some kind—all these had demonstrated a degree of potential, which meant that they were henceforth indispensable in modern war.

In 1919 most of the western world preferred to forget about war if at all possible; demobilization went on at a pace too rapid for professional soldiers, but all too slowly for the millions of civilians in uniform and the governments that were paying for their sustenance. The process was perhaps most dramatic among the forces of the United States, for the huge and unwieldy machine that was still getting ready to fight the war now was thrown into reverse. Contracts for material were immediately canceled, men who were still going through the confusion of induction into the service were suddenly thrown back out, and the waste and mismanagement were enormous. In France, where the U.S. Army had hundreds of the already obsolete and now totally surplus D. H. 4's, the air service simply stripped whatever was regarded as useful out of them, heaped the tangled airframes up in open fields, and touched off what critics called the "Billion Dollar Bonfire." In the army's view, the planes were not worth shipping back home.

Britain, France, and Italy did not have the problem of distance that the Americans did, so their solutions were a little less dramatic, but their armed forces shrank the same way. On Armistice Day, the French Aéronatique Militaire numbered 127,630 officers and men, with 3,222 operational planes. There were 66 fighter squadrons, 34 bomber squadrons, and 154 artillery observation and reconnaissance squadrons. The Aéronautique Navale, or Aéronavale for short, remained independent, unlike the Royal Air Force. With the coming of peace, the air-force establishment was reduced to about 180 squadrons, or roughly two-thirds of its wartime strength. As the French were so distrustful of the Germans, they maintained their forces with a greater effort than did the other victors, but as the twenties wore on, they too began to slack off their effort.

After Versailles, the French government undertook the rationalization of the air establishment, and set up a command and organizational structure that lasted for a decade. There was no doubt as to the primacy of the French army; indeed, throughout the interwar years it was universally regarded as the finest in the world, and the aerial forces, whatever their permutations, were not seen as challengers of this fundamental order. But both the air force and the naval air service were put on a sound footing that worked well until the thirties.

In Great Britain the situation was rather different. The British army was always perceived by most Englishmen less as a major force in its own right than as a weapon to be projected by the navy onto some foreign shore. The Royal Navy was the "senior service," and, in the British tradition, World War I was actually a military aberration. The norm for the islanders was that they should subsidize the lesser Continental powers against the greater and commit their usually small army only in a supportive role in a secondary theater. The mobility and flexibility that command of the sea conferred on them made up for the lack of numbers in the army. For them, the tragedy of World War I was that their allies on land proved unequal to the task of defeating Germany, and therefore Britain was drawn into a major land commitment.

With the war over there was little intention of remaining in this new mold. There was in fact little perceived need for any kind of defense at all; after the distressing upheavals of war even the professional military men wanted to return to what the services were really about—close-knit, elitist little family groupings in which everyone who counted knew everyone else, from back in the good old days out in India or on the China station. Through the twenties and thirties the Royal Air Force was called "the finest private flying club in the world," and that nickname was not entirely facetious.

For the army, demobilization came rapidly at the end of the war. Four million men went out of uniform, and by September 1920, the great British army was back to its almost ludicrous peacetime figure of a quarter of a million men. Most of them were discreetly kept out of sight, in Egypt, India, or other assorted colonial garrisons. The navy's turn came a bit later, but it, too, rapidly reverted to peacetime ways. In 1922 the Washington Naval Conference conceded maritime parity to the United States, a move dear to the budgetary authorities and bitterly opposed by senior naval officers. But as there appeared to be relatively little for the navy to do—armed forces need enemies, after all, and the Royal Navy had none—there also appeared to be little demand for the navy.

There was even less need for a Royal Air Force. In Lloyd Geroge's 1919 coalition government, Churchill became Secretary of State for War and combined the position with that of Secretary of State for Air. In 1921, when the latter became a separate ministry, the minister ceased to have a seat in the cabinet. Air simply was not that important. Ever the man of action seeking like fellows, Churchill called Trenchard out of a short-lived retirement to become the first peacetime Chief of the Air Staff, just as he had been the first wartime one. This time Trenchard lasted for ten years, until 1929.

Through those ten years there were endless squabbles with the army and the navy over who was to get what from the constantly shrinking budgetary pie. Of the three services, the navy did passably well, the air force rather less well, and the army came in a poor last. The great English historian A.J.P. Taylor commented that in the interwar years the navy had plans and some equipment, the RAF had plans but no equipment, and the army had neither plans nor equipment. What Trenchard actually concentrated on, aside from fending off the claims of the other services, was building an infrastructure of bases and organization. He recognized that aircraft technology was evolving much more rapidly than maritime or land-war equipment, and he managed to avoid, partly through government parsimony but also partly due to his own policy, saddling the service with antiquated and outdated material, a mistake the French made. By the end of Trenchard's tenure he had managed to retain good officer material—in 1919 he told Sir John Salmond his intention to resign was disgusting—and he had created a base structure that made life in the RAF surprisingly attractive.

The business end of the force remained small. At the Armistice there had been 188 operational squadrons, 99 of them in France, 34 in other theaters, the rest at home, and just under 300,000 men in the service. Six months later there were only 23 squadrons officially operational, and of these only 10 could actually be employed, not for lack

of pilots or machines but rather because the logistical and maintenance men had been discharged. Civvy street paid good wages for experienced fitters and engine mechanics, and throughout their histories,
the siren song of private industry has been the bane of the air forces,
who train expensive and highly skilled technicians, only to see them
siphoned off into the better conditions and higher wages of civilian
life.

During his decade Trenchard set up the Royal Air Force College at
Cranwell and a staff college for senior officers at Andover. He also
established the idea of the short-service commission, which saw young
officers train as pilots or aircrew, serve for five years, and then be released into a reserve. This avoided clogging the ranks with officers
who wanted only to fly and had little interest otherwise in the force
as a profession. He also set up the Royal Auxiliary Air Force, the aerial equivalent of the Territorial Army. He insisted on his old idea of
offensive air war, and also on strategic bombing, to which he had now,
after his experience in the closing months of the war, become converted. By the mid-twenties, the squadron establishment had risen from
the dismal twenty-three to fifty-four, eighteen of them for home defense in Britain itself, the rest scattered about in overseas basis. The
government looked forward to having a full fifty-two squadrons just
for home defense by 1930. Trenchard's ideas on aerial war meant that
three quarters of them would be bomber squadrons. But as with the
other British services, with no enemies in the offing the whole matter
was a bit academic. The Royal Air Force was still seeking a responsible role in the national life when Trenchard retired in 1929, when
the Depression threw everyone's plans into the trash basket.

The process of finding a place for military aviation in the United
States, the third of the three great surviving victors, was substantially
different from that in Great Britain. For one thing, the American air
force had not achieved independence before the end of the war; for
another, both geography and the political system were different; finally, American air power's advocate, Billy Mitchell, was as publicity
conscious as Hugh Trenchard was inarticulate. The American air force
might not get off the ground, but the fireworks rose to the heavens.

Bounded by Canada and Mexico, and more important by the Atlantic and the Pacific, the United States rapidly beat its swords into
plowshares. There had never been before, and certainly was not after
1918, any disposition to maintain a large standing army, and by the

mid-twenties, the U.S. Army was no bigger than the one fixed by treaty on the defeated Germans. Public discussion and congressional hearings were less interested in the role of an air service than in the kind of army the United States ought to have, and the National Defense Act of June 1920 decided upon a small, essentially professional regular army, with the air service firmly under its control. Budgets were cut appropriately, and the U.S. Army Air Service, which was to have had eighty-seven squadrons, was cut instead to twenty-seven. It was, by way of compensation, recognized as a combat arm, and definitively separated from the Signal Corps, but that was hardly enough for a man such as Mitchell. He began extensive propagandizing and proselytizing for a greater role for air power, for the creation of an independent service.

His grasp exceeded his reach. In 1923 the report of a board headed by General William Lassiter took a very qualified view of Mitchell's ideas. It was essentially more interested in tactical air support than in strategic operations, and though it did go so far as to recommend a semiautonomous force for the latter, that was still not enough. Mitchell was eventually court-martialed and suspended from the service for insubordination in pushing his views. The furor created by the famous court-martial of Billy Mitchell, which has become one of the set-piece scenes of twentieth-century American history, prompted President Calvin Coolidge to appoint yet another board, the Morrow Board, to look once again into aviation questions. Men whom Mitchell castigated as blind, but who regarded themselves as more balanced than he, recommended minor increases in army aviation, and in 1926 the service became the Army Air Corps, with an Assistant Secretary of War for Air. By the end of the twenties the air force, by whatever name, was still small, still subordinate, still looking for a mission, and still frustrated.

Other countries went through variations on these themes, depending upon geography, politics, and past experience. The Italian aircraft industry had begun to make substantial progress just at the end of the war, but that was cut short by the Armistice, and virtually nothing was done about the air force for another three or four years. These immediate postwar years were very bad in Italy; the people were frustrated by the sacrifices of the war and felt cheated out of their just rewards—as they saw them—by the Allies. In 1922 dissatisfaction led to dictatorship, when Benito Mussolini gained power for his Fascist Party after the highly dramatic March on Rome. Against this backdrop, the needs, desires, and ambitions of the Italian air service were of little importance, but that was soon to change. Mussolini was a man of considerable ambition; he intended to make a splash in the world, and if necessary he would do it by force. In March 1923 the Regia Aeronàutica became an independent service and, spurred by the dynamic new government, the aircraft industry in the peninsula began a real revival. There was a revolt in Libya in the mid-twenties that gave the Italians some operational flying time, and into the thirties Italy was one of the more air-minded countries.

By the middle of the decade, every country had something of an air arm. Portugal, for example, possessed an Arma de Aeronáutica and an Aviação Naval, both dating back to the Great War, in which the country was a little known but sorely suffering participant. Even though Portugal had always been a virtual satellite of Great Britain, its aircraft for the first decade were almost all French, and the major types in the twenties were Spads, Breguets, and Caudrons. The British made some headway in the Portuguese aircraft market as France's leadership faltered, and by 1924, Fairey, Vickers, and Avro types were in service.

Another small country in similar state was Denmark, and its first military aircraft, both for the army and the navy, were derivative French types, followed by small production of indigenous designs. There was a series of fatal accidents in 1919, and the Danish War Office grounded all planes with underpowered or unreliable engines. Unfortunately, this left only six planes flying, and the air service languished. In 1922 an Army Air Corps was formed, followed the next year by a Naval Air Service, but through the thirties both establishments together seldom operated more than fifty aircraft, most of them foreign or license-built designs.

The British and French continued to dominate the European market, and the Americans slowly took over the South American one. Out in the Far East, Japan imported foreign experts, both British and French, and quietly began to build both an air force and an aircraft industry.

The situation in Germany was quite different, for development of the air service there was completely conditioned by the overriding demands of the Treaty of Versailles. Part of the punitive nature of the peace was that severe restrictions were placed on the German armed forces. Both the navy and the army were limited in numbers of personnel and types of equipment; the army was to have only one hundred thousand men, the navy to be denied submarines and dreadnought-type battleships. There was to be no air force whatsoever. The treaty came into force in January 1920, and in April, the Chief of Staff of the Army, General Hans von Seeckt, ordered the few residual air squadrons to be disbanded. Aircraft were either sold, broken up, or taken abroad by the victors as reparations. The German aircraft industry was forbidden for several months to build anything at all, and for some time after that it labored under restrictions that were supposed to make construction of potential military types impossible. Former pilots and air-service technicians were discharged, though a fortunate and chosen few were retained in the armed forces on other duties. But by the mid-twenties, the Germans could look any foreign critic in the eye and say, "We have lived up to the Treaty; we have no air force in Germany."

They did, however, have an air force; it was in Russia. At the Treaty of Rapallo, signed in 1922, the two outcasts of the western world, defeated Germany and Communist Russia, went to bed together, to the intense disgust of the other countries who had driven them to do it. Officially the Rapallo agreement was a trade and diplomatic affair, but it also laid the foundations for surreptitious cooperation between German and Soviet forces over the next decade and a half. Under a misleading name, the Germans set up a virtual air inspectorate in their military administration, and they then established training bases in the Soviet Union, the most important of them at Lipetsk, north of Voronezh. This was operational in 1924, stocked with the current Fokker fighter-trainer, the D. XIII, and manned by German pilots training other German pilots and offering services to the Russians as well. The Lipetsk school was later followed by a tank warfare school at Kazan and a gas warfare school on the lower Volga, all officially denied the Germans by treaties. So although it was technically correct to say there was no air force in Germany, it was not correct to say there was no German air force.

This was all pretty small pickings, but it was an earnest of greater things to come. At home the Heinkel aircraft works was designing planes that were carefully hidden from prying or inspecting western eyes; Dornier was doing the same, and so were other manufacturers.

The great German vogue for sports flying, so notable a feature of the early thirties, received official blessing a decade earlier. From 1925 on, the army, the Reichswehr, kept a very careful and up-to-date register of personnel who had aviation experience or were qualified fliers. In 1926 the aircraft stipulations of the Versailles Treaty were amended, and Germany was openly permitted to build, as the felicitous phrase had it, "aircraft conforming to the aeronautical performance of current types of fighter aircraft"; these were to be in small numbers only, and were purely for sports competition. Most of the military air forces of the day won popular support and government funding by participating in air shows and races, and it would have been truly vindictive to have denied the Germans this simple, artless pastime. Heinkel, Dornier, and Junkers, as well as several lesser manufacturers, all began to produce suitable airplane types, some of which looked remarkably like reconnaissance seaplanes or even potential fighters. By the end of the decade, the foundations had been laid both for a naval air arm and for an army air service. Air-minded German military men could see light at the end of the tunnel.

The new German air force was born in secrecy; the Soviet air force was born in war. During World War I the Tsarist air units had been hampered constantly by lack of equipment and poor maintenance and training facilities. By the time of the Russian Revolution in 1917 they had largely lost their usefulness, and they collapsed in the general disintegration of the Russian armies. People such as Seversky fled to the west, and Russia's greatest ace, Captain Alexander Kazakov, also went over to the Allies. The western Allied powers all launched interventions in Russia, first of all supporting the Provisional Government, which tried to keep Russia in the war, and, when that was overthrown, then supporting the White Russian counterrevolutionaries fighting against the Bolsheviks. From Murmansk and Archangel, from Odessa on the Black Sea, and from Vladivostok on the Pacific coast, British, French, and Japanese all either staked out claims of their own or backed White forces under various Tsarist admirals and generals.

In late 1917 the revolutionaries, on their side, organized the Workers and Peasants Air Fleet, which eventually became the Red Air Force. They started out with about 150 derelict aircraft, a fair number of ground workers who had joined the Revolution, a few pilots who had done so of their own volition, and several who had been given the choice between the Revolution and a bullet in the head. When the World War I Armistice came, the Reds quickly grabbed whatever the Germans had left behind, and through the ensuing period of the civil war, Red Fokkers fought White Camels, Spads, and D. H. 4's. This was a bitter kind of conflict, as civil wars often are, with little mercy shown on either side. The Reds eventually won as much by the failings of the Whites as by their own resources.

At the same time there was a vicious little Russo-Polish war in 1920. The Poles, having been partitioned and suppressed for more than a century, emerged united after World War I and advanced exorbitant territorial claims, which they immediately asserted by force of arms. They put together an air force of about two hundred German planes, and advanced into Russia under the leadership of Marshal Pilsudski. The Reds found it difficult to resist them, and there was a good deal of tactical employment of air power, with the Poles attacking Red transport centers and rear areas. Unfortunately for the Poles, they could barely keep their aircraft flying, for lack of spares, ground personnel, and general know-how, and when the Reds counterattacked after a few weeks, they soon wrested air control from the now debilitated Poles. They got nearly to Warsaw before the French intervened on Poland's behalf; France sent a military mission under General Maxime Weygand, and a large number of aircraft as well, many of them excellent British Bristol Fighters. The Poles rallied and soundly thrashed the Reds, and went sweeping back east a second time. Finally both sides gave up and signed a treaty in October. The Reds then finished off residual White forces, and by late 1920 they were largely masters in their own house. They had also learned the value not only of an air force but also of the indispensable ground organization and facilities without which an air force was just dead weight. By the end of the civil war, the Red Air Force had 325 aircraft in military and naval detachments. They soon set up an Aviation Research Institute, undertook state planning and implementation of an aircraft manufacturing and development program, and opened competitions for their own designs. A young Russian named Nikolai Polikarpov was turning out his first drawings. Over the next twenty years, the Russians learned a lot from the Germans, but they also learned a lot that would surprise the Germans, and the rest of the world as well.

To justify the existence and expense of airplanes and air forces, especially in a world more or less at peace, it was necessary to define some reasonable missions they could perform better than the already long-established services. It proved difficult to do.

One thing in their favor was the fact that airplanes made news. The public had an almost insatiable appetite for deeds of aerial daring, and nearly everyone involved in the business of flying recognized that this need could be used to aviation's advantage. There were races and trophies to be won, long-distance and altitude records to be set, and, in however tangential a way, all of these advanced the cause of the airmen. They not only gained popular support but also encouraged research and development.

This was recognized very early on. In 1919 two British airmen, Captain John Alcock and Lieutenant Arthur Whitten-Brown, made the first nonstop crossing of the Atlantic. They took off in a Vickers Vimy bomber from Newfoundland on June 14 and reached northern Ireland the next day. They had vicious weather, and at several points looked as if they would not make it, but sixteen hours after takeoff they crash-landed in a bog in Galway. At the end of the year two Australians, Lieutenants Keith and Ross Smith, flew another Vimy from England to Australia in twenty-eight days. The Italians, meanwhile, planned a multiplane flight from Rome to Tokyo. This was another of D'Annunzio's ideas, and eleven planes, seven Ansaldo Scouts and four large Capronis, took part in the venture. Their eleven-thousand-mile route took them across the Middle East and the top of India, through China and Korea, and across to Japan. One by one the planes faltered and dropped out; all the Capronis were gone through the Levant. Two Ansaldos made the whole trip, only the one piloted by A. Ferrarin getting the entire distance by air. In 1920 an Italian military mission in South America undertook the first flight across the Andes as well.

In the United States the air service was equally well aware of the value of publicity. A Martin bomber flew around the perimeter of the country, nine thousand miles. A Lieutenant Conet flew a D. H. 4 from San Diego to Jacksonville in twenty-two hours, landing and refueling on the way. Lieutenant James H. Doolittle then flew the reverse course, and cut nearly an hour off the flying time. In October 1922 the army decided to try for a nonstop coast-to-coast flight. They used a bulky high-wing single-engine transport, the Fokker T-2. The brute had so much gas and oil aboard, she couldn't get over the Rockies, so the pilots flew her up and down the West Coast and set a new endurance record instead, thirty-five hours and eighteen minutes in the air. A month later they did manage to get her over the mountains, but a ruptured cooling system forced the T-2 down in Indianapolis. The third try was lucky, and in May 1923, flying from east to west, they made it.

Perhaps the most significant flight after the Wright Brothers came in 1924. A relatively new firm, Douglas Aircraft Company, was building biplane torpedo carriers for the navy. Four of these were bought and specially modified by the Army Air Service, and on April 8 they took off from Seattle for an attempt to fly around the world. Their 26,000-mile route took them from Washington to Alaska, out along the Aleutians to Japan, down the coast of Southeast Asia, and across the Indian Ocean to the Middle East. Then they flew over the Mediterranean and across Europe, across the Atlantic to Boston, and from there on to Seattle. The first of them went down on a mountain in Alaska, but the crew walked out 10 days later. The second was lost in the Atlantic, west of Iceland, but the other two settled back in Seattle 5 ½ months and 388 hours' flying time after they had left. It was a monumental achievement, inevitably earning its fliers the press nickname of "Magellans of the Air." Three years later a young man name Charles Lindbergh became an instant hero by making the first solo flight from New York to Paris.

All these events made headlines, but what did they prove? Were they enough in themselves to justify an air force, or were they still just a promise of some importance at some future date? The British found a mission for their air force. They sent Trenchard's boys out after the Mad Mullah.

Worldwide empires tend to acquire strange characters in out-of-the-way places, and few have ever been stranger than the Mad Mullah. He appeared in 1898, half bandit chief and half religious cult leader, in the Horn of Africa, at the time divided into British and Italian Somaliland. Eventually he generated a punitive expedition that chased him around the bush for three years and finally broke up his followers, losing several hundred men and spending several million pounds in the process. The Mullah, however, would not go away, and year after year he and the British sniped at each other. By 1919 he was a real pest, and the government reluctantly decided on a full-scale campaign to be rid of him once and for all. The thought of sending two divisions, and building a rail line of supply into the interior, caused heartburn among the treasury officials, and thus the Colonial Secretary, Lord Milner, called in Trenchard. There was a minor argument; the army did not want to do the job, but they would rather do it than have the air force do it. But in January 1920 a single squadron of bombers flew down from Cairo to Somaliland, and in three weeks they bombed the Mullah out of successive strongholds. His followers rapidly lost enthusiasm, and finally, as a single fugitive, he crossed into Abyssinia, where he was killed. The squadron went back to Cairo, various battalions of ground troops returned to their stations, and the Colonial Office rejoiced at "the cheapest war in history." The Royal Air Force had a peacetime mission: It could serve as Britain's frontier police force.

When a full-scale revolt blew up in Iraq a few months later, the government decided to pull out its army garrisons and let the air force patrol the country and keep the tribes in order. This turned out to be a very difficult job, and not a very rewarding one for the men involved. How effective it actually was is a matter of argument, and it undoubtedly looked better to the accountants in London than to the pilots and gunners who were bombing tribal villages and all too often, when their planes were forced down by mechanical trouble, getting their throats cut—if they were lucky—by Iraquis or Afghans whose concept of war did not include the so-called civilized niceties.

Yet the business had its triumphs. In the winter of 1928–29, six hundred Europeans were caught in the midst of a civil war in Kabul. The RAF organized the first-ever major airlift, and in the course of nine anxious weeks they flew out all six hundred with no losses, the transport aircraft flying over the notorious Hindu Kush whenever the weather let them do so. This certainly contrasted favorably with one of the famous disasters of British imperial history. In 1842, during the First Afghan War, sixteen thousand British soldiers and their dependents had been massacred while trying to get over the mountains away from Kabul; only one survivor had staggered into India to tell the tale. However effective they actually were, Trenchard's squadrons at least avoided events such as that.

In the United States the problem of finding a mission was largely jurisdictional. Traditionally, the army had taken care of everything on land and the navy had taken care of everything on the water. The advent of aviation, at home over either element, violated this comfortable division of labor. A naval air service was not likely to bother the army too much, but an army air service potentially impinged upon the navy's role as the first line of defense. If army planes could range far out to sea, and perhaps sink an enemy fleet as it approached, what did that do to the navy's situation? The navy answered that planes could not do the job anyway, but in 1921 Mitchell used his bombers to sink the captured German battleship *Ostfriesland,* at anchor off the Virginia Capes. Two years later, two obsolete American battleships went the same way when army bombers destroyed the *New Jersey* and the *Virginia.* Mitchell had not really played fair, in that he had violated the conditions the navy set for the tests, but the navy had not played fair either, for the conditions that they set were designed to prevent Mitchell from succeeding. Both sides put the interpretation they chose on the events, Mitchell saying the battleship was now useless, and the navy insisting that bombers still would not sink fully operational ships maneuvering at sea. Eventually the army had to agree that it would not have airplanes that could fly more than a hundred miles out to sea, no matter how far they might fly over land. It was a decision with which neither side was happy, and which therefore was as reasonable a compromise as anyone was going to get.

But Mitchell's problem, and that of his supporters, was more fundamental than an interservice boundary dispute. It was bluntly stated by the Morrow Board in its report: "Is the United States in danger by air attack from any potential enemy of menacing strength? Our answer to this question is no. . . . The fear of such an attack is without reason. . . ." In spite of all Mitchell's fulminations, he could not alter this basic situation. A country that had no enemies, that had two great oceans between it and any conceivable trouble spots in the entire world, did not need an air force. The U.S. Army Air Corps, newly created from the old air service in 1926, languished throughout the late twenties.

Until air forces could find a viable reason for their existence, they were going to remain stepchildren of the older services. Tactical air power left them still in a supporting role, and true independence would come only when air power was seen as capable of dominating naval and military forces, not simply of supporting them on a tactical level. This was the question addressed by the great visionary theorists of air power in the years immediately after the Great War.

The answer was, of course, strategic bombing. It had to be the answer; it was the only other thing that air forces could do. But it was more than that; visionaries do not think in negatives. To men who both believed in the future of the airplane and had gone through the hell of the Great War, the strategic employment of air power was the panacea that would avoid future senseless slaughters. A number of men arrived at these conclusions more or less independently at about the same time. In Great Britain, men such as P.R.C. Groves, who had been director of flying operations, a British planning position, in 1918, F. W. Lanchester, and Sir Frederick Sykes, who was Trenchard's archenemy in the early days of the RFC, all meditated and wrote on the question. Trenchard himself was more a doer than a thinker, and his ideas of strategic bombing were more limited in scope than those of the others. Mitchell was more a propagandist than a real thinker. Writers in France who advocated strategic bombing, such as Colonel Pierre Vauthier, largely accepted the ideas of the first true prophet of air power, an Italian by the name of Guilio Douhet.

Douhet was born in 1869, and he was already near retirement age when Italy entered the Great War in 1915. At that moment he was Chief of Staff of an infantry division, but he had already been attracted to aviation, and even before the war had begun, he was thinking and writing about its possible uses. Influenced by Count Caproni, he was soon proposing an independent bombing force of five hundred of the latter's big bombers. He was actually court-martialed and sentenced to imprisonment after Italy's humiliating defeat at Caporetto in 1917 for criticizing the army high command, but in 1918, upon his release, he was named head of the Central Aeronautical Bureau of the army, and remained in service until his retirement in 1921. That year he published *Command of the Air*.

Here was a full-grown theory of air power and its potential. Douhet had extensively considered Italy's prospects and its problems, and he recognized, as his later readers often did not, that his ideas were conceived in response to his country's peculiar situation. Italy was poorly suited to be a naval power; the country lacked resources and had a long and vulnerable coastline, while none of Italy's potential enemies had anything absolutely vital within reach of the Italian navy. Militarily, the Italian condition was even worse. Any land offensives must be made through and over the Alps, and the repeated and ghastly battles along the Isonzo had shown what a futile proposition that was. The only way, therefore, that Italy could exert effective offensive pressure on an enemy was through the use of long-range air power.

In the airplane Douhet saw the perfect offensive weapon; it had none of the limitations of ground or naval power—it was indeed ubiquitous. Based on his own wartime experiences, both positive and negative, Douhet concluded that the airplane was capable of inflicting overwhelming destruction. Fleets of airplanes appearing over the enemy's capital and industrial centers would cause chaos; the enemy's government and industry would collapse immediately. There could be no effective defense against the airplane; the bomber would always get through. What had been done in the last war by blockade and slaughter on the battlefield would be done in a future war by strategic bombers, independently of the other services. Armies would have done no more than mobilize while air forces would have destroyed the will of their masters to continue the war. Douhet's dreams of masses of bombers was like Marshal Saxe's dream of masses of citizen soldiers, who at the first threat of war would leap to arms and dash among the enemy, utterly destroying his will to fight. Saxe's eighteenth-century dream was his Enlightenment answer to the sterility of the formal war of his day; Douhet's twentieth-century dream was his technological answer to the futility of modern mass warfare.

Defense was useless. A country should organize passive measures only, for building fighters merely detracted time and effort from the all-important bomber. Armies and navies might try to retain tactical air power for themselves, but the impact of the independent strategic air force would make even this use of air power unnecessary. Tactical air power, even armies and navies themselves, would simply wither away. Douhet stated emphatically, "the fundamental principle of aerial warfare is this: *to resign oneself to endure enemy aerial offensives in order to inflict the greatest possible offensives on the enemy.*" He pointed out that in the long run, his idea of war, brutally conducted but quickly over, was far more humane than what society had recently gone through.

With Douhet, air power had a coherent philosophy at last. Air forces need no longer be mere auxiliaries; they should rather be a country's primary military system. Their possession would deter an attack; and if it did not, it would ensure the prompt and inexpensive collapse of the attacker. As Mitchell said in his memoirs of the Great War, first appearing in *Liberty* magazine, "Air power is the great determining influence in the world's development. . . . Air power . . . conquers the opposing state in war by paralyzing its nerve centers. . . . Those of us in the air have had a vision of the future which we believe to be unquestionably correct."

In fact, as with most prophets, Douhet's greatest influence came long after he was dead. Not too many people read him during the twenties, and when he died in 1930, he had attracted no more than a few disciples. But those few were influential; his work was known in a translation at the U.S. Army Air Service Field Officers School at Langley Field in Virginia, and the American air doctrine enunciated in the manual *Employment of Combined Air Force* in 1926 borrowed heavily from Douhet's theories. Yet a popularly available English translation was not produced until 1942, and it was only then that most people discovered in Douhet a retrospective philosophical explanation for what air forces were trying to do in World War II. For the generation of the twenties, air power was still searching for a soul. Outside the fraternity of true believers, Billy Mitchell's arrogant assertion of an "unquestionably correct vision" was regarded as a pipe dream.

VIII

EXPERIMENTS IN
TERROR

At the end of the 1920s the western world was in an economic tail-spin. Millions were unemployed, industries were failing in every country, governments appeared powerless to alter or redirect the blind forces of the market. The world seethed with frustration. The infant aviation industry was grounded; hopeful veterans of the Great War who saw themselves taking hordes of passengers aloft into the heavens now sold their three or four airplanes and then went to selling shoes or life insurance. But in the midst of the chaos different orders were emerging. Soon a new American president would declare a New Deal, while a new German leader would proclaim the New Order. In 1929 the stock market crashed; in 1939 the world went to war.

Within the confines of the aviation world itself, the fermentation of ideas and techniques continued. There were the same old arguments about jurisdiction over land and water, about the fighter versus the bomber, about tactical versus strategic uses of air power, about who was the enemy, about private enterprise or state-run industries, and on and on and on. But airplanes got bigger and better and faster, and the men who started out as carpenters and auto mechanics were now thinking about all-metal construction, better aerodynamic streamlining, retractable undercarriages, rotatable turrets, leakproof gas tanks, and a thousand and one other ideas, none of them so terribly remarkable in themselves, but all of them together making a revolution in the industry.

Military aircraft were more or less standardized in the late twenties. The classic fighter was a biplane, with either a radial or an in-line engine. It had a fixed undercarriage, an open cockpit, and it carried two rifle-caliber machine guns. It had a top speed of something between 150 and 200 miles per hour, and a range of perhaps 250 miles. In the United States the beautiful Curtiss fighters and the sturdy little Boeings, in Britain the Bristol Bulldog and the Hawker Fury, all fit within these limits. They were lovely aircraft, carefully crafted and lavishly maintained, painted in bright squadron colors, and brought out for display at air shows and inspections; they were flown by pilots who in some cases still quoted their Great War scores after their names. For many, this was the golden age of aviation, and antique aircraft fanciers still vehemently insist that *real* airplanes have two wings and round engines.

Various designers were toying with monoplanes; the French favored parasol designs, with the single wing above the fuselage on struts, the Italians liked the Warren truss, a system of vee-shaped struts. Even back during the war, German manufacturers such as Junkers were producing tough, boxy, all-metal monoplanes with a characteristic corrugated metal skin. But these remained exceptions to the general acceptance of the biplane type.

The period may have been the golden age for fighters, but no one looking at the larger aircraft of the interwar period would say that designers had been preoccupied with aerodynamic qualities. Manufacturers resolutely ignored the old adage "If it looks good, it'll fly well," and they draped spars, struts, wheels, gun bins, and other protrusions on their planes with total disregard of drag and wind resistance. The 1929 Handley-Page Hinaidi looked like an angry bulldog; the 1932 American Keystone bomber looked like a flying barn with a question mark on the rear end for a fin; and the British Blackburn Iris looked very much like a blue whale with wings attached, which may have been appropriate as it was a flying boat. The absolute prize for ugliness probably went to the French, however, for they produced a whole series of bombers—Blochs, Potezs, and Loire et Oliviers, all slab-sided, square-winged, engine nacelles, and turrets and landing gears sprouting everywhere—whose very appearance typified the French aircraft industry's slide into mediocrity.

In the mid-thirties the revolution began, and designers, with new materials and manufacturing techniques, and new engines being developed, began the transition to the next generation. There was a quantum leap forward, and factories started to turn out the designs that would fight at least the early stages of World War II. The Martin B-10, entering service in 1935, was an all-metal, mid-wing, twin-engine monoplane, with enclosed cockpits, retractable landing gear, and internal bomb-carrying capacity. It was a marvel for its day, and even it was soon outclassed by bigger and better airplanes. The Douglas B-18, a military derivation of the company's famous DC-2 commercial transport, entered service in 1937. That year also saw the advent of the Heinkel 111, which served as a bomber for one or another of the world's air forces for thirty years.

Many of the new bombers did come from commercial aircraft, for by the thirties, in spite of the Depression and what it did to travel generally, there was a slowly growing market for air travel. Planes got faster, more comfortable, and, especially, more reliable. Douglas, Boeing, and Lockheed in the United States; De Haviland and Short Brothers in Britain; Breguet, Caproni, Fokker, Dornier, and Heinkel on the Continent—all were in the airliner business, and a plane that could carry twenty or thirty passengers several hundred miles could equally carry bombs, especially if, as in the case of some of the German planes, it was designed with that specific conversion in mind. "Flying Down to Rio" with Pan American Airways had both strategic and technological implications that could not be ignored. Airline routes also had potential military uses, and the major aviation countries were quick to stake out claims. In France and Germany no secret was made of this; Air France and Lufthansa were both overtly state owned and run. The Dutch, as usual, took a halfway stance with KLM, and the British, also as usual, ran Imperial Airways on the old boy network— ostensibly private industry, but with everyone who counted in the airline a relative or classmate of the necessary political opposite number. The United States' major overseas airway, Pan American, lambasted this bitterly, but Juan Trippe, its president, Yale '21, never hesitated to use the Old Blue connection in the corridors of the State Department, which not at all incidentally happened to be stocked with fellow Yale graduates.

It was ironic that naval aviation made very real strides in the interwar years, because it was naval air that stood most determinedly in the way of land-based air power. This was a battle the British had already lost, with the amalgamation of the Royal Air Force, and the Royal Navy's air component suffered for it throughout the period. But in the United States, the establishment of a Bureau of Aeronautics in the Navy Department, and the presence of a dynamic and forceful political admiral named William A. Moffett, ensured that naval air was not going to play second fiddle in some military corporate merger.

Billy Mitchell contended that navies were now of value only in an auxiliary role: They could transport planes and troops to islands which would then become air bases, after which aircraft would totally dominate the waters. In this as in so much else, Mitchell's vision overreached itself. He neglected the basic fact all sailors know, that oceans are very big, and the corollary, that islands in the middle of them are merely hostages to command of the sea. Mitchell thought that command of the air entailed command of the sea as well. Naval air people went at it in the other direction: If you commanded the sea, then you could command the air. Their answer was the aircraft carrier.

The advent of the carrier was assisted by the Washington Naval Treaty of 1922. It severely restricted the tonnage available for battleships and battle cruisers, but it permitted development of aircraft carriers. These might be a maximum of 23,000 tons, and the United States and Britain were allowed 135,000 tons' worth of them; Japan, 81,000 tons; and France and Italy, 54,000 tons. Even more important, battleships that were presently under construction, and which otherwise would have had to be scrapped, could be converted to carriers, and these were allowed to be as big as 33,000 tons, an exception to the first rule. This was the kind of escape clause beloved of diplomats, and in this case it was big enough to sail a battleship through.

At that time there were already aircraft carriers of a sort in existence. The British had HMS *Furious,* converted from a large, fast, and flimsy battle cruiser, and HMS *Argus,* converted from the hull of the liner *Conte Rosso,* which they had been building for Italy. With the first complete flying deck and no superstructure, she was universally known as "the flatiron." They also had a conversion from a battleship; laid down in 1913 as the Chilean *Almirante Cochrane,* this was bought by the Admiralty, altered to a carrier, and finished in 1923 as HMS *Eagle.* This was the first ship to have the characteristic "island" superstructure on the starboard side, a feature subsequently copied by virtually all navies. The first British carrier built as such was *Hermes,* and though small, at only 10,850 tons, this was a useful vessel incorporating experience to that point. The British undertook two more conversions during the twenties, *Courageous* and *Glorious,* from cruiser hulls, but they did not get another purpose-built carrier until *Ark Royal* in 1937.

This was all a bit of a hodgepodge, but it still was sufficient to show the British leadership in this aspect of naval war at the time. The United States had only the converted coal collier *Jupiter,* which entered service as an aircraft carrier, renamed *Langley,* in 1922. At the time of the treaty, however, there were two huge battle cruisers on the building ways; these were *Saratoga* and *Lexington,* and they were basically the American answer to the British *Hood.* They were now converted to carriers. At 36,000 tons, they were too big and heavy even for the escape clause, but a little judicious fudging with figures reduced their "published tonnage" to 33,000 tons. They were launched in 1925, and the Americans did not produce their next carrier, the little *Ranger,* for eight years.

The Japanese also had naval ambitions, as evidenced by their third place in the Washington treaty. A British naval air mission was at work in Japan at the time, and it soon bore fruit, ultimately bitter, as twenty years would show. Their first carrier was a converted oiler, the *Hosho,* of only 7,000 tons, completed late in 1922. But in 1925 the Japanese launched a battleship conversion, the *Akagi;* they said the tonnage was 26,900, but in fact it was over 30,000, and at the time of her entry into service, she was the biggest, fastest, and best-armed carrier in the world. A second conversion followed shortly, with the *Kaga.* Japan was staking further claims to the dominance of the western Pacific and east Asia; what the Americans and British saw as a generous treaty allowance, Japan saw as a humiliating second-class status. The simple truth was that no one in the outside world really understood what was going on in Japan in those days, and that included the British training mission, who found the young Japanese students willing and eager, but somewhat clumsy, imitators of things western.

None of the other powers did a great deal. The French were bitterly insulted by their treatment in Washington, less at being allocated fourth place than at being regarded as merely equals of the Italians, but they did not produce an aircraft carrier until 1927. This was the *Béarn*, a conversion from a battleship hull that had rusted on the stocks since 1915. They authorized two more in 1938, but neither was completed. The Italians, with an independent air force, never produced a carrier, though they began conversion of two ships during World War II. Germany never commissioned a carrier either, though she did build one, the *Graf Zeppelin;* this vessel was accompanied by all the usual trumpet blasts of propaganda, but it never weighed anchor. For practical purposes, therefore, aircraft carrier production and development remained a monopoly of the three great naval powers.

With the largest number of carriers between the wars, it might have looked as though the Royal Navy would have been the unchallenged leader in this field, but that was not the case. Naval air power was virtually stifled by the crushing embrace of the Royal Air Force, and for the crucial middle decade of the interwar years, this component of British naval power wallowed about, caught up in the bitter argument over who controlled what. The RAF insisted upon the "indivisibility of the air" and therefore of air forces. The navy insisted equally vehemently that it had special needs. Only very slowly did it make any headway. In 1921 the RAF reluctantly acknowledged that naval officers might be trained as observers—all the pilots of the old RNAS had had to transfer to the RAF if they wished to continue to be pilots. In April 1924 the Admiralty won another concession when the Fleet Air Arm was set up, though it was still a part of the Royal Air Force and remained so until 1939. Once when Trenchard addressed a group of graduating naval fliers, he said, "I congratulate you on becoming pilots—but I'll be damned if I can understand the color of your uniforms!"

The shortage of trained, and especially senior, air officers was equaled by the equipment problems. Aircraft procurement was securely in the hands of the Royal Air Force, and it was not about to make concessions in this vital area. The Fleet Air Arm did get some of its own planes, including the delightful Fairey Flycatcher biplane fighter, one of the true gems of the twenties with a jaunty look and sprightly performance, as well as the reconnaissance Avro Bison, arguably the world's ugliest aircraft in its day. But by the thirties, naval aircraft design was faltering in Britain, and the Fleet Air Arm entered World War II—and indeed with one type ended it—still flying biplanes.

American naval aviators might have had to fight the battleship admirals, but at least this was a family fued, and that made a great deal of difference. American carriers were fewer, but bigger, than the British. In fact, the entire Fleet Air Arm complement in 1930, 141 aircraft, could have been operated with room to spare by the *Lexington* and the *Saratoga,* each of which was capable of handling 90 aircraft. The normal complement for these ships was four squadrons, one each of fighters, scouting, torpedo bombers, and something new that the Americans were developing—dive bombers. The fighters were usually Curtiss Hawks and Boeings of one type or another, with Curtiss and Glenn Martin designs used for bombs and torpedos. The Martin torpedo bomber was capable of carrying either a torpedo or a bombload, and naval pilots, by judicious experimentation, discovered that aiming a plane at a ship and releasing the bomb in a dive was somewhat akin to aiming the plane as the best way to shoot the machine gun. It was to prove a discovery of enormous significance—its origins have been argued at great length—and was destined to become the standard naval attack procedure. Metamorphosed for land warfare by the fledgling Luftwaffe at the urging of Ernst Udet, it was also used with devastating effect by the Germans during their blitzkrieg campaigns in 1939 and 1940.

In 1929 the U.S. Navy undertook a series of maneuvers known as Fleet Problem IX. The exercise was an attack and defense of the Panama Canal. While the battleships steamed all over the place and "sank" each other with impressive enthusiasm, the *Saratoga* loafed at anchor in the Galapagos Islands. On the last day of the exercise, with only two hours left to go, she steamed over the horizon and launched eighty planes in one strike. These flew over the canal, "bombed" it and all the army planes in the area, "sank" most of the opposing fleet, and went home happy as lambs. The concept of the independent carrier strike force was born. The Fleet Air Arm might have been poor, second-class members of "the finest flying club in the world," but in the U.S. Navy, pilots who had less than a thousand hours' flying time were accepted into some crack squadrons on a trial basis only until they were considered competent.

* * *

Airplanes in the early thirties were almost an escape mechanism for a public that was eager to find any color and fun in a drab world of depression and unemployment. Schoolboys built delicate models of balsa wood and paper, and devoured *Flying Aces* and *Air Trails*. Hollywood churned out movies that catered to the demand for vicarious flying thrills. For pilots, there were almost too many thrills, not at all vicarious. In 1933 President Roosevelt responded to charges of monopoly-mongering by the commercial airlines. He canceled their contracts to fly the mail, and substituted the Army Air Corps instead. The results were a disaster, with eight planes wrecked, six pilots hurt, and five pilots killed in the first week of operations. This was the instrument with which Mitchell and like-minded men were proposing to replace the rest of the world's armed forces.

The fiasco resulted in yet another board, headed by former Secretary of War Newton D. Baker, and it recommended a General Headquarters of the Air Force. This was set up in 1935, but rather than address itself to the force's immediate needs, it started playing with the concept of the heavy bomber. Mitchell's apostles, exiled after his suspension to the dust of Texas, had thought long and hard about his ideas, and now, with a modicum of power, they were determined to play the strategic game. Their ruminations, translated into development specifications, eventually led to the B-17 Flying Fortress, which was one of the classic World War II bombers, but this also left the air corps, and the army, without any first-class fighters or tactical support aircraft in 1941 and 1942.

Far more portentous events were taking place simultaneously in Europe. On January 30, 1933, Adolf Hitler became chancellor of the German republic, and immediately began the transformation of his country, not only into a one-party state but into a militant and aggressive bully. One of his chief stalking points on his path to power had been total repudiation of the restrictions of Versailles, the hated *Diktat,* and he rapidly cast off the shackles. He did, in fact, exactly what he had always said he would do, and no one moved to stop him.

In 1930 the German army high command had stuck its toe in the water, and hinted that Germany needed a military and naval air establishment of twenty-two squadrons, for defense purposes only, of course. But with Hitler, all hesitation was swept aside. His right-hand man, Hermann Göring—twenty-two victories in the Great War, commander of the late von Richthofen's Jagdgeschwader No. 1, holder of the Pour le Mérite, the most prestigious convert to Nazism—became Minister for Air. Things happened quickly. The rest of 1933 saw the butterfly of a whole air-force command structure emerge from the cocoon of the army, and on April 1, 1934, the former Reichswehr advertising flights were transformed into Fighter Squadron 132. This was quickly followed by two more fighter squadrons, five reconnaissance, seven bomber, three naval, and a couple for general-purpose. The Germans began practicing dive-bombing, and the school in Russia was peremptorily closed down. Antibolshevism was another of Hitler's points, and there was no longer any need for disguises anyway.

All of this was overtly in violation of the existing Versailles Treaty system, but no one was willing to tell the Germans to stop. On March 16, 1935, Hitler issued a formal denunciation of the treaty's disarmament clauses, and announced that as France and Russia had never disarmed, the presuppositions of the whole system were invalid. He said there was going to be a German army of thirty-six divisions, there was going to be conscription for military service, and there was also going to be an air force, the Luftwaffe. The other European powers fluttered aimlessly and wrung their hands at this ungentlemanly conduct, but the British, ever sportsmanlike, left their supposed French friends in the lurch and signed a naval agreement with the new regime within three months. As long as Germany's navy was no more than 35 percent of Britain's, the French could solve their own problems.

On March 1, two weeks before the Versailles denunciation, the Luftwaffe became an independent service in its own right. The day was officially declared to be Air Force Day, Fighter Squadron 132 became Jagdgeschwader Richthofen No. 2, and its Heinkel 51 biplanes put on a flypast in Berlin to show the world there was already an air force in being. Indeed there was. In the last year the available strength of the still surreptitious service had increased ten times. In the six months of its open existence it trebled again, so that by August there were forty-eight operational squadrons. The German Air Sport League, which had become the National Socialist Flying Corps, now changed its initials once again and became the training establishment of the Luftwaffe; the Lufthansa airliners suddenly became auxiliary bombers. As if all this were not sufficiently threatening in fact, the Germans shouted their new power to the skies, grossly inflating their numbers and the performance figures of their aircraft. The Nazis operated on the thesis that if the lie is big enough, and repeated often enough loudly enough, people will believe it. People did.

The drive for immediate power entailed long-range sacrifices. It meant taking what was useful now rather than waiting for what might be better later on. As the Luftwaffe air staff counted up its possible enemies, it considered that a war with either France or Poland, or both, was likely, war with Belgium and Czechoslovakia possible, and war with the Soviet Union or Great Britain quite out of the question. Given this assessment, plus the drive for equipment at the first possible moment, the Luftwaffe was almost inevitably bent in the direction of tactical and medium-range operations, rather than long-range strategic air power. Its leaders concentrated on fighters, Heinkel 51 and Arado 68 biplanes, dive bombers such as the new Junkers 87, and twin-engined bombers such as the Dornier 23 and Junkers 52, then the Heinkel 111 and Dornier 17. Development began on four-engined, long-range aircraft, but this was going to take too long and use up too many scarce resources; the programs were shelved or canceled in favor of the bird in the hand, a decision made by Göring himself, and one which ultimately cost the Luftwaffe dearly.

During 1935 the Luftwaffe was preoccupied with expansion and training of new units. Exercises late in the year demonstrated profoundly that the force would not be ready for any real conflict until it was shaken down into a viable system. Hitler was not disposed to wait for perfection, however; he was ready early in 1936 to begin moving. It was his assessment, after all, that no one would try to stop him anyway.

The French might have done so, but their problem was more one of national will and morale than of material. The great armed force of 1918 had stagnated in the intervening years. Massive numbers, huge fortifications, and generals who believed they knew all about how the next war would be fought because they had suffered so badly in the last one provided only the illusion of security. That illusion collapsed in a sordid welter of pusillanimity and recrimination the first time it was challenged.

On April 1, 1933, as Hitler was fitting into the chancellor's job in Germany, the French air force became independent, as the Armée de l'Air. It completed the transformation to full autonomy a year later. Its problem was not organization, however, but outdated equipment. The

French aircraft industry and design had led the world in 1918, but had done little since then. To keep up their numbers against the Germans during the twenties, the French stayed with obsolete types and continued making aircraft as they had during the Great War. Some of their fighters were good, but their bombers were heavy, clumsy things, able, they hoped, to fight their way through to German targets and drop the minimal loads they could carry. Production methods were antiquated, and it took nearly twice as many man-hours to make a French plane as it did to make a German one. In 1935 the French aircraft industry delivered only 698 planes to the armed forces. The next year, under the threat of a resurgent Germany, a socialist government nationalized the industry to inject new life into it. In that year it delivered 702 aircraft.

In 1933 the French air minister, Pierre Cot, had introduced Plan I, which envisaged an air force of 1,000 planes, a reserve of 200 more, all to be replaced every five years, so that the French need produce only 250 new planes a year. Cot soon went out of office, for those were the years when French politicians played musical chairs with the country's destiny. He did not return until June 1936; by then the Germans had militarized the Rhineland, a crisis one French officer summed up by remarking with a shrug, "We have just lost the next war." Plan I was still in effect. In fact, at the end of 1935, the Armée de l'Air was actually in better shape than Cot's scheme would indicate. It had 437 fighters, 357 bombers, 1,368 reconnaissance aircraft, 1,632 trainers, and 559 planes in reserve. In other words, with 2,162 combat aircraft, however good they were, it was still more than a match for the nascent Luftwaffe. The point was academic, however, as the French chose not to use it.

Hitler's remilitarization of the Rhineland, on March 7, 1936, retrospectively assumed enormous significance as the first step on the road to World War II. But at the time it was just one crisis of several, for by then the whole world was marching resolutely but blindly forward to war. The Italians had invaded Ethiopia, the Japanese were flexing their muscles in China, and Spain was about to burst into civil war. The development of air power, kept on a short rein since 1918, was soon to be given its head once again.

No one knew what to make of Mussolini and Italy. Was he one of the great leaders of modern history, or was he a swaggering charlatan? It was impossible to be certain which, and sometimes he appeared to be both at once. And his country: Was it the greatest of the smaller powers, as its resources seemed to imply, or the smallest of the great powers, as its role in recent years proclaimed? Only Mussolini and a few of his more ardent and self-deluded followers thought it might be the greatest of the great powers, but in pursuit of this grandiose dream, Italy set out on a path of colonial empire. Late in 1935, after a series of engineered border clashes, Italian forces invaded Ethiopia in East Africa, one of the last remaining independent African states and long a target for Italian economic penetration. The campaign that followed, lasting for several months, was not much of a test for air power.

Ethiopia, whose Emperor Haile Selassie appealed in vain to the League of Nations, put up a valiant struggle, but he did not have a great deal with which to wage it. Several hundred thousand tribesmen mustered to fight, with antique weapons and outdated tactics. It took the Italians seven months to overrun the country and disperse the native armies, after which there were unending guerrilla operations, but there was never much question about the final outcome.

Nonetheless, the Italians did not really do very well. Their regular forces were slow and clumsy. The Fascist militia, which "volunteered" in large numbers for the campaign, proved to be totally incapable of waging war, even against primitive tribes. To break the back of enemy resistance, the Italians resorted to policies of what was regarded at the time as deliberate terrorism, and these especially involved the use of the Regia Aeronàutica, for the Italians were virtually unchallenged in the air. They sent about five hundred planes to East Africa, while the Ethiopians could reply with only a half dozen outdated French Potez biplanes. Ironically, the best aircraft they had was a single Breda transport that had been presented to Haile Selassie by the Italian government. One measure of the almost total lack of opposition is that Italian planes in Ethiopia were painted off-white with large bright red fan patterns on their upper wings; it was more important that they be visible if forced down by mechanical failure than that they be camouflaged against enemy action.

Most of the Italian aircraft were bombers and transports, as few fighters were needed. Caproni trimotored bombers were followed by Savoia Marchetti trimotors, and these, with no opposition, proved effective machines. Count Galeazzo Ciano, Mussolini's son-in-law and later Italy's foreign minister, flew in a bomber squadron in the cam-

paign. The air force was busy bombing and strafing Ethiopian positions in the early days of the action, and then carrying out what were
really terror attacks against towns and villages that held out against
them. They not only dropped high explosives in considerable amounts
but employed poison gas as well, a fact that they took enormous pains
to deny to the rest of the world. Terrible as it occasionally was, it was
not especially effective, and on balance was hardly worth the effort to
cover up the whole matter.

Few valid lessons could be drawn from a war in which air power
met practically no opposition, and in which it also had very little to
attack. There was no question of the bombers fighting their way
through to targets, but neither was there any question of using them
in a strategic sense, to destroy the enemy's industrial base, for he had
no industrial base. About all the war demonstrated was that air power
did indeed exist (though just how good Italy's was remained argu-
able), that it was potentially very nasty, and that that nastiness was
not going to provide much of an inhibition against its use.

The flagrant aggression of Italy in Ethiopia was a body blow both
to the League of Nations and to the general concept of collective security, and it moved Italy more and more toward Hitler's Germany
and away from the western democracies. But it was still essentially a
colonial war in the nineteenth-century fashion.

Far more crucial to the period, and also to the development of modern military technology and practice, was the civil war in Spain, which
broke out in July 1936. Here, the country was split between radical
left and reactionary right, and after a long series of riots and abortive
risings, a bitter struggle finally broke out. The Spanish army rose
against the Republican government, and was supported by most of
the navy, the Church, and the landowners. General Francisco Franco
emerged as the major leader of the rebels, who called themselves the
Nationalists; the government, or Loyalists, was supported in their turn
by large masses of urban workers. In the opening days of the war, the
country was more or less split in two, with the rebels controlling the
northwest-central part of Spain and a small area in the southwest, and
the Loyalists holding the Basque country on the Bay of Biscay, the
eastern part of Spain, and Madrid, the capital. The rebels also held
Spanish Morocco, across the Straits of Gibraltar, and this fact led to
a significant innovation in the use of air power right from the beginning.

The Spanish air force, like that of most of the lesser states, was both

small and out of date. It had about forty Nieuport NiD. 52 sesquiplane fighters, perhaps sixty Breguet Br. XIX light bombers, and a
few other odd planes. The naval air arm had twenty Vickers Vilde-
beest torpedo bombers, and there were a few experimental types, such
as the three Hawker Fury biplane fighters modified for Spain and
known as the Spanish Fury, which some authorities consider the most
beautiful biplane ever built. None of these aircraft types alone, nor all
of them together, would have had a significant effect on the war, even
if, at its outbreak, the force had remained united. Instead they split,
and units or planes usually ended up on the side that happened to
take over any given base.

It was less the Spaniards themselves than the foreign intervention
that became significant, and in this the air war rather reflected the
entire conflict. The Spanish Civil War, terrible enough in itself, became the great testing ground of political ideals in the thirties, thereby
assuming an importance beyond that justified by its actual military
activities. Germany and Italy intervened blatantly on the side of the
Nationalists, France sided surreptitiously and the Soviet Union sided
openly with the Loyalists, and the British wrung their hands ineffec-
tually around the edges.

For the Nationalists, the first great success came with the trans-
porting of their regular troops, especially units of the Spanish Foreign
Legion and African colonial soldiers, across the Straits of Gibraltar.
The Nationalists, flying the Douglas DC-2 and having Fokker transports at hand, appealed for assistance, and in late July, ten days after
the uprising began, the first Germans arrived to help. Flying Junkers
Ju 52 trimotored transports, they began to ferry men and equipment
across the Straits. Twenty planes, carrying about 22 men per trip,
carried more than 13,000 men, 36 field guns, 127 machine guns, and
well over 500,000 pounds of stores, enough to tip the balance in the
Nationalists' favor in the south.

Early in August the first German "tourists" arrived, and were soon
establishing a full-fledged air operation, which by November became
the Condor Legion, commanded by Generalmajor Hugh von Sperrle.
From then until the end of the war, the Germans rotated men and
equipment in and out of Spain, gaining extremely valuable combat
experience. With a field strength of about six thousand men, the Legion had bomber, fighter, reconnaissance, and coastal-patrol units, plus
signals and operations staff, and an antiaircraft artillery unit, which

in German service was habitually part of the Luftwaffe rather than the army. The pilots and ground-support people got combat experience that stood them in good stead later on. For example, most of the World War I tactics of air combat had been neglected during the twenties and early thirties, and pilots concentrated on formation flying to the exclusion of other skills. In Spain the Germans learned that if they were busy watching their leader's wingtip, they could not watch for the enemy. They quickly abandoned their tight, formal flying for loose gaggles of planes, and set up tactics calling for cooperation between leader and wingman, but not much more than that. These were lessons that British and French fighter pilots still had to learn in 1940.

The Germans also tested and refined new equipment. The Junkers 52 did not make a great bomber; the Heinkel 51 was an elegant biplane fighter, but it proved woefully inadequate in plane-to-plane combat; and the Heinkel 70 was an equally elegant, and equally inadequate, light bomber and reconnaissance aircraft. By the end of the war, all these had been replaced, with Heinkel 111 and Dornier 17 bombers, the Messerschmitt Bf 109 fighter, and the Junkers Ju 87 "Stuka" dive bomber, in other words, by the German planes that would fight much of World War II.

Mussolini was even more anxious to help his fellow aspiring dictator than Hitler was. Hitler wanted to keep the war rolling along and everyone preoccupied with it while he fished in troubled waters; Mussolini actually wanted to win it, and to that end he sent more than fifty thousand men to Spain—infantry and armored units, and a very substantial air contingent as well—numerically about the same size as the Condor Legion. Italian equipment in the early stages of the war was better than German; the little Fiat Cr. 32 fighter was a fine aircraft, and so well known that it was referred to simply as "the Italian fighter." Savoia Marchetti S. M. 81 trimotor bombers were followed by the even better S. M. 79 trimotor, and these were widely used throughout the war. Older Italian types such as the Meridionali biplane light bomber and reconnaissance aircraft did useful work; indeed, the success of Italian aircraft in the war led them to the erroneous conclusion that the biplane fighter was here to stay, and the Italians were building and using them, with decreasing success, after other countries had passed on to more modern designs. More than 400 of the Fiat fighters were used in Spain, out of the 763 aircraft Italy sent to the war.

The Nationalists were not the only ones courting foreign aid, though they were more successful at getting it, largely because the sources to whom they applied were less scrupulous. The Italians and the Germans, while openly sending men and machines to Spain, also sat down with the democracies to discuss ways to prevent the very intervention they were supplying. In 1936 a Socialist government was in power in France, and though it would not intervene openly, it was willing to help the Spanish Republic around the edges. French fliers organized units across the Pyrenees, and several deals allowed the Loyalists to obtain French aircraft. André Malraux formed an Escuadra España at Toulouse, and managed to get Dewoitine D. 372 parasol winged fighters for it. The French government also released Potez 540 twin-engined bombers; in 1937 this was the main type of bomber for the Loyalists, comprising about fifty of the roughly two hundred aircraft that France provided during the war.

The big foreign supplier to the Republic was the Soviet Union. Unfortunately, its aid was so hedged with political constraints that the Russians were often working at cross-purposes with the people they were helping. Nonetheless, Communist aid was still the greatest external factor in the prolongation of Republican resistance. There is some dispute over figures, but the Russians are generally agreed to have supplied 1,405 aircraft to Spain. Most of these were the Polikarpov I-15 biplane fighter, known as the "Chato," or "Cat." A good aircraft of its type, it was soon outclassed by newer western types, and then the Russians supplied the I-16, which they called the "Fly" but the Nationalists called the "Rat." Cat and Rat together accounted for 1,025 of the Russian aircraft sent to or built in Spain. The Rat, a tubby monoplane with a retractable undercarriage, was an advanced and agile little plane showing just how surprisingly modern the Soviet aircraft industry was. The other major type was a medium bomber, the Tupolev SB 2, an excellent aircraft and really the first modern bomber to be used in Spain, ahead of the Dorniers and Heinkels.

Ironically, the Nationalists habitually regarded many of the Russian aircraft as American, regularly referring to the Tupolev bombers as "Martins" and to the Polikarpovs as "Curtiss fighters." In fact, the Americans had little to do with the air war, except for a few foreign volunteer pilots. The only American plane to be used in any real numbers was the Grumman G-23; this was an export version of the U.S. Navy's FF-1 fighter, built in Canada by the Canadian Car and

Foundry Company, ostensibly for Turkey; about forty of these ended up in Spain.

Given the usual wastage of operations, there were never masses of aircraft available. The Loyalists peaked at about 470 planes late in 1937; the Nationalists were then outnumbered, but they continued to receive increasing amounts from Italy and Germany. The role of air power was never really decisive, though some advocates have said the Nationalists would have lost without the early airlift across the Straits. Beyond that, however, air power was still an auxiliary, though an increasingly important one. Condor Legion aircraft successfully bombed and put out of action the Spanish battleship *Jaime I,* an incident successfully ignored by battleship admirals. In the same month, August 1936, the Germans managed to drop two tons of supplies to the besieged garrison of the Spanish military academy, the Alcazar, in Toledo.

Tactical use of aircraft continued to demonstrate its value. In March 1937 two Italian divisions, supported by fifty light tanks, attempted to break through the Loyalist lines in Guadalajara and surround Madrid. March is not a good month in Spain, so the Italians were forced by the mud and rain to advance along the roads in column. Caught by surprise by Russian divebombers, the Italians were mercilessly pounded until they broke across country, losing most of their equipment and all of their cohesion. It was a classical attack, launched by the Loyalists from usable fields while Nationalist aircraft sat in the mud on improvised strips behind their advance.

The use of tactical air power was not especially exciting to the world at large; far more shocking was the widespread bombing of cities. Though neither side could muster large numbers of bombers for this type of work, both used what they had as much as possible. For a large part of the war Madrid was held by the Loyalists, at the end of a long salient reaching out from the east coast. The rebels repeatedly attacked the city, usually with only a few planes but occasionally in heavier numbers. Madrid became the first western city to suffer this sort of bombardment, and watchers of *News of the World* in movie theaters were awed by the sight of bomb bursts on the white buildings of Madrid's University City. But the Loyalists held on grimly and life went on; people adapted surprisingly quickly to the new rules of life necessitated by bombardment, and the incongruities of civilized life in the middle of war soon ceased to shock.

Both sides bombed whenever and wherever they could. The Loyalists struck at Seville and Valladolid, and Barcelona, the major Republican city aside from Madrid, was repeatedly attacked. A raid in late January 1938 by nine S. M. 79's killed 150 people; in March a three-day series of raids killed 1,300. But the most horrifying attack of this type had already come earlier in the war, when in April 1937 the Condor Legion hit the small Basque town of Guernica.

At the time, the Nationalists were trying to conquer the province of Vizcaya and the Bay of Biscay coast, and were advancing on the major city of Bilbao. General Mola, one of Franco's chief rivals, later killed in an air crash, was conducting the campaign with a relentless fervor that typified the war in general and this part of the country in particular. At the end of March the Nationalists had bombed and strafed the town of Durango, but the 7,000 people of Guernica were caught by surprise on Monday, April 26, a market day, when German planes appeared overhead. It was late in the afternoon, and the town was repeatedly bombed and strafed by Heinkel 111's, followed by Junkers 52's. The planes dropped high explosives and incendiary bombs, then came in low with machine guns blazing. Attacking in waves every twenty minutes for three hours, they reduced the town to rubble. Some 1,654 people were killed, another 889 wounded. The town was occupied without resistance a couple of days later.

World opinion was intense; investigations were launched, appeals made, protests penned. For a while the Germans attempted to deny that they had done the bombing, and concocted all sorts of stories that contradicted each other. Some said it was a mistake, some said it was an experiment, some said the Republicans had done it, some denied that it had ever happened. Research is still going on about Guernica, and so many facts have been revealed that the truth of it will probably be obscured forever. It inspired Pablo Picasso to produce his masterpiece, and *Guernica* became the most famous painting of the modern world. Once a German officer viewing it asked Picasso, "Did you do that?" And he replied, "No. *You* did that!"

Gradually the war burned down. The Nationalists slowly improved their strength and their territorial holdings, while the Loyalists fought bitterly among themselves. Catalonia in the northeast was isolated in the middle of 1938, and from then on it was but a matter of squeezing. The foreign volunteers and International Brigades went home, Barcelona fell, and in March 1939 Franco and the Nationalists stood triumphant but exhausted over the wreckage of their country. Spain was bankrupt, and about 750,000 people had died, some 15,000 of them in air raids. By the time it ended, the Spanish Civil War was back-page news, a mere proving ground for greater things to come.

The thirties saw one other area of conflict that would have been of even greater significance than Spain if anyone had known much about it. Japan took giant strides in the aggressive and expansionist policy she had followed ever since her emergence into the modern world in the mid-nineteenth century. Overpopulated, militaristic, disciplined, and industrious, the Japanese had adopted and adapted what they wanted of western technology and used that to preserve and enhance their essential easternness. They borrowed aircraft technology just as they had earlier borrowed naval and military technology, and they then made it their own. The first generation of postwar Japanese pilots were trained by the French or the British, but they then trained their own people. One of the typical aircraft of the period was the Mitsubishi 1MF; it was designed by Herbert Smith, better known as the creator of some of the best British aircraft of World War I, for he was chief designer of the Sopwith Company. He went to Japan in 1923 as an adviser. But by the thirties, indigenous designs such as the Nakajima 91 were replacing license-built French types, and the Japanese aircraft industry reached maturity just as the country embarked on the Chinese phase of its expansionist career.

In 1931 the Japanese took over Manchuria, which they set up as a puppet state the next year, withdrawing from the League of Nations. In 1932 they attacked and temporarily occupied Shanghai when the awakening Chinese organized a boycott of Japanese imports. For several years there was growing tension as Chinese Generalissimo Chiang Kai-shek tried to pull his faction-ridden country together. In July 1937 open if undeclared war broke out, and the Japanese launched a full-scale invasion of north China.

The Chinese could oppose this with manpower, but not much else. They had little modern industry, no navy, only a few obsolete aircraft flown as often as not by foreign mercenaries whose claims of experience would not bear very close scrutiny. They had nothing of the substructure that enables air power to function. The Japanese, by contrast, had modern and effective naval and army air forces, and the industrial and logistics backup necessary for their support. By the end of 1937 they had overrun most of China north of the Yellow River.

They had fought a fierce battle for Shanghai, in which their troops had been so badly pressed that they had had to fly air support all the way from Japan itself, which they did very successfully. They took the old capital of Peking and the new one of Nanking, where they bombed and strafed British and American gunboats in the Yangtze River, sinking the USS *Panay*. The Chinese moved their capital to Hankow, and when that was threatened, to Chungking, in the southwestern mountains. Everywhere the Japanese bombed and strafed, their airplanes usually unhindered in the sky. To meet the occasional Chinese fighter opposition, they developed long-range escort fighters and hacked out emergency forward airstrips where the fighters could quickly refuel and rise to fight again.

By the end of 1938, they controlled most of the coast and all of China's great ports; they were starving the Chinese of outside help, but they could not finish off the war. There were simply too many Chinese to control or kill them all, and by 1939, the Japanese were forced to change their strategy to one of occupation and attrition. They had learned valuable lessons on the uses of air power, how to coordinate it, and what it could do. They had developed new aircraft and new techniques; the Mitsubishi A5M fighter or the G3M2 bomber were as good aircraft as anything in the world, and Japanese high-level bombing and fighter tactics were more than a match for anything being done in Spain. Japan was on the march, and if she was a bit frustrated in China, she had a long way to go yet.

War was in the air by the late thirties. Everywhere the totalitarian powers were aggressive and demanding. Air power and its potential for destruction was a hot topic, and an overtly employed propaganda tool. While the citizens of Madrid or Shanghai stood up to aerial bombardment, democratic politicians were sure their own people could not do so, and therefore must not be offered the chance. Some of air power's most crushing victories were won in battles that were never fought.

IX

FALLACIES OF FEAR

When German troops moved into the Rhineland on March 7, 1936, it was all a gigantic bluff. Militarily it was not even gigantic, for the operation was carried out by a total force of three infantry battalions and two squadrons of fighter aircraft. The soldiers were instructed to retreat and give up the effort if one single shot was fired at them. But, of course, not one single shot was fired, and the French, who were the biggest losers in the affair and the most resentful of it, were easily talked out of any firm action. They had at the moment a caretaker government, and when they consulted with Great Britain, the British were unwilling to go to war just because Hitler had "walked into his own backyard." Prime Minister Neville Chamberlain consistently found homely and innocuous phrases to disguise actions that he did not wish to perceive as dangerous.

It was this employment of air power that Hitler understood best. Indeed, he had little conception of the major problems or limitations of aerial warfare, a shortcoming he compounded by leaving direction of the Luftwaffe largely in the hands of Hermann Göring, who did not really understand it either. In spite of occasional flashes of insight, or of the presence on the air staff of farther-seeing men, the Nazi leadership shaped the Luftwaffe for its own limited ends. Those ends were more psychological than military. Hitler was willing to use his armed forces, but he did not really intend to use them, at least not in the immediate future. Hitler was like a poker player winning several hands on the strength of his bluffing. The other players did not call him until he had almost won the game.

For the next three years Hitler forced the pace, scaring not only his enemies but his own military men as well. He had assessed the opposition and decided that it was weak and vacillating, as indeed it was, and he therefore consistently overrode the cautions and hesitations his own commanders voiced, until he had established a complete moral ascendancy over them. In October the Berlin-Rome Axis was formed, and Italy and Mussolini fell under the sway of Germany. In March 1938 German troops moved into and occupied Austria. Italy was wrapped up in Spain, France was in the midst of yet another cabinet crisis, the British again determinedly saw Hitler taking only what was his own.

In May there was an affair that has been known as the First Czech Crisis. German nationals within the hybrid state of Czechoslovakia were agitating for union with Germany. Refusal of some of their exorbitant demands, and rumors of mobilization of German troops on the border led Britain, France, and Czechoslovakia itself to take a strong line with Hitler. He at the time, and some German writers since then, protested innocence in outraged terms, and the minicrisis blew over. But whether or not this was a false alarm, Czechoslovakia was indeed next on Hitler's shopping list, and in September the problem flared up again. There were feverish negotiations back and forth. France was allied with Czechoslovakia, and pledged to come to her assistance. But the French would not move without the British, and the British were determined not to fight. Eventually Premier Daladier of France and Prime Minister Chamberlain not only agreed to all Hitler's demands but also did his dirty work for him, forcing acceptance of those demands on the reluctant Czechs at the Munich Conference. Germany got the mountainous Sudetenland region of western Czechoslovakia, which made the rest of the country virtually defenseless. This was largely academic, for in March of the next year Hitler took over the remainder of the state anyway.

Munich and the Czech crisis was probably the greatest victory of air power to date, for one of the major factors in the whole equation was the question of air warfare, and what might happen to those countries foolish enough to resist the will of Hitler and open themselves to attack by his invincible Luftwaffe. Politicians possessed both an exaggerated fear of the potential of air warfare in general and of the Luftwaffe in particular. This the Germans assiduously fostered. In the midst of the crisis, for example, they invited General Joseph Vuillemin, Chief of the French Air Staff, to make an inspection visit to Germany. The French government was foolish enough to insist that Vuillemin accept, against professional advice, and he was therefore exposed to a very impressive display of German legerdemain. It looked like a quick—and deceptive—peek at Hitler's hole card. The Frenchman was taken to German air bases, where impressive numbers of bombers were lined up; he visited factories and saw how diligently the Germans were turning out war planes; he saw a demonstration flight of the Heinkel 100, a souped-up prototype machine that had just won a world speed record. Vuillemin was led to believe that this was but one of hundreds of German fighters; in fact, it was but one of a dozen, and the type never reached first-line squadron service. Vuillemin went home to France full of German hospitality and dire prophecy. His conclusion that in war the Armée de L'Air would not last two weeks against the Luftwaffe reinforced the government's already well-developed desire to capitulate.

Nor was this the only counsel of surrender. Both American Ambassador to Britain Joseph Kennedy and Charles Lindbergh were skeptical about chances of standing up to Hitler. Kennedy did not matter much, as his opinions were those of an obstreperous amateur, but Lindbergh was a different character altogether. Universally accepted as an aviation expert, he and his wife were just back from a visit to Germany. He had been asked by the United States government to observe whatever he could, and the Germans, playing their bluffing game to the hilt, had shown him everything to strengthen their case and nothing to weaken it. What he did see was enough to cause him serious alarm, and neither he nor anyone else at the time really knew what aerial bombardment could or could not achieve, or how much of it civilian populations could withstand. In London his mood and his message were both pessimistic; his dire pronouncements reinforced ideas many leading British figures already held, enabling them to follow a path they were all too anxious to pursue already.

The facts, of course, were rather different. Just who had what when, and what it was capable of doing, is a matter of endless argument. The French were indeed in dire shape; in Telford Taylor's phrase, their air force had been "victimized by a combination of parsimony, lethargy, and senility." At the end of 1936 the Armée de l'Air possessed 4,447 aircraft; during 1937, as a result of changeover in the industry, they accepted only another 528. Of this 5,000 total, about 1,300 were fighters or bombers, and most of these were qualitatively inferior to German types.

The Royal Air Force had rather fewer aircraft available than France did, but they were almost invariably better and more modern planes. There were approximately 4,100 aircraft on squadron strength, but 3,600 of them were relatively new and useful planes, with only about 500 in the reserve category. The majority of British planes in service were bomber types, but the RAF was then in the midst of a doctrinal shake-up that arrived just in time to prepare it for the coming war.

Against these 9,000 planes of the two western allies, the Germans could muster just about 4,500 in first-line service. This left them outnumbered two to one in the west, if indeed they had had to fight. The Czechs did not have much of an air force; their best plane was a biplane fighter, the Avia B-534, of which they had something over 400. Nonetheless, in the event of war, the Germans proposed to use most of their available strength on the Czech front, where they allocated an air fleet of more than 1,200 first-line aircraft. This would have left them very little with which to flatten London and Paris.

What mattered was not what anyone had, but rather what one side thought the other had. The British and French leaders, and their advisers, thought the Germans had a great deal more than they did. Figures of anywhere from twelve to twenty thousand aircraft were bandied about, and horrendous visions of terror from the air filled the press. For men who were already defeated in their own minds, air power and the threat of destruction was a major excuse. Though it was only dimly recognized at the time, the Munich crisis proved the last best chance to stop German aggression short of another major war; by surrendering to Hitler, the western democracies ensured the very thing they sought most diligently to avoid.

After Munich, and especially after the takeover of the remainder of Czechoslovakia early in the next year, the pace of rearmament increased frantically. By now, important technological and doctrinal decisions had already been made, decisions that were vitally to affect the way in which air power would be used, and World War II fought and won, and lost.

Everyone had by now accepted that air power and air forces were an integral part of a war-making capacity. But different governments had varying conceptions of what air power was capable of, and they therefore had different doctrines of its employment. These in turn conditioned the technological evolution of the machines, so that views adopted in 1935, say, were still being worked out in their consequences in 1945.

Most countries took the view that air forces were still basically auxiliary to other forms of armed force. Even if they possessed an independent air service, as the French and the Germans did, they accepted the primacy of another service—the army in both these cases—and therefore saw their air forces as providing essentially tactical support for army operations. They built fighters, ground-attack aircraft, and reconnaissance planes. They also built bombers, but though these might have been considered heavy bombers at the time, they were in fact medium, usually twin-engined, and with relatively limited ranges and bomb-carrying capacities. They still saw strategic bombing as being in direct if more distant support of actual military operations.

The Japanese did not possess an independent service; their army and navy each had their own private air force. The Italians had the Regia Aeronàutica, and they paid homage to the theories of Douhet, but their industry and economy were such that they were never able to put this into practical effect. The Soviet Union had a huge air arm, but it was relatively clumsy and possessed types that were fast becoming obsolete. Though they did eventually produce a small number of strategic bombers in the true sense of the word, they employed them very little, and essentially they took the same stance as the French or Germans did: Air power was best used for tactical support of ground forces.

Of the major powers, then, only Great Britain and the United States went beyond this limited conception of the use of air power, and began working toward a fully independent strategic striking force. There was a variety of factors at work here, and it was not simply a matter of the independence or otherwise of the arm of service, for the Royal Air Force was a separate service while the Army Air Corps was not.

More important were the philosophical underpinnings of the forces' leaders, the question of geography and what that meant for defense problems, competition from the other services and the forms it might take, and, above all, the possession of the technological and economic substructure that encouraged and enabled a long-term investment of time, money, and expertise. The great bomber fleets of 1944 hardly sprung full-grown from the war itself.

In both air forces, the commanders had grown up with the idea that bombing, and strategic bombing at that, was the end purpose of air power. Trenchard and his successors, Mitchell and his disciples, had all accepted the view that air power was indivisible, that it was ubiquitous, that command of the air was achieved not by shooting down the enemy's bombers but by destroying them on the ground at their own bases or, better yet, in their own factories before they were built. Only large bombers could do that, and in Great Britain during the thirties there were better than two bombers built for every fighter, in spite of the far greater expense of building, maintaining, and flying bombers. Air power was exercised offensively, and, so it was thought at the time, this was done by bombers.

Though it did not look it on the map, the countries were geographically similar in the sense of strategic air warfare. Britain was an island compared to Europe, the United States was an island compared to the world. Both were relatively immune from invasion, and both needed, in the event of a war, to project force abroad rather than concentrate it for defense at home. The British would want to exert pressure on the Continent, the United States would want to extend protection to and beyond its offshore holdings—Alaska, Hawaii, the Panama Canal, the Caribbean. These factors combined with the situation of the other armed services. Both countries possessed navies that were only partly rivals to the claims of air power; the Royal Navy was still living with the subordination of the Fleet Air Arm to the RAF, and the United States Navy, having adopted the airplane and the aircraft carrier, was reluctantly resigned to an expansive role for the Army Air Corps. More important, neither country possessed a major army to which the air service could be subordinated, as was the case in France, Germany, and the Soviet Union. If military power were to be projected on land beyond the homeland, it was not going to be by the British army, which was little more than a colonial police force in the mid-thirties, or by the United States Army, which in 1935 consisted of 135,000 men, and which three years later did not possess one combat-organized division.

Finally, it was in the United States and Britain, and only in those countries, that the industry, economy, political system, indeed, the entire ethos of the two countries was such that it could afford and sustain the kind of effort needed to produce a fleet of four-engined, heavy strategic bombers capable of acting independently and exerting an influence on the war to come. This was no short-term, quick-fix matter, and it took a major effort extended over a good decade to develop the end product. Japan could not do it, neither could Italy. France probably could not, given the wrong turns of the twenties and early thirties, and Germany and the Soviet Union, though capable of such an effort, chose a different path because of the other determining conditions.

The painful course of development is best illustrated by the design history of three of the famous heavy bombers of World War II—the American Flying Fortress, the British Lancaster, and the German Heinkel He 177. All three became legends; each in its way typified its country's air effort.

In the early 1930s the U.S. Army Air Corps finally won its battle for priority over the navy in matters of coastal defense. As a result the Material Division issued a specification for a new bomber to carry a ton of bombs at 200 mph for 5,000 miles. This was called Project A, and the aim was to get a plane that could reinforce Hawaii, Alaska, or Panama via a direct flight. In response to this the Boeing Aircraft Company of Seattle, Washington, designed a four-engined airplane called the XB-15. But it did not go into production, for the air corps revised the specification, calling simply for a multiengine bomber. Several designers entered twin-engine designs, but Boeing stayed with four, and submitted a proposal based on a slightly scaled down XB-15, which they now called the Model 299. Boeing was a dynamic company, already a world leader in commercial aircraft design, and their Model 247 transport had been a huge technical success. The methods of all metal construction used on the 247 were applied to the 299, and the result was a marvel of aeronautical engineering. It was also a great risk, for it was the only four-engined plane in the competition. With a wing spanning 103 feet, and four Pratt and Whitney engines, it could fly 235 mph at 10,000 feet, with a ceiling of 25,000; it could carry more than a ton of bombs, and the demonstration model flew 2,100 miles nonstop from Seattle to Wright Field in Ohio for its military tests.

From this impressive beginning it was an uphill battle for the strategic bombing advocates to get the bomber they wanted. The air corps intended to buy 65 Boeings, but an accident to the prototype changed their minds; they could get 185 other aircraft for the same price. Instead they bought 13 test models. By August 1937 the 2nd Bombardment Group of the General Headquarters of the air corps was fully equipped with the big new Boeing bomber. The group, commanded by Colonel Robert Olds, flew testing missions, and then long-distance demonstration flights, to Buenos Aires, Rio de Janeiro, and back and forth across the United States. However good the plane might have been, strategic theory still had an uphill fight, and when in 1937 the Boeing bombers, B-17s as they were now known, intercepted an Italian liner 700 miles at sea on a training exercise, the navy made such a fuss that the air corps agreed to mind its manners and buy only tactical planes for the next several years.

Munich changed all that. With the threat of war, development accelerated, and by 1939 production was gathering momentum. There were still a mere 23 in service when war broke out in Europe, but they were the only combat planes in the air corps' entire inventory still operational by the time of Pearl Harbor. All the time there was a constant process of refinement and design improvement; power and weight both went up correspondingly. In 1941, 20 went to Britain under Lend-Lease; more went out to the Philippines as the U.S. Army tried to build up a credible presence in the Far East. The first truly combat-worthy model, the B-17E, the first of the series with the characteristic huge tail, appeared in September 1941. From then on, Boeing never looked back. The early B-17's were great performers, but not really capable of modern air combat, of living up to the name "Flying Fortress." But with the E model, after six full years of development, the B-17 was ready for war and for a place in aviation legend. From July 1940 to the end of the war, 12,677 Fortresses served with the air corps, and though it was eventually outclassed by bigger and better aircraft, it became the embodiment of America's air effort and the best-loved plane in American history.

What the Fortress was to Americans, the "Lanc" was to the British; as the former exemplified American design vision, the latter typified the British ability to adapt to changing demands and circumstances.

The Lancaster was a successful derivative of a resounding failure. Its original, the Avro Manchester, was designed to meet Air Ministry specification P.13/36, which called for a high-performance twin-engine medium bomber. The criteria set meant a major advance in airplane development, which A. V. Roe met, but they encountered two problems. One was that they had to install untried engines, the twenty-four cylinder Rolls-Royce Vulture; the other was that development was so pressed by panic rearmament after Munich that the plane was ordered off the drawing board and put into quantity production without time to work out the kinks. For neither the first nor the last time, the British found themselves saddled with an inadequate aircraft by the pace of events. By mid-1940 the new Manchester was reaching squadron service, where, largely thanks to its unreliable engines, it was a disaster.

It was, however, an excellent airframe, and by early January 1941 Avro had successfully mated the basic type with four Rolls-Royce Merlin X engines. The Merlin was one of the great engines of all time, powering among others the Spitfire and Mustang fighters. With this combination, the new machine, now named Lancaster, was ordered into production. It proved both a tractable and highly versatile aircraft. It carried greater payload with less crew than the Flying Fortress, it was docile enough to take a large number of modifications, including one that enabled it to carry the incredible 22,000-pound "Grand Slam" bomb, the biggest of the war. Flown by almost sixty squadrons of Bomber Command, Lancasters dropped two thirds of the RAF's bombs on Germany. In all marks, 7,374 were built, and it was probably just what the British claimed it was, "the finest bomber of the war."

The story of the Heinkel He-177 "Greif," or "Griffon," by contrast, illustrated exactly what was wrong with German aircraft development and air-war theory. The first Chief of Staff of the Luftwaffe, General Walther Wever, was actually a believer in strategic bombing; he wanted Germany to have long-range aircraft that could deliver useful payloads on British targets and harass British shipping out in the Atlantic. Had he gotten his way, World War II might have taken a somewhat different course, but Wever was killed in an air crash in 1936, and for two years his ideas appeared to have died with him. Then in 1938 the Luftwaffe decided that it probably did need a long-range heavy bomber after all, and it commissioned the Heinkel firm to design and build one. Heinkel's response was radically innovative; it called for four engines, coupled in two nacelles and driving only two huge propellers. So the Greif, though it was a four-engined bomber, looked as if it were twin-engined. The cooling system was to be by surface-evaporation radiators, which would further reduce drag, and defensive armament was to be in remotely controlled barbettes, again reducing drag more than manned turrets would.

Unfortunately none of these innovations was sufficiently tested to work well. Conventional radiators had to be installed with an aerodynamic penalty; the engines still overheated and often caught fire, to the extent that in service the plane was known disgustedly as the *Luftwaffenfeuerzeug,* or Luftwaffe fire lighter. Meanwhile, the air authorities kept changing the specifications, calling for the plane to be able to act as a dive bomber and do other quite impossible feats. As if that were not enough, between bouts of changing their minds they simply shelved the program altogether.

The prototype flew on November 19, 1939, but did so for only twelve minutes, as the engines overheated alarmingly. The second prototype disintegrated in midair as a result of flutter, the third was used for engine testing, and the fourth crashed in the sea when it refused to come out of a shallow dive. By now the monster had become so heavy that special landing gear had to be devised for it; weight kept going up, performance down. Not until late 1941 were production aircraft built, and several months later the Luftwaffe was still testing, and still complaining about and demanding changes in, the prototypes. The first thirty production types were used for testing, many were lost in accidents, and all were returned for repair after each flight.

By now it was 1942, and Hermann Göring, who had hitherto thought the whole heavy-bomber effort a waste of time and resources, was loudly demanding that the Greif enter service. At the end of the year, when schedules called for 70 aircraft a month, Heinkel was delivering 5. The first Greifs used operationally were flown as transports to the surrounded German Sixth Army at Stalingrad, hardly the use intended for them. In 1943 Heinkel produced 415 machines, many of which were modified for use as torpedo bombers, and they were largely used over the Atlantic, where they were lost at such an alarming rate that by the end of the year the Luftwaffe ordered all the surviving ones scrapped. This was ignored, and the Germans used Greifs with other types in an attempt to revive the London Blitz early in 1944. So they soldiered on until the end of the war, still undergoing modifications and corrections intended to make up for their original flaws. Altogether about 1,000 were built, but a mere 200 seem to have seen operational service. The rest were written off in one accident after another, and their remains were found on airfields all over Germany at the end of the war, testimony both to the shortsightedness and vacillation of the German leadership, and to the German aircraft industry's inability to fulfill its promises.

The idea that "the bomber will always get through" was an article of faith among the proponents of strategic bombing, and it was that faith that produced the "heavies" of World War II. But ironically, just as those large aircraft were becoming a reality, the foremost supporters of the idea were having second thoughts. In the later thirties the British began thinking of aerial defense. This trend coincided with a whole rash of new developments. In terms of aircraft, a new generation appeared. The first fighter monoplanes came into British service—the Hawker Hurricane and then the Spitfire. With these the RAF possessed machines at last capable of meeting and overwhelming the bomber—if they could find it.

The answer to that was provided in a roundabout way, by the offshoot of a search for some sort of death ray, a concept beloved of science-fiction writers of the period. It was impossible to develop a death ray; but it was possible to build a machine that would bounce an electronic echo off a target, a Radio Direction Finder, subsequently known as radar. By 1939, barely in time, the British were developing a chain of radar stations that gave them advance warning of enemy aircraft heading toward them. They also had a device, IFF, or Identification Friend or Foe, that told them which of the dots on their radar screens were their people and which were not. Equally important, they had connected the whole system together in a communications net that provided their fighters with the essential control and information that enabled them to put their knowledge to good use. All these things together—the three-hundred-mile-an-hour, eight-gun fighter, the early detection by radar, and the control network—suddenly and very quietly meant that the bomber was *not* always going to get through. This was an idea that flew in the face of the established policy of the RAF, which went right on building bombers just when it was preparing to shoot them out of the sky, and it was a contradiction that air officers chose to ignore in their discussions with politicians, especially at budget time. Ultimately, of course, the British had their cake and ate it too. Because of the wealth of their material, and the vision with which they used it, they proved the bomber could not get through to Britain, and they proved it could get through to Berlin.

Rearmament went on rapidly after Munich and the absorption of Czechoslovakia, but there was relatively little time left to accomplish much. There turned out to be just enough time for Britain, and rather too little for France. Twenty years of neglect could not be recovered in a few months. The French aircraft industry went to three shifts a day, and the government now voted millions of francs for airplanes, but lavish expenditure of money could not buy time. It could, however, buy foreign aircraft, and French purchasing missions followed a British lead and went to the United States with blank checks. There they bought a hundred Curtiss Hawk fighters, an export equivalent of the U.S. Army Air Corps' P-36 fighter, and, in early 1939, practically the only modern fighter type serving in the Armée de l'Air. The French in fact were so desperate that they bought anything, from brand-new designs that never got to France before their collapse to already obsolete types such as the Vought Vindicator naval scout bomber, known to its crews as the "Vibrator." The Army Air Corps objected vigorously to the release of new aircraft to a foreign power when it was still flying old planes, and the purchases were in violation of American laws prohibiting the sale of war material abroad. But President Roosevelt was strongly in favor of aid to the democracies, so the laws were circumvented and eventually amended, and the air corps quickly realized that French money could revitalize the American aircraft industry far more easily than American money that had to be fought through an isolationist Congress. That was precisely what happened; that it happened too little and too late for France was her hard fortune.

So, in the midst of uncertainty, fear, and frantic efforts to prepare, the European powers stumbled toward war. At the end of March 1939 the British and French gave a joint guarantee to Poland, and in July RAF and Armée de l'Air aircraft joined in combined exercises over the French countryside. The politicians twisted and turned; then in August Hitler scored another great coup, with the Russo-German Nonaggression Pact. That made war a certainty. September 1 saw German dive bombers shreiking over Polish skies, and two days later,

France and Britain declared war on Germany. There could be no more buying time.

The Germans attacked Poland with unprecedented speed and ferocity. Germany was not prepared for a long war, or a big one. Hitler's intent was to gobble up Poland, presenting the western Allies, whom he had not even expected to declare war, with a *fait accompli;* he had not thought very far beyond that. To achieve this, he possessed an excellent but still relatively small war machine, backed by an economy that, in spite of the frantic rebuilding of the preceding years, was very shaky and not really geared for the demands of a large war. What he did have was quite enough for Poland.

Everyone, even the Poles, recognized this, and they hoped only to hold the Germans at bay long enough for the western Allies to honor their earlier pledge and attack Germany from the rear. France, however, had constructed her military forces solely for defense, and it was no part of the French plan to attack anyone at all. The French mobilized, let their army sit in the fortifications of the Maginot Line, and watched Poland go under. Britain sent the British Expeditionary Force over to France, accompanied by its Advanced Air Striking Force, neither of which was anything more than a minuscule appendage of the great French war machine, and they conformed perfectly to the French view of affairs. The Allies did not expect Poland to last long, and they did not expect to give her any help; both expectations were perfectly fulfilled.

Under these circumstances, who had what is far less important than who used what. The Armée de l'Air is said to have possessed 3,600 aircraft; of these, 1,364 were combat types, and only 494 of them were modern designs. The Aéronavale had 253 aircraft. None of these French planes need be considered in the equation, as none were used in the campaign. The Royal Air Force had 1,466 aircraft, of which about 1,000 were modern types. The Fleet Air Arm, which had come under the navy's control once again, had 232 planes; 18 of them were modern types, which demonstrates the plight of naval aviation under RAF control. Once again, as none of these British planes were used in the campaign, they need not be considered.

The war was thus fought out between the Germans and the Poles. The Poles possessed an air force of 745 planes, almost equally divided between combat types, 397, and training and reserve aircraft, 348.

Their best were the P. 11c fighter, a gull-wing indigenous design, and the P. 23 Karas light bomber. Both were out of date. Figures for the Luftwaffe depend upon which authority is grinding which ax; Allied writers have tended to inflate German numbers to exlain away their own passivity; German writers have deflated their numbers to show their victory was one of skill rather than of material. As everyone has his own definition of *first-line, obsolete, reserve,* and other qualifying terms, this is easier to do than it ought to be. One example will suffice to illustrate this tendency for the rest of the war. The German writer Cajus Bekker, in *The Luftwaffe War Diaries,* points out that the official British history of the war gives Germany a strength of 4,161 first-line aircraft on September 3. The "actual" figures, he then says, attempting to prove the Luftwaffe was weaker than this, were 1,929 in the east, which he calls two thirds of Göring's entire strength, and 2,775 aircraft, which he calls the "remaining third," in the rest of Germany. This gives a "humble" total of 4,704; it also gives the Luftwaffe more than 500 machines above what the British gave them. The only real conclusion one can draw is that the reader must be very skeptical of figures.

In any case, the Germans seem to have disposed of about 1,900 aircraft over Polish skies, and in first-line figures outnumbered them by roughly 5 to 1. As the attack was opened without warning, large numbers of Polish aircraft were destroyed on the ground, though most of these were second-line machines, the combat types already having been dispersed to operational fields. Nonetheless, there was little the Poles could do. They fought heroically to break up German bomber formations heading for Warsaw, but the P. 11 could not catch the German fighters, and had to settle for slower, clumsier victims. The Messerschmitt had a speed advantage over the Polish fighter of very nearly a hundred miles an hour, so it was hardly an equal contest.

The Germans therefore controlled the air almost immediately, and with minor interruptions were able to do as they wished. They used their dive bombers, the infamous Stuka, the Junkers Ju-87, as mobile artillery, bombing Polish concentrations and communications points, breaking up troop formations, and disorganizing the Poles before they were even mobilized. The back of Polish resistance was broken within a week, Warsaw was surrounded by the end of the second week, and the desperate Poles went down fighting. While their western Allies sat and watched, Hitler's newfound friend, Soviet Russia, intervened.

On September 17 the Red Army advanced into Poland from the east. Warsaw was repeatedly bombed from the air—here was Madrid revisited in the newsreels, sirens wailing, bombs bursting, men, women, and children running or wandering dazedly in the rubble—and surrendered on September 27. By the first week of October, Poland was gone from the maps of Europe again. In a brilliant campaign against admittedly second-class opposition, the Germans had shown the world a new type of lightning war, blitzkrieg. The tank on the ground, and the airplane above it, had restored mobility to war once again.

Hitler would now have liked to turn west, to deal with the supine French and British and end the war once and for all. They had done nothing for Poland, but they refused to make peace and accept his gestures of satisfaction and good will. So he would take care of them as well. He ordered redeployment of his forces. His generals wisely dragged their feet. They were not as convinced as he of his military genius, they believed that France would be a far tougher nut to crack than Poland, and they had had major losses and deficiencies that must now be made up. Even against Poland, the Luftwaffe had lost 285 aircraft and had another 279 written off due to accidents and damage. The ground forces had similar problems. The Mark I and II tanks had proven totally inadequate, army-issue horseshoes had been too small for the farm horses requisitioned for the campaign, and so on and so forth. By careful lack of enthusiasm, the generals delayed operations in the west until the fall rains began. Then, while the French army mildewed in the Maginot Line, everyone could relax.

During the winter attention shifted to the north. The Russians, having had close experience of German prowess, decided they needed a bit more buffer than they had. They took over the three Baltic states of Latvia, Lithuania, and Estonia, and suggested a rectification of frontiers with Finland. When the Finns resisted, the Russians invaded, and through the late winter of 1939–40 there was a bitter little war in which the Finns threatened to trounce the Russians before they were overwhelmed by weight of numbers. Helsinki was bombed, like Warsaw, like Madrid, like Shanghai, to mixed reaction from the rest of the world. Britain and France considered intervention on the side of Finland, seeing important benefits for themselves in the ensuing control of northern German iron-ore sources, but, as usual, they did not quite get around to it.

Hitler did. He could read a map as well as his enemies, and once his attention was drawn north, he decided he might as well have Denmark and Norway, thus creating a glacis behind which the Baltic would be secure for German domination. On April 9, 1940, the Germans launched another blitzkrieg. The Danish government, informed that planes were on the way to bomb Copenhagen, surrendered precipitately. The Norwegians fought. German troops landed from warships at all the main Norwegian ports. The Royal Navy spotted them by aerial reconnaissance, but misinterpreting the move as a raid against convoys, they sailed off into the Norwegian Sea, leaving the Germans free to secure their initial landings. At Fornebu Airport outside Oslo, and Sola near Stavanger, streams of Junkers Ju 52 Trimotors swept in, disgorging German airborne troops. Insisting they came as friends, they quickly seized the airfields and set up perimeters, opening the way for fighters and bombers of the Luftwaffe. Within a few hours the Germans had operational airbases in southern Norway.

This was really the key to the campaign. The Allies landed thirty thousand men in central Norway, where they linked up with the remnants of the pitifully small Norwegian army and tried to fight their way south. They quickly proved incapable of doing it. The Germans completely dominated the air. Attacks on the British-held ports forced their ships to withdraw, and strafing and dive-bombing constantly harassed the soldiers. The British tried to operate fighters off some of the frozen lakes in the center of the country, but this was a haphazard effort at best, doomed from the start against the well-organized and combat-tried Luftwaffe. No. 263 Squadron of the RAF, for example, flew its antique Gladiator biplanes onto the frozen Lake Lesjaskog; there was no ground crew, and a runway was trampled out of the snow by willing Norwegians. The ice of the lake began to melt, but the Gladiators' carburetors began to freeze. Within three days the squadron has lost all but four of its aircraft, and the Germans had ruined the lake airfield by bombing it. The pilots went all the way back to Britain, got more Gladiators, and returned to try again. It was not all disaster. Pilot Officer L. R. Jacobsen took off on June 2, intercepted a flight of German bombers, and shot down four Heinkel 111's and possibly two Junkers Ju 88's in one glorious sortie. He won an immediate Distinguished Flying Cross, but he was killed four days later on his way back to England, when the aircraft carrier *Glorious* was sunk by German battle cruisers.

Obsolete British aircraft flying from improvised strips, no matter how daring they were, could not compete with the Luftwaffe in full cry. Central Norway was soon evacuated, and the Royal Navy took severe losses in its light units from the German aircraft. Only up north, where air power could not reach, did the Allies make any headway, and that, too, soon had to be abandoned. Air power and its aggressive tactical employment had proved the key to another campaign, and added new laurels to German arms. They were beginning to look invincible.

By May 1940 a good deal of the Germans' work had already been done for them. The French army, greatest in the world a few months ago, had been sapped by inactivity, defeatism, public apathy, and political confusion. The country as a whole was torn between extremes of right and left, and both used the army as a target and stalking horse. Conscripts and reservists alike resented the disruption of their lives to no apparent point, and their leaders totally failed to use the breathing space that winter had given them. When the avalanche hit, there was very little to resist it.

The French plan was to use the Maginot Line as a shield, concentrating their mobile forces north of it on the Franco-Belgian frontier. When the Germans advanced into the Low Countries, the French would move forward to meet them; the battle would thus be fought on someone else's soil, to a presumably satisfactory conclusion. The original German plan more or less conformed to this French view, but during the winter they reversed its main thrust. They opened what looked like their main drive through Holland and northern Belgium; then, when the French and their British allies advanced to meet this, the Germans sliced an armored spearhead through the Ardennes Forest in southeastern Belgium, cutting in behind the Allies. Virtually unopposed, this new "Sicklecut" went all the way to the Channel, cutting off the northern armies, destroying French communications, and leaving the entire front in an uproar. The French had kept no reserves back, their armor was all trapped in the north, and French military leadership, typified by General Maurice Gamelin, responded to the crisis by throwing up its hands in despair. Many of the troops followed this lead and threw up their hands in surrender. The cut-off northern armies ended up in a defensive perimeter around the little port of Dunkirk, from which the Royal Navy successfully evacuated 338,000 of them, about two-thirds British, but they lost all their armor, vehicles, heavy weapons, and in most cases even their personal weapons. It was a military disaster unmatched since Napoleon over-ran Prussia in two weeks in 1806.

The Germans then turned south, while new French generals has-tily tried to set up a line of defense forward of Paris. They still thought in World War I terms, of linear and static defense, but they now lacked enough formations to create a solid front, and the Germans rapidly broke through. Once this secondary line, or attempt at one, was breached, it was but a matter of time. German armored columns roared through the countryside; occasionally they encountered pockets of determined French soldiers, but these they either sideslipped or over-whelmed. More often they found dazed mobs of leaderless men, only too anxious for the war to be over and eager to surrender. In the towns the civilians wanted to be spared the ravages of war, and soon the countryside blossomed with white flags and declarations that such-and-such was an "open town": "We won't defend it; please don't attack it!" The government fled from Paris to Bordeaux, and then col-lapsed in an ignominy of accusation and recrimination, presided over by France's Medusa, Countess de Portes, Premier Paul Reynaud's mistress. Marshal Pétain, the hero of World War I, was called to power; he met the challenge by announcing, "The fighting must cease," and in six weeks it was all over. The French surrendered in the same rail-way car in which the Germans had signed the Armistice twenty-two years earlier.

The brilliant campaign was a victory for a World War II–style army over a World War I–style army. The French believed in fortifications, infantry, and artillery preparation, and they still moved at the pace of a marching man. The Germans believed in mobility, armored vehi-cles, tactical aircraft support, and they moved at the speed of a fast tank. It was a victory of doctrine and daring over material and cau-tion. The Allies outnumbered the Germans in all major categories ex-cept one. Though they were roughly the same in numbers of divisions, the Allies had about 4 million men versus 2 million Germans. The Germans, of course, had unity of command, while the Allies were split among the French (94 divisions), the British (10 divisions), the Bel-gians (22 divisions), and the Dutch (9 divisions). The Germans had approximately 2,400 tanks, while the Allies possessed nearly 2,700; the difference here was that the Allies used their tanks as infantry support vehicles, parceling them out in penny packets, while the Ger-mans used theirs in concentrated armored attack spearheads. The

French alone had far more artillery than the Germans, but much of it was permanently sited in the Maginot Line and never used.

Only in first-line aircraft did the Germans have superior numbers, and those were marginal. They outnumbered the Allies about 4 to 3, 3,200 planes to 2,400. The latter figure includes all the French, Belgian, and Dutch machines, plus those the British committed to France, which was roughly 600. The Germans had better types of aircraft, and they employed them to better effect. Large numbers of the French planes, for example, were reconnaissance aircraft, intended to scout and spot for artillery but not much good for anything else, and extremely vulnerable to the German fighters that dominated the sky. French fighters were not very effective. The Morane M. S. 406, France's most numerous modern type, was already dated, and seriously outclassed by the Messerschmitt Me 109. The newest fighter, the Dewotine D. 520, was available only in small numbers; incredibly, many of those that were ready for service were held back at supply depots by administrative officials who did not want to see them damaged. The Curtiss Hawks gave a good account of themselves, but there were not that many around. The French were reluctant to use their bombers; those that they did employ were ineffective in the face of German superiority.

The British fared little better. They had sent two distinct groups across to France. The Advanced Air Striking Force consisted of fighters—the Gladiator and, by the time of the campaign, the Hurricane; and medium bombers—twin-engined Blenheims and the totally inadequate single-engined Fairey Battle. The second group was the Air Component of the BEF, again fighters, plus army cooperation aircraft. Neither accomplished much against the Luftwaffe. The Battles especially were committed to a series of suicidal attacks against German bridges and river-crossings; within the first three days, half of the 135 available British bombers were gone. On the evening of May 14 the British threw 71 bombers, all their remaining Battles and Blenheims, into a desperate effort to stop the crucial German crossing of the Meuse at Sedan. In this one operation 40 planes were lost. The French pleaded abjectly for the British to commit more of their squadrons held back for the defense of Britain itself. Reluctantly the British agreed, and several more squadrons were fed into the fire. It was all to little and too late; eventually they had to stop. It came a point where the prime minister, now Winston Churchill, appealed to

Air Marshal Dowding for more squadrons for France and Dowding simply refused. This was the "Stuffy" Dowding who had once dared to beard Trenchard on behalf of his weary men. Now he told Churchill straight out that if one more plane were sent to France, he would no longer be responsible for the defense of Britain. That was plain speaking with a vengeance, but no matter how sympathetic the British were to France, it was obvious the French were going under, and Britain was not going to join them, not if Dowding could help it.

The Germans, of course, took heavy looses too. On the first day of the campaign they wrote off 304 aircraft. But they infinitely outclassed the bewildered and demoralized Allies. Losses were quickly replaced: The German ground organization improvised far better in the advance than the Allies did in retreat, the Germans possessed the experience of past victory and the homogeneity of a single command structure, and, class for class, their aircraft were marginally superior to the Allies. They quickly won dominance of the air; with it, they could employ to excellent advantage their tactical support aircraft, such as the Stuka. This ugly, angular beast was a sitting target for any reasonable enemy fighter, but few of them were around to challenge it. The sight of Stukas hurtling out of the sky almost vertically, like so many vultures, and the sound of their screaming sirens, totally unnerved overage French reserves and untrained Belgian conscripts. They flattened pillboxes and strafed retreating columns of troops and refugees both. German planes roaring seemingly unopposed overhead were a constant feature of the battle, and several RAF men were beaten up by resentful survivors of the BEF back in Britain.

There were few independent operations for the Luftwaffe in the campaign. Largely it was a matter of tactical cooperation with the armored spearheads. But there were some notable occasions when aircraft were employed in startling ways. The great Belgian fortress of Eben Emael, linchpin of the entire northern defense system, a mere five years old and the strongest fortress in the world, was knocked out on the first day by eighty-five German engineers. Towed by Junkers Ju 52's, they made their approach and landing in silent gliders, and took the fortress by surprise in what would now be called vertical envelopment. It was one of the most daring coups of the entire war, fully deserving of its unprecedented success.

Equally useful, if less startling, was the Luftwaffe's deployment of antiaircraft batteries. In Germany everything to do with aircraft was jealously guarded by the Luftwaffe, including the right to shoot them down. The Germans rapidly brought up their flak batteries to protect their bridges and crossings, and it was largely these that decimated the British and French bombers trying to stem the advancing tide.

However, when Hitler gave the task of finishing off the Dunkirk perimeter to Göring, calling off his panzers, the Luftwaffe stumbled. Depleted by the preceding weeks' operations, flying at long range from even their forward airfields, the Germans could harass and infuriate, but they could not halt the evacuation. The RAF fought gamely and effectively, though largely out of sight of the long lines of patient troops waiting for shipping, and in the end the Luftwaffe did not quite have the stuff it needed to destroy the British Expeditionary Force. The British got away to fight once agian, and Hermann Göring's boast that his Luftwaffe could take care of the matter went unfulfilled. It was not the last time that would happen.

But what could a few unarmed British, mere flotsam of the greatest victory in modern history, matter? France was totally prostrate before the victors, and French politicians hastened to show that they were really in sympathy with the New Order. In the face of complete domination of the Continent, from the North Cape to the Pillars of Hercules, from Lisbon to the Pripet Marshes, what could a handful of decadent and effete Englishmen do? The war was over. If the British did not realize that, a few short weeks of summer should suffice to bring them to terms with reality. The Channel might have kept out Napoleon, but Napoleon did not have an air force.

X

THE BATTLE OF BRITAIN

In the midsummer of 1940, some of the great questions about air power were at last going to be answered. At least so it was thought at the time, as the British girded themselves to meet the full brunt of German might. They knew exactly what they had to do, for in war, as Napoleon said, everything is simple; it is only the doing of it that is difficult. The British had to control the Channel and keep the Germans from getting across. If the enemy did get ashore on the island, it was all over. Churchill might inspire his people by saying they would fight on the beaches and in the hills, they would never surrender, but the truth, as he well knew, was that they had precious little to fight with. If the Germans managed to secure a Channel crossing and a beachhead, they would probably win the war.

The Germans, however were not quite certain how to go about this, and in their uncertainty, no one wanted to be the first to try. Had the Channel been the Meuse River or even the Rhine, the army would simply have taken it on the run; the German army knew all about opposed river crossings. But the Channel was rather more than that.

The army, still gasping for breath after its incredible victory, turned thankfully to the navy and said, "Well, now it's your turn." The navy did not want to do the job either. The Kreigsmarine had taken a beating in Norway, and it had not expected to challenge the Royal Navy for another five to ten years, if at all. To take its relatively few ships into the narrow waters of the Channel and go up against the greatest navy in the world was suicidal, and German naval officers knew it. Yet the Channel *was* salt water, after all; it was their job. So their buck-passing had to be a little more sophisticated than the army's. They said, "Only when there is complete air control over the Channel can we attempt a crossing." In this way both senior services neatly sidestepped the issue and handed it to the junior service, whom some authorities say they would not be sorry to see fail.

The Battle of Britain thus became the first independent air battle in history, though it was not intended to be that; it was regarded by both sides as the prelude to invasion. Only when the Germans failed was it seen that the air battle was going to be the whole of the campaign.

It may well be that the issue was already won and lost before it was fought, in the thirties, when the Germans failed to develop a large strategic bomber, and when the British belatedly adopted the idea of aerial defense, but if men were willing to let mathematical calculation and rational analysis govern their affairs, there would not be wars. The men who fought the American Civil War did not say the South was doomed to lose because it was so greatly outnumbered, and therefore refuse to fight. It is only after the test of action has proven them so that we discover our theories or philosophies are invalid. So the triumphant Luftwaffe prepared to take on the Royal Air Force and wrest from it command of the air.

Most foreign observers, including American Ambassador to Britain Joseph Kennedy, were betting on the Germans. The British, after all, looked to be already shattered in the wake of France's defeat. If the greatest army in the world had not been able even to slow down the Germans, what could the British expect to do? But this David versus Goliath, Spartans at Thermopylae vision, which was strongly fostered by the British and by Churchill's magnificent oratory, was a bit delusory. The British were stronger than they looked, and the Germans were weaker.

This was not simply a matter of numbers, as some people, including Göring and Hitler, thought at the time. The idea of the knockout blow was still current in military thinking about air power, as if by suddenly hitting all the airplanes on all the bases at one time, one could suddenly win the war. After Poland and France such a view might well have seemed a reasonable proposition, but against a modern power it was incorrect. Air warfare between industrialized states, like the World War I fighting it was supposed to replace, was in fact a battle of attrition. The enemy's air force might well be worn down and knocked out once, but while that was being done, his aircraft industries would probably have made good the losses, so then it had to be done all over again. It was only when the loss rate could be made to exceed the replacement rate, and do so for long enough to have telling effect, that the necessary attrition could take place. The process was remarkably similar to the one by which modern governments, through deficit spending and debt servicing, drive themselves into bankruptcy. It is a complex process and it takes a long time, but it can be done.

Had it been solely a question of numbers, the RAF would have been in serious difficulties right from the start. Before the war the British had believed they needed a minimum of 52 fighter squadrons for home defense against Germany. Now, in June, they had only 32, as a result of the campaign of France and especially the effort to protect the evacuation. Seven of those 32 were equipped with inadequate types— the Blenheim, the Gladiator, and the Defiant, a heavy-gunned turret fighter (a fine-sounding concept that did not work in practice). That left a mere 25 squadrons of Hurricanes and Spitfires, or less than half the strength the British themselves thought necessary.

But that was in June. More important than numbers then was the fact that the British got a breathing space, while the Germans had to redeploy their forces, replace their losses, and get organized for the onslaught. They skirmished through July and were not ready for the main event until August. By August 8, the day the full-scale battle began, they had 60 squadrons, disposing in all of 654 aircraft. Only 565 of these in 49 squadrons were Spitfires or Hurricanes, but that was still a major improvement over the situation six weeks earlier.

The replacement rate was due to the fact that the British aircraft industry, revitalized especially by the appointment of Max Aitken, Lord Beaverbrook, as minister of aircraft production, was achieving wonders. "The Beaver," a Canadian businessman pulled into the government by Churchill, was one of those ruthless men of affairs the British throw up in times of emergency. Possessing an enormous capacity for work, he was both universally disliked and universally respected. His motto was "Action this day," and he rode roughshod over civil servants, air marshals, and everyone else who got in his way. In the thirties this would have meant endless trouble with organized labor especially, but now, under the equally forceful dominance of Aneurin Bevan, British labor worked ten-hour shifts and seven-day weeks. Factories had been dispersed before the war broke out, and shadow organizations set up which were now fleshed out; the final result was that at the end of the Battle of Britain, the RAF had more aircraft than it had had at the beginning.

The Germans did not match this degree of effort; indeed, they did not even try. The German aircraft industry's spurt of growth had come in the mid-thirties, earlier than the British, and now they happily loafed along on what was really a peacetime routine. British women went to work in munitions and airframe factories; German women stayed home. British factories worked around the clock; German factories worked only a daytime shift. While the British tried frantically to eliminate production anomalies and produce the most useful aircraft in the shortest possible time, the Germans played about, confident that military skill, of which they thought they possessed a monopoly, would outdo mere industrial activity. The war was all but won, after all. Their poor intelligence could not tell them what the British were doing, and they would not have believed it if they had known. One of the most thoughtful authorities on the air war, R. J. Overy, sums up the differences between the two powers by noting that Churchill surrounded himself with scientists and industrialists, Hitler with astrologers.

For the moment, it was the sharp end of all this effort that mattered. On August 8, the day that the RAF had 654 aircraft in Fighter Command, the Germans had 1,971 planes, including 594 of their best fighter—the Messerschmitt Me 109E. The rest were assorted types of bombers, either Dorniers, Heinkels or the Junkers dive bombers, or twin-engined "escort" fighters such as the Messerschmitt Me 110. They thus outnumbered the British Fighter Command strength by roughly 3 to 1.

As all this was being done for the first time, there were totally unanticipated difficulties. Chief among them was the simple question of what to attack. Here was a weapon to which the old limitations of a linear, ground-bound front did not apply. The airplane could strike at anything it wanted to. What then should it hit? The spectrum of possibilities ran all the way from the first enemy airplane encountered to the enemy civilian population, that is, from the most purely military target to the most purely nonmilitary one. Did the attacker wish to adhere absolutely to the conventions of contemporary war, or did he wish to follow the ideas of the more outlandish air-power prophets and break his opponent by terror bombing? Theoretically, both of these extremes, and everything in between, lay open to the bomber. Target selection arose as a problem, and became a major one for the entire war.

The Germans came down strongly on the military end of the range. They began by attacking the Channel convoys and ports in the month of July, attempting with considerable success to draw the British into battle on even terms. The convoys took such a beating that eventually the British had to change their shipping patterns, and several Royal Navy destroyers and other lighter units were put out of action. This was something of a red herring, however. Bombing ships might be useful for the German navy, if it ever attempted its crossing, but air command was the precondition for that, and it was the RAF that had to be the Luftwaffe's real target. The Channel battle served a purpose only in that it cost Fighter Command planes the British could not well afford to lose. Again Dowding went to Churchill and said he could not hold the Channel; he must conserve his resources for the main attack he knew was coming.

This was an attack for which the British were prepared. Around Britain they had two radar nets, a high-level one that could cover the enemy coast from Rotterdam down to Cherbourg, and a low-level one that reached perhaps thirty miles out to sea. Fighter Command was divided into two, later four, groups. The most important of these were 11 Group, covering London, Kent, and the other southeast counties. It was commanded by Air Vice-Marshal Keith Park, with his headquarters at Uxbridge. North of him was 12 Group, commanded by Air Vice-Marshal Trafford Leigh-Mallory, at Nottingham. These two, who were both absolutely vital to the success of the defense, disagreed openly on the best way to conduct the campaign. Park believed in sending up small groups of interceptors that could be kept tightly under control, while Leigh-Mallory was firmly in favor of an all-out response. The radar net and the visual observers were all tied into the headquarters and the airbases by the well-developed and largely bomb-proof, because it was underground, communications net. All three elements proved vital to the RAF.

Against them the Germans disposed of three air fleets, or Luftflotten. Luftflotte 5 was based in Norway and Denmark, and took but a marginal part in the battle. Luftflotte 3 was based roughly south of Le Havre, and the main effort was by Luftflotte 2, commanded by Albert Kesselring, newly promoted to field marshal; it was based in northern France and the Low Countries.

While the airmen skirmished over the Channel, Hitler postured in Berlin, offering peace, ordering preparations for invasion, beginning to toy with what to do about Russia, and uttering dire threats about destroying great empires. But the real work was going on at Luftflotte 2's airbases, where sweating groundcrews tuned engines, loaded ammunition belts, checked bombs, and polished windscreens. By the end of the first week of August, the Luftwaffe was at last ready to go. On August 8 the attacks took a quantum leap in intensity, though they were still directed against shipping. Three heavy attacks were made on a hapless coastal convoy; the Germans sank several ships in spite of Fighter Command's best efforts. Twenty-six German planes were shot down for a loss of eighteen British. It was a loss ratio the Germans could sustain and still win the battle.

The Luftwaffe kept up the pace over the next week, and began also to shift targets. Free-flying fighter patrols, independent of the bombers, went out looking for trouble and generally found it. The bombers themselves began hitting the British airfields, taking on Fighter Command directly. On August 13, as a preliminary to their main assault, the Germans sent up a major attack against the fighters. The weather was chancy, some of the flights were canceled, and the operation proved a fiasco, though it still did substantial damage to fields in 11 Group area.

The Germans had not yet unraveled exactly how the British were running their battle. Though possessing radar themselves, they did not fully understand its critical importance as an early-warning system; nor did they realize the extent to which British commanders, especially Park, were both conserving their resources and rotating different squadrons in and out of the battle zone. On August 15 they launched their main attack, code-named "Eagle Day," designed as the culmination of their efforts, the great knockout blow. It turned out to be a disaster. Thinking all the British defenses had been drawn south, Luftflotte 5 flew over unescorted from Norway, to be pummeled unmercifully by the British squadrons along the Scottish east coast. But in the south the Germans swamped the defenders, and hit airfields in 11 Group so badly that some were temporarily put out of action. In the fiercest day's fighting so far, the Germans lost seventy-five aircraft; the British lost thirty in the air and, more tellingly, another twenty-four on the ground.

This fighting went on for three more days, with losses too heavy to bear on both sides. Fighter Command won its only Victoria Cross on August 16, when Lieutenant J. B. Nicholson stayed in his burning Hurricane to shoot down a Messerschmitt. The highly touted and much feared Ju 87 Stuka proved such an easy mark for the British fighters that it was withdrawn from the battle, and by August 18 the Germans had to pause for breath.

No one could tell how he was doing. By accepting pilots' claims, the Germans thought they should already have destroyed the British, yet obviously they were still there. Every time the Luftwaffe flew a raid, there were a handful of Hurricanes or a pair of Spitfires coming down out of the sun to meet them.

The last week of August and the first week of September proved the crucial period for the RAF. In those two weeks the Germans finally got their priorities correct and went after the whole structure of Fighter Command—the radar stations, the airfields, the control mechanisms. They also increased the number of free-fighter sweeps, and, by unremitting pressure, they began to win. Some of the radar went out, a couple of the most forward airfields were untenable, and, most important of all, pilot attrition was wearing down the fighter strength. Dowding was scrounging pilots from Coastal Command, the Fleet Air Arm, any place he could get them. The British were feeding in Polish and Czech refugee pilots who could barely understand English commands over the radio, and by September 7 they were palpably losing. In two weeks they lost 264 fighters, and though many of their pilots parachuted or crash-landed on their own territory and lived to fight again, many did not. They went into the sea, they were burned, shot, or invalided, and their places had to be taken by younger, less experienced, and more vulnerable fliers. The attrition rate was just as bad for the Germans, worse, in fact, as they were fighting over enemy territory, but there were more Germans to get through. In a war of attrition the side that can stay longer wins. The Germans were now winning. Dowding believed that three more weeks would destroy his command, thereby opening England to invasion. The Germans were collecting barges along the coast.

On September 7 Göring threw victory away. Believing the exaggerated claims of his pilots, steadfastly misunderstanding the nature of his enemy, and indeed of air war, he decided the British were already finished. He thought Fighter Command was a broken reed; the battle was won. On September 7 he ordered the coup de grâce for England. The army and the navy were all but ready to go; moon and tide would be right from September 8 through September 10. The British had put out an invasion warning, and on the afternoon of September 7, more than a thousand aircraft took off from bases across the Channel, formed up in massive units, and droned out toward England.

Park and 11 Group watched them come with grim determination. They knew it was all over; the thin blue line was fraying out into invisibility. Waiting for their last best shot, they watched for the Germans to break up and head for the airfields and factories; while they did, the huge armada droned stolidly on, disdaining targets in the flat green countryside below. Incredulously, almost too late to do anything to stop it, the British realized the Germans were heading straight for London itself.

While Park called in every fighter he could find, the Germans bombed the London docks and the East End. Immense fires piled up into the sky, to last all night and be seen a hundred miles away. Hermann Göring, whose pilots sometimes unkindly called him "Nero" in reference to his pretensions and pomposity, stood on the cliffs at Calais and warmed himself with the glow of London burning. His cup ran over. He did not know he had just lost his war.

It was, of course, hardly that clear-cut at the time. The RAF took such heavy casualties in the first daylight raids on London that the slackening of the pace was almost indiscernible. But the change was nonetheless there. The radar stations were repaired, the runways on the airfields bulldozed back into service, the repair shops functioned again. The Germans were now making the same mistake the French had made two hundred years ago: Unable to defeat the Royal Navy, they had developed a strategic doctrine of "the ulterior motive," convincing themselves that British command of the sea was acceptable

as long as they could occasionally get a squadron out to take an island or two. The Luftwaffe now did exactly the same thing. Had the
Royal Air Force been beaten in the air, everything else would have
followed as a matter of course. Instead of that, with the RAF still alive
and kicking, the Germans now went after an ulterior objective, the
morale of Britain, thinking to destroy that and win the war. To be fair
to them, they thought the RAF already finished, so their error was
less blatant than the same one made by the Allies later in the war. It
was still costly beyond calculation.

The London Blitz is like the Terror of the French Revolution, one
of those episodes in history whose importance and image transcend
statistics. The Terror killed about twenty thousand people, hardly
enough to make Napoleon bat an eye. About thirty thousand died in
the Blitz; set against Leningrad, Tokyo, or Dresden, that is hardly a
major figure. The Blitz was in that sense a mere portent of things to
come. Yet here was one of the great cities of the world under attack
from the air; here was what the prophets and preachers had cried
about; here was air power doing its worst. For the whole of the western world, the images filled the mind: St. Paul's silhouetted against
the fires, the Thames aflame, the wail of sirens and the crump of
bombs, Edward R. Murrow and "This is—London," streets full of rubble
and the broken shop front with the BUSINESS AS USUAL DURING REN-
OVATIONS sign propped against the bricks, and always Londoners carrying on.

The Blitz was the best thing that could have happened to the Royal
Air Force, for respite meant survival. But again, this was something
the British were not really prepared for, in spite of trenches in Hyde
Park and the universal issue of gas masks. What the British needed
were night fighters, and they had few of those.

The Germans began bombing on September 7, striking by day and
by night. They hit London every night from then until November 14.
No one, including the Germans, was entirely sure what they were
trying to do, and what began as a preliminary to invasion was kept up
for lack of a sensible alternative and ended as an exercise in frustration. They did a lot of damage. They destroyed or severely hurt three
and a half million homes, they bombed out the House of Commons,
they ranged beyond London itself to attack other industrial cities. A
major strike hit Coventry, for example, making the city, like Rotter-

dam earlier, a symbol of German barbarity. Yet Coventry was the home of important aircraft industries, and a perfectly legitimate target. The British played up the destruction of its famous cathedral and said little about the factories, which were back to work five days after the strike. The story that the British knew through code interceptions of the Coventry raid, but chose not to react to to protect the secret of their code-breaking, has now been discounted.

After the first few raids, to which the RAF reacted very strongly, the Germans were forced to go to bombing by night. This could be seen only as an admission of weakness, of defeat during the day. With the direct attacks on Fighter Command abandoned, the Luftwaffe could no longer take the daytime punishment. Hitler postponed the invasion indefinitely and lost interest, leaving the matter of the British to Göring and the air force

Night bombing was notoriously inaccurate—which meant it was even less accurate than day bombing—but London was an immense target, clearly indentifiable on most nights, and the Germans were bound to hit something. For more difficult or sophisticated efforts they had a radio-beam system of navigation. The pilot flew along one beam until it was intersected by another one, at which point he then released his bombs. The British were baffled by this for a while, but then they discovered a way to send up contradictory signals, which had the effect of warping the beams. For quite a while the Germans happily bombed open spaces. This was what Churchill, with his great fascination with gadgets, called "the wizard war."

What the British really needed was night fighters, and those they had were not much good. The twin-engined Blenheim bomber had been converted for night use, and so had the Boulton Paul Defiant, the turret fighter that had not worked during the daytime. The ubiquitous and indispensible Hurricane was also pressed into service as a single-seat night fighter, but none of these was entirely adequate. British fighter control techniques could send these planes aloft into the general area where a bomber was flying, but were not sophisticated enough to bring the interceptors into visual contact with the target. British pilots thus knew the Germans were out there somewhere, but they had to depend on luck for the contact and then the kill. The Germans had to be caught by moonlight, or by the glow of fires on the ground, or by making the mistake of being silhouetted against a river, or something. Luck was really not good enough in a war depending increasingly upon science. Through the winter months, twice as many Germans were shot down by antiaircraft guns as by night fighters, though neither scored significantly.

But once again science was coming to the rescue. Better planes, most notably the Bristol Beaufighter, a fighter rebuild of the Blenheim, were entering squadron service. More important, the British were developing more precise radar, and a technique known as GCI, for Ground Control Intercept. Antiaircraft and fighter scores were now reversed. In January 1941 the fighters got 3, the guns 12, in February, 4 and 8. But in March the fliers got 22 to the gunners' 17, and from then on the total climbed rapidly; 48 to 39 in April, and in May, 96 for the aircraft and 42 for the ground defenders. On May 12 the Germans called off the campaign.

Even the May losses were hardly prohibitive, and the whole campaign worked out to a loss rate of a little more than 3 percent of aircraft per missions flown. That was, ironically, very close to what British Bomber Command and the American Army Air Force suffered later in the war. It was clear that if the Germans wanted to, they could keep going.

The real question was, What were they achieving by the effort? What did the raids do that made the losses worthwhile? The answer to that, the Germans eventually concluded, was very little. Given the fact that the German aircraft industry was still not producing for a long war—indeed would not do so for years to come—Luftwaffe strength was slowly but steadily eroding away. The British, by contrast, going flat out, were much stronger in early 1941 than they had been in early 1940. Seen as a war of attrition, the Battle of Britain and the Blitz were thus both losing propositions for the Germans, unless they were to put a great deal more into their war effort than they were then prepared to do. In 1940 the Germans produced a mere 1,870 fighters to 4,283 built by the British; the Germans were simply still not serious about their war effort.

Obviously, just from this one statistic, the German campaign was not having a substantial effect on British industrial production. This marked a second failure for the Luftwaffe. They had not been able to wrest tactical command of the air from Fighter Command, and now they had proved inadequate to a strategic attack against British industry. The other thing air power was supposed to be able to do was demoralize the civilian population and throw it into such a panic that it would demand surrender. Even the Germans could easily see that this idea was ridiculous. Except for the actual physical destruction, and the tragedy of personal losses and attendant grief, almost every effect of the Blitz was beneficial for Britain. The always exuberant London humor blossomed under attack, and Englishmen seldom felt as good about themselves before, and never since, as they did during the period from Dunkirk to the spring of 1941. Shared adversity evoked a conscious feeling of nationalism and pride in Britain, epitomized and capitalized on by Churchill. Further, it won the embattled islanders the sympathy of the outside world, not just the Commonwealth and Empire that already stood beside them, but neutrals such as the United States as well. The Germans had almost no moral capital before the Blitz, and none after it; having sown the wind, they would reap the whirlwind.

Dimly concluding that air power had failed to live up to its larger promises, the Germans turned away from it. Hitler was increasingly preoccupied with his forthcoming invasion of Russia. The army was his war-winner, and the Luftwaffe, after the western adventure, was firmly fixed as a tactical support force. The Germans would never again seriously assay strategic employment of air power.

The British, partly by force of circumstances, chose a different path. As they had looked farther ahead in the thirties and opted to build a strategic bomber force, so now they chose to employ it. Germany might turn to her army; Britain did not have that option. There was no way the British army, even with wartime expansion, could match the German. The Royal Navy could not vitally affect affairs on the Continent in any immediate sense. If Britain were to stay in the war, play an effective role, and eventually win it, she had to do so with air power. The Germans concluded air power could not be decisive, and downgraded it. The British concluded that it could be decisive, and set out to make it so.

XI

TOWARD THE BIG RAIDS

By the end of 1940 Britain's air defense had proven itself, and the islanders had survived everything the Germans could throw at them. That kept Germany from winning the war in the west, but it did not win it for Great Britain. It is one of the axioms of modern military thought that the defensive may prevent defeat, but it is the offensive that actually wins wars. Britain's problem now was what kind of offensive she could wage.

One answer was already at hand, and as it was not simply the only one available, but the only one likely to be available for some considerable time, the British grasped it with both hands. They embarked on a strategic bombing campaign against Germany. For four years it was their most direct way of bringing pressure on Hitler's empire, and for the first three of those four, it was highly debatable whether it was even worth the effort.

Until the fall of France, the British employed Bomber Command sparingly and without substantial effect. Flying the available heavy bombers of the period, the twin-engined Whitley and Wellington, they attempted to convince Germans of the futility of the war by dropping leaflets over the Rhine. Presumably the Germans, waking up in the morning and seeing British paper scattered across the countryside, would realize they could have been hit with bombs instead, and be correspondingly alarmed and depressed. Not surprisingly, there was little reaction to this effort.

There was more response to the other main activity of this early period, and it was very unpleasant. The British did carry out a maritime campaign, undertaking aerial reconnaissance over German naval bases and occasionally trying to hit their ships. The most famous of these episodes came in December 1939. On December 18, a force of twenty-four Wellingtons took off to reconnoiter and bomb the bases at Wilhelmshaven and the Schillig Roads. The Wellington was one of the great planes of the war, and the first production machines had entered squadron service late in 1938. Bomber Command had six squadrons of them when war was declared, and they dropped the first bombs on German shipping on September 4. With power-operated turrets in the nose and tail, and their crews practiced in formation flying, they were considered more than a match for the fighter defenses of the Luftwaffe. That delusion lasted until the December 18 raid.

This, which is known as the Battle of Heligoland Bight, perhaps in conscious imitation of a naval battle in the same area in World War I, should have disproved once and for all the contention that the bomber could get through. Of the twenty-four planes, two turned back with engine trouble. The rest droned on over the German bases without dropping any bombs, and were then pounced upon by a large number of German fighters of various types. The results were catastrophic for the British: Ten of the twenty-two were shot down, and three more were so severely damaged that they crashed back in Britain. Those that returned sat, shattered wrecks, on their airfields, with gas pouring out of their shot-up tanks, not yet self-sealing, while their surviving aircrew were frantically hauled off to the hospital or to debriefing. Bomber Command immediately withdrew the Wellington from daylight operations over Germany.

Until May 1940 the British government forbade attacks on German land targets for fear of retaliation. But once the German assault was launched, there could be no further reason for restraint. The government then authorized Bomber Command to undertake operations against German industrial targets in the Ruhr, providing the usual stipulation that only military targets were to be hit. Efforts were next distracted by the all-consuming battles, first of France and then of Britain, so that the bombers found themselves trying desperately to support land operations; and then, during the summer of 1940, they were diverted to bombing the German invasion ports and their concentrations of barges.

This was to be one of the recurrent themes of the champions of strategic bombing. Time after time throughout the war the general needs of the moment would override the commanders' desires or plans for their operations. They would always insist that if left alone they could achieve significant results, and the fact that they never were left alone became the excuse for the failure to achieve those results. There is some justice to the complaint, though there is, equally, a great deal of naïveté to it as well. There has never been, after all, such a thing as a "pure" war, where one or the other side was left free, either by the enemy or by its own leaders, to do exactly what it chose. To demand those sorts of conditions was merely to display a vast ignorance of the nature both of war and of human affairs.

During the Battle of Britain the bombers struck occasionally at German air bases and tried to hit the aircraft industry, but Bomber Command, now led by Air Marshal Sir Charles Portal, did not regard that as its true function. Just what the true function was remained a matter of dispute. Churchill himself wanted widespread attacks against the German population, in answer to the Blitz, and there were some among the Air Staff who supported this view. The official position, however, remained that attacks against transport, communications, and especially oil were the most rewarding efforts. Here was a second theme to be replayed again and again throughout the war: What target type paid the most dividends, and how often and how long did it have to be hit?

The search for the "panacea" target became obsessive. The problem, which was never realized through the war itself, was not that such a target could not be found; in fact, the Allies found several such vulnerable items in the German machine, and their very first assessments, oil and communications, were among them. The difficulty was rather that the airmen overestimated the damage they were doing, and underestimated both the adaptability of the German economy and the amount of fat on it. Just as the Germans threw away victory in the Battle of Britain by prematurely giving up their attack on the RAF itself, so the Allies, by switching too early from one panacea to another, made the same error. Several times, with the Germans on the verge of strangulation, the Allies abandoned one target system and moved on to the next one. Theirs was not a failure to find the magic answer, but rather a failure to pursue it to fruition, and that in turn was engendered by their overestimation of their own accomplishments. Ultimately this more than anything else made the air war one of attrition.

All this was to be played out in the future, over the course of years of unremitting, and long unrewarding, effort. In the fall of 1940 Portal's resources could produce little more than pinpricks. In response to Churchill's desire for retaliation, even though the airmen believed the effect of this was minimal, they dutifully sent a few planes as far as Berlin. Throughout the early years of the war, in spite of politicians flirting with the theme of revenge, both sides insisted that they were aiming at purely military targets, but as neither side achieved any reasonable degree of accuracy, and as a bomb is totally incapable of distinguishing between a soldier and a woman or a child, the whole question of who did what to whom first is a futile one. By 1941 Portal professed to believe that civilian morale was not only a legitimate military target but also the most vulnerable part of the German system, which was one way of dodging the fact that his bombers were inadequate to strike at anything more concrete than that.

There were repeated attacks on Berlin and on the industrial areas in western Germany; there were even longer-range raids, such as those in 1940 that struck at Italian factories in Milan and Turin. This was a staggering accomplishment for the period, with Whitley bombers flying 1,500 miles to deliver the raid. The ugly old Whitley, known to its crews as "the Flying Barn Door," could carry only a thousand pounds of bombs that far, but the raids caused a widespread reaction and fear in Italy. Indeed, if Germany had been Italy, with the latter's marginal economy and less-disciplined population, this type of effort might have been the war-winner it was supposed to be.

Such was not the case, and Germany was going to require a great deal more effort before results were discernible. But the British were looking ahead. In late 1940 the first of their four-engined bombers, the Stirling and then the Halifax, entered service. Armed with these, the RAF might at last expect to achieve real results against German targets. The Stirling, as the first heavy bomber in the modern sense to reach squadron service, represented a quantum leap forward. A huge, ungainly beast that sat immensely high off the ground on a stilty undercarriage, it was the only one of Britain's wartime bombers designed from the start for four engines. Yet that very fact told against it, for the restrictions placed on the design betrayed peacetime origins. By the middle of the war, designers were allowed to produce pure killing machines; when the Stirling was first conceived, the RAF could still insist that the big bomber have a fuselage cross-section wide enough to take the standard government packing case, and a wingspan short enough to allow the plane to be parked inside the regulation aircraft hangar, whose doors at the time were a hundred feet wide. Limitations that seemed reasonable enough in peace killed crews in war, and the Stirling was eventually judged to be a disappointment. This did not prevent the British from building 2,375 of them, though by the time the last came off the production lines, the type was already being relegated to second-line duties.

The Halifax, third of the trio that made up the bulk of Bomber Command's machines, was better than the Stirling but not as good as the Lancaster. It could be seen as the lineal descendant of Trenchard's bloody paralyzer of World War I. Like the Lancaster, it started as a twin-engine design, and was subsequently modified to four engines. It went through the usual long gestation period, and eventually emerged as a powerful and dependable weapons system, neither quite as aesthetically attractive nor as beloved as the Lanc, but a thoroughly useful aircraft, of which 6,176 were built.

The two new machines began operations in the spring of 1941. The British also began flying missions with Lend-Lease American B-17's. Bigger machines meant bigger bombs as well, and during the year the bombs increased in size from the standard 500-pound bomb to 1,000-, 2,000-, and eventually 4,000-pounders. Sir Charles Portal became Chief of the Air Staff, and was replaced by Air Marshal Sir Richard Pierse. As the summer came on, Bomber Command appeared ready for large-scale efforts at last. The new heavies first hit targets along the French coast, then gradually extended the range of their strikes, getting as far as the Ruhr during the short summer nights.

The techniques employed, which seemed radically innovative at the time, appeared incredibly amateurish by later standards. Planes took off largely at their own discretion and plotted their own routes to the target. Higher direction consisted chiefly of telling the aircrew what the destination was and providing some casual weather information. There was still little systematic target analysis. On any given night, something over a hundred bombers would take off from airfields scattered in the Midlands, make their way across the Channel or the North Sea, try to pick up some navigational marks, find something that looked promising, drop their bombs on it, and head for home.

There were real if ill-defined constraints on what could be hit. Because the Germans enjoyed such a great geographical advantage, occupying all of northern France, the coast, and the Low Countries, the British bombers had an uphill struggle. The high command was reluctant to strike targets in the occupied countries for fear of hitting friendly civilians. During summer they could not get to Berlin and back in the dark, so they were limited essentially to those targets in the western part of Germany. Flying by night was an admission of failure, but after earlier disasters the British had to admit that daylight raids were beyond their capacity. In 1941 they tried individual daylight sorties with the high-flying B-17's, only to take prohibitive losses. These were the early models, with no guns in the tail; the Americans had said they must be flown in formation for mutual protection, but they enjoyed such a high ceiling that the British thought they could get through on their own. They were mistaken, and the survivors of this error were eventually withdrawn and used for maritime reconnaissance.

In spite of the haphazard nature of operations, Bomber Command still deluded itself that it was achieving a high degree of accuracy, to the extent that aircraft were assigned individual buildings in target cities as their dropping points. There was, however, growing suspicion both among the airmen themselves and also, more importantly, in the ranks of their political superiors that bombing was not proving very effective. There was also a series of distractions and demands that threatened the very existence of Bomber Command.

First of all, there was the heating up of the eastern end of the Mediterranean. There, through 1940, the British had handily beaten the Italians in Egypt and Libya. But when the Germans entered the fray in April 1941, invading Yugoslavia and then Greece, the British overstretched their thin resources, with the result that they lost Greece and Crete, and threatened to lose Egypt as well. Then in June, Hitler invaded Russia, and though the overall effect of this was enormously beneficial to Britain, the immediate one was less positive. For five months the Germans looked as if they would do to Russia what they had already done to France and so many other countries. British assistance to the Soviet Union again served to disperse her own efforts.

Finally, most immediate and important of all, in 1941 the British were losing the Battle of the Atlantic. With their U-boats and their relatively few but very effective long-range reconnaissance aircraft, such as the Focke-Wulf Fw 200 Condor, the Germans were strangling Britain. The Royal Navy was fully extended trying to stop this, but was fighting a losing battle. One of the most efficient answers was increased antisubmarine patrols by long-range aircraft, and this was what the navy demanded. The RAF resisted; it regarded bombing as the way to win the war, and saw the diversion of heavy aircraft into Coastal Command as yet another waste of precious resources. The fact remained, however, that if the convoys could not fight their way through to Great Britain, then Bomber Command's aircraft were going to be grounded for lack of fuel and all the other elements that ultimately had to be imported by ship into the British Isles. So the claims of the navy and Coastal Command had to be met too, and once again the bombing advocates saw their resources siphoned off to other tasks.

Faced by these problems, Bomber Command reached a crisis in the fall of 1941. The government began to lose faith in it, it began to question its own effectiveness, and the Germans began improving their defenses. Churchill and the War Cabinet were now looking at the bombers much as the boy who cried wolf. The prime minister was a man of enthusiasm, and his support was waning. In October he wrote a memo to Portal in which he severely qualified the kind of optimism he had previously expressed, opening with, "We all hope that the air offensive against Germany will realize the expectations of the Air Staff," and then going on to explain why this was a hope and no longer any certainty, before refusing to put all Britain's eggs in the bombers' baskets. The Air Staff had too often promised results and then had to explain failure to enjoy any automatic acquiescence in their demands for equipment and scarce resources.

Unfortunately for them, when the bombers got around to a scientific examination of what they were achieving, as opposed to the guessing game that had earlier been played, they found that the government's skepticism was thoroughly justified. It was autumn of 1941 before they were able to get useful photographs of targets after strikes; they also developed cameras that would take pictures of the actual bombing attacks. Analysis of a hundred raids was devastating, not to the Germans but to Bomber Command. Intelligence experts looked at photographs taken by 4,065 aircraft whose pilots and bomb-aimers claimed they had hit their targets. The evidence was that not one bomb in three had hit within five miles of its designated target, and there were extreme errors of up to a hundred miles. In a few bizarre cases the aircraft had not even bombed the right country, being over France or Switzerland when they thought they were over Germany. Knowing how readily they had been able to bend and distort the German radio beams, the British had been reluctant to rely on electronic aids to navigation, preferring star sights, piloting by ground features, or mere dead reckoning. The end result was simply wasted effort on a gigantic scale.

Finally, German defenses were improving. Hitler, who took a personal interest in the nuts and bolts of his war machine, was adamantly opposed to fighter defense; he regarded the Luftwaffe as purely an offensive arm, and seemed almost to think it a slur on his own prowess as a war leader to suggest that the Reich needed defending. But in spite of him the Germans slowly managed to build up, almost surreptitiously, a night-fighter defense organization. Large numbers of flak batteries were stationed in the paths of the bombers, and increasingly efficient night-fighter groups, supported by a radar net and control system similar to Britain's in 1940, began to challenge the British in the night skies. The normal operational loss rate was about 2 to 3 percent, but on the night of November 7, the British sent out 400 planes and lost 36 of them. A 9 percent loss was too high to sustain, and by the approach of winter, Bomber Command was at a crossroads. Either they had to find better ways to fight their war or they had to give it up altogether.

Bomber Command was not the only element of the Allied effort suffering disaster at the time. The Germans in November were gearing up for what looked like the capture of Moscow and the collapse of the Soviet Union. The situation in the Near East was parlous, and in the Far East it was perilous. And on December 7, the Japanese navy struck at the U.S. Pacific Fleet at anchor in Pearl Harbor; the door of conquest swung even wider.

A week after Pearl, Churchill and his top advisers and military men were on their way to Washington aboard the new British battleship

Duke of York, sister to *Prince of Wales,* now lying in fifteen fathoms in the South China Sea. With time to think, the prime minister wrote up a series of papers on the course of the war as he now saw it. He was optimistic, for he knew that the entry of the United States into the war meant ultimate victory, but the trials and disappointments of the last eighteen months had tempered and sobered his view. He asked for twenty American bomber squadrons to assist the British effort in Europe, saying, "Our own bomber programme has fallen short of our hopes . . . its full development has been delayed." But he then went on to speak of developing "the Anglo-American bombing of Germany without any top limit from now on until the end of the war." So the bombing offensive would continue, but more because it might eventually have "internal reactions upon the German government" than because it could hope to win the war in and of its own right.

American bombers in the future were one thing, but more immediate changes were in store for Bomber Command. In February 1942 it got a new commander, Air Marshal Arthur Harris, and with his appointment dramatic events were in the offing. One of the most controversial commanders of the war, Harris was a very tough nut. Shipped out to Rhodesia at the age of sixteen with five pounds to his name, he had grown up fast. He started World War I in the infantry, and transferred from there to the RFC. He then climbed painfully up the peacetime ladder, spending several years commanding squadrons. Moving into higher echelons, he got involved in the interservice battles of the thirties, and his caustic wit became one of the service's heavy weapons. He once remarked that the army would never understand the tank "until they could modify it to eat hay, and shit." At the start of the war he commanded No. 5 Group of Bomber Command, and then, after a couple of staff jobs, he got the top bombing position. It was ideally suited for him, for he was a fervent believer in the RAF in general, and the value of bombing in particular. He thought, in fact, that it could win the war, and he never once wavered. Build enough bombers, and drop enough bombs on the Germans, and by God, sooner or later they would crack.

Harris's arrival at Bomber Command Headquarters at High Wycombe coincided roughly with a new directive issued to the RAF by the Air Staff. The British had now recognized the great degree of inaccuracy they were suffering in their attacks. They had in the pipeline new navigational aids and techniques that they hoped would remedy this problem. In the interim before those arrived, they changed their policy. Abandoning the futile attempt to strike at individual targets, they said, "operations should now be focused on the morale of the enemy civil population." This meant adoption of what the British chose to call area bombing and the Germans called terror bombing. It was a conscious, albeit supposedly temporary, acceptance of the thesis that if you could not hit the German worker's factory, you could lessen his efficiency by bombing him out of his house. It was going to take a lot of bombers and an immense backup effort to do it. Harris was just the man to try.

At the time he took over command, there were less than four hundred aircraft in Bomber Command, whose requirements had taken a backseat to Coastal Command and other needs. But one thing was in Harris's favor. The majority of his planes were twin-engined bombers—Wellingtons, Whitleys, Hampdens, and Blenheims. These were slowly being downgraded, and through the next year would be replaced by Stirlings, Halifaxes, and eventually Lancasters. Under Harris's incessant prodding, the force was to grow mightily. To do so, of course, it had to show results. Within three months it had done so in a most dramatic way. At the end of May Harris staged his first thousand-plane raid.

This was obviously something of a conjurer's trick, for Harris himself did not have that many planes available. But the very thought of it was awe-inspiring, and that was just what Harris wanted. Through the first couple of months of his tenure, the bombers practiced. With a new radar aid to navigation, known as Gee, they improved their accuracy. Over the old German towns of Lübeck and Rostock they experimented with incendiary bombs, trying to find the right mix of fire with high explosives. In May they were ready. Harris and his staff combed their resources; they called up instructors and trainees, and culled planes from the Operational Training Units. They borrowed back the bomber crews and their aircraft that had been sent off to Coastal Command. Harris would have liked to hit Hamburg, but was persuaded to stay with a target that could be reached by the Gee system. They chose Cologne.

On the night of May 30, the mightiest force ever to leave the shores of Britain groaned into the air. In all, 1,134 aircraft took part in the operation, counting decoys, fighters, and intruders. Of bombers themselves, about 910 came in over the city and dropped their loads. They did this in a pulsating stream, culminating in three waves designed to swamp the defense system on the ground, and the entire bombing phase lasted only about an hour and a half. Forty-four aircraft were lost—most shot down, a few in collision—a percentage rate of 3.9, slightly higher than average but still within acceptable limits. Harris had expected 5 percent; Churchill, when approached with the plan, said he thought even 10 percent would not be too great.

What did they accomplish? In Germany less, in Britain more, than they had hoped. Harris had wanted to wipe Cologne off the map, not because he was a vindictive Hun-hater, as he has often been painted, but because he was a single-minded man doing his job. That task proved beyond the capacity of even a thousand aircraft. Some twenty thousand homes were destroyed, along with two thousand businesses and factories. Nearly half a million people were bombed out of their homes, but only about five hundred were killed. The German police and air-raid defense functioned efficiently. Industrial production and transportation were both disrupted, but neither for as prolonged periods of time as the British had expected. The authorities kept a tight rein on rumor and news reports, and morale did not suffer to any appreciable degree, though there was some lurking recognition that if the British could do this, and especially if they could *continue* to do this, Germany was in for real trouble.

Whether the British could continue the effort was of course the whole point of the issue. In an immediate sense they could not; for the moment, Cologne was a one-shot effort, and big raids shortly thereafter on Essen and Bremen were failures. But the important thing was that the thousand-plane raid enormously raised Bomber Command's stock with both the British public and government. The average Englishman had dined on a diet of defeat since 1939; the thought of the same dish being fed to the Germans cheered him tremendously. Bomber Command was suddenly popular.

Even more important, Churchill and the government had some of their earlier faith restored; in a congratulatory telegram, the prime minister stated that the raid was but a "herald" of things to come. Bomber Command would get the support it needed, Harris and his ideas had weathered the late-1941 crisis of confidence, and the strategic bombing offensive would continue. Harris—"Bert" to his old friends, "Butch" or "Butcher" to his aircrew—was now permanently "Bomber" Harris to press and public. He began looking for new targets, and for better ways to hit them.

This led in the fall to the development of the Pathfinder force. Harris was adamantly resistant to ideas expressed by those outside the magic circle, that is, those who were not bombers, but he could be persuaded to adopt useful ideas by insiders, and the more experimental and imaginative—and successful—of his commanders often came up with new tactical wrinkles to improve accuracy. While the research scientists constantly sought to give the fliers better weapons, the fliers themselves searched for better ways to employ them; a man who was putting his life on hazard every time he left the ground wanted to think he did so to the best possible effect. The Pathfinder idea was the simple one that if the best pilots and navigators could be employed to find and mark targets accurately, then the average aircrew should be able to bomb that much more effectively. Some group commanders were opposed to the concept, but its results eventually proved undeniable. Slowly and painfully, the British were learning the complex business of the most technologically and tactically advanced war yet fought.

While the Royal Air Force was making this halting progress, the Americans were getting ready to take part in the air offensive. The whole idea of such an attack dovetailed with thinking about the uses of air power in the United States, and as the Army Air Forces had gained a measure of autonomy in the American command structure in 1940 and 1941, they had produced plans on the assumption that they would do just what the British were trying to do. Roosevelt had spoken of the United States as "the arsenal of democracy"; his military men knew that, however carefully he skirted the issue, sooner or later it would be Americans who used the weapons produced in the arsenal. When the president called for the production of 50,000 aircraft a year, many people thought he was crazy. In 1939 the country had built less than 6,000 planes, and in 1940 less than 13,000. Yet Roosevelt's figure, which in fact was pulled out of the air much like Harris's thousand-plane raid and for much the same purposes, was exceeded as America mobilized for war and threw her vast resources and energies into action: 26,277 in 1941; 47,836 in 1942; 85,898 in 1943; and a staggering 96,318 in 1944, the peak year. In 1944 the United States alone built nearly as many aircraft as Britain, Russia, and Germany combined.

Discussions between American and British military leaders had long preceded the war, though this was not stressed for an isolationist public in the States. In March 1941 planners agreed that, should the Americans enter the war, there would be an ongoing air offensive as a prelude to invasion of the Continent. When the U.S. Army and Navy developed their own war plan, known as Rainbow 5, they accepted this view. An adjunct to Rainbow 5 was the air corps' own plan, AWPD-1, or Air War Plans Division-1, and it stated baldly that the primary mission of the air forces was to wage "a sustained and unremitting air offensive against Germany and Italy." The only difference in the plans was that the air corps was looking to win the war all by itself, seeing the air offensive as a means of victory and not just a harbinger of invasion. In June 1941 General H. H. Arnold, the same man who had once gazed at the Blériot cross-Channel flyer in Paris, became commander of the Army Air Forces. He was legally subordinate to General George C. Marshall as Chief of Staff, but in fact he acted as a chief of staff himself, and the AAF functioned virtually as a third service with the army and navy for the duration of the war.

With the planes rolling off the assembly lines, with a command structure in place, and with a general view of how to conduct the war, all the Americans had to do now was go on and fight it. That, as always, proved easier to say than to do. No one is ever really ready for war, military men least of all, and the sudden Japanese attack faced the Americans with one of their perennial military problems—fighting a war and expanding and training their armed forces to do it at the same time. The confusion was enormous; the fact that they succeeded as well as they did was little short of miraculous.

Roosevelt and Churchill had long ago agreed that Germany was the most dangerous foe of the democracies, and must have priority over Japan. The Pearl Harbor attack threatened this view, for most Americans, including the formidable and influential Admiral Ernest J. King, wanted to charge out into the Pacific and beat up the Japanese. It was thus essential to get Americans in action in Europe as soon as possible. One result of this was the acquiescence of the Americans in Britain's Mediterranean strategy. Another was the acceptance of a buildup of strength in Britain, for the eventual invasion of the Continent. But the quickest way to get into action was to join in the bombing campaign.

To command the Eighth Air Force, the American air effort in Britain, Arnold appointed General Carl Spaatz, universally known as "Tooey." He was an outstanding choice, and may well have been the most brilliant air commander of the entire war. A quiet and self-effacing man, he diligently resisted the best—or worst—efforts of the Army Air Force publicity people, and remains even now a relatively little-known person. He had a wide-ranging background of command, staff, and operational roles, going all the way back to his service as a pilot in the Mexican border expedition of 1916. A Billy Mitchell disciple, he believed in strategic employment of air forces, and he believed that American aircrew could fly over Europe in daylight and attack precision targets.

In this he was wrong, but it took a long time to find out. Almost the first thing Americans learned when they got to Britain was that the war was not going to wait for them. They planned to have a thousand bombers operating from England by early 1943, but their program had to be downgraded from the start. The U-boats were demanding attention, and bombers had to be diverted off for antisubmarine work, some to the air force's own Anti-Submarine Command, bitterly resented by the U.S. Navy, and some to the navy itself, bitterly resented by the air force.

Even more disappointing to American hopes for Britain-based operations was Roosevelt's agreement to the British view that the war in the Mediterranean should be pursued first. From Marshall down, American commanders desperately resisted what they regarded as an unnecessary distraction, and the decision was made, and enforced, right at the top. There was a congressional election in 1942—Roosevelt *had* to get American troops in combat with the Germans; on November 8 Anglo-American forces invaded French North Africa, and once again the buildup in Britain was set back. The Mediterranean even drew off Spaatz himself, who for a time in 1943 directed tactical air forces there under General Dwight D. Eisenhower, the overall commander.

In Britain, Spaatz's bomber commander, General Ira Eaker, found himself starved of men and planes. His first bomb group, the 97th, no sooner arrived than it was ordered off to North Africa. Two of the next three across went the same way. As General Marshall was a strong believer in tactical air support, the Americans deployed eight fighter groups to Britain during the summer of 1942; seven soon went to the Mediterranean. Arnold complained that North Africa had delayed his British schedule by at least four months.

Nonetheless, the Americans made a beginning. On June 12, 1942, their heavy four-engined Liberator B-24's, the Flying Fortresses' rival, bombed the Romanian oil fields at Ploesti, a two-thousand-mile mission from Egypt. The refineries suffered little damage, but this was the first intimation of things to come. On July 4 twin-engined Boston bombers flew a low-level sweep over Holland, just to celebrate the day, and on August 17 a dozen American B-17's made their European combat debut in a raid on Rouen, with Eaker himself flying the mission.

The Americans thought big. They intended to create a force larger than the whole Royal Air Force in Britain, thirty-five hundred aircraft in sixty combat groups by April 1943. Though they fell behind schedule, the Eighth Air Force eventually grew to become a mighty armada. Squadron after squadron came across the Atlantic on the long Greenland-Iceland-Scotland route to settle at their new, rough bases in East Anglia. Through August and September they did their familiarization flights, then slowly, a few at a time, they took off to bomb French ports and factories. It would be some time yet before they were ready for operations over Germany itself. Meanwhile, they were out to prove that they could fly by day, and that they could bomb precisely defined targets, two points on which the British, with their greater experience, remained thoroughly skeptical.

In mid-January 1943, Prime Minister Churchill, President Roosevelt, and their top military advisers met at Casablanca to plan the future course of the war. Things looked brighter for them than at any time since Pearl Harbor. The Russians had survived a second deadly summer, and were now surrounding masses of Germans at Stalingrad. The tide had already turned in the Pacific, and the Americans were beginning the long, painful slog up the island chains to Japan. In the Mediterranean, General Montgomery's Eighth Army had definitively defeated the Germans at El Alamein, chased them all the way across Libya, and were nearing Tripoli. The North African landings had brought France back into the war, and the Allies had pushed east into Tunisia. The leaders could now look forward to the invasion of continental Europe itself.

This state of affairs was satisfactory for the progress of the war as a whole, but it was less than that for the extreme proponents of air power. It tended to mean that strategic bombing would do what the overall directors of the war had originally thought it would do, and not that it would win the war by itself. The pace of events was just too rapid for the bomber offensive to fulfill its largest claims. On January 21 the Combined Chiefs of Staff issued a new order, the Casablanca Directive, to the British and American bomber commands. They called for continuous air operations aimed at hitting precision targets, breaking German morale, and wearing down and destroying German fighter strength. But they also made it clear that this was all a prelude to a ground invasion. This directive was supplemented by another one in May, which in its allocation of target priority gave a good indication of how well, or ill, the bombers had fared so far. First on the list was submarine construction. The U-boat was still a menace; attempts to destroy the huge Atlantic Coast U-boat pens by bombing had failed, so now the bombers must go after the building yards. Second was the German aircraft industry itself, a reluctant and belated recognition that Germany's fighter defenses were too formidable to be ignored any longer. Then came the various choke points of the German economy: ball bearings, oil, synthetic rubber, and transport vehicles.

The man who got most out of the discussions at Casablanca was probably Ira Eaker. Churchill was so disillusioned with American daylight bombing promises that he was about to abandon his support; even more important, Eaker thought his own commanders were moving in the same direction. During the course of a long and intense discussion with the prime minister, who pointedly told him that after all these months of effort the Americans had still not dropped one bomb on Germany, Eaker pleaded his case so forcefully that Churchill turned around and supported the bombers' claims in the full sessions. Even as late as Casablanca, belief in bombing was still a matter of faith.

By the summer of 1943, the two bomber commands, British and American, were at last ready to justify that faith. They had new types of navigational aids, the most important being H2S. The code name for this was the chemical combination for hydrogen sulfide, and the story is that when this new type of radar was suggested, the initial response was, "It stinks." H2S was able to give the bombers a picture of the terrain below, enabling better navigation and more accurate bombing; eventually it was perfected so that planes could bomb not only by night but through thick cloud as well. This was followed by Oboe, a system that enabled planes to determine their positions by measurements from ground stations. Only a few aircraft at a time could use this, so it went to the Pathfinder squadrons. Using these new aids, and the increasing numbers of heavy bombers available, RAF Bomber Command flew series of missions against targets in the Ruhr. Four times in March and April they struck at Essen, where the great Krupp factories were located. Then they hit Duisberg, then Düsseldorf, leaving an increasing swath of destruction behind them. Then they began shuttle missions, flying from Britain to North Africa and back, hitting targets in Germany on the way out and in Italy on the return. By late summer, Harris was ready for his biggest effort yet, the Battle of Hamburg.

Meanwhile, to give the lie to Churchill's complaint that no American bombs had yet been dropped on Germany, the Eighth Air Force's Bomber Command at last bombed targets in the Reich itself. Having perfected its methods over France, the American force now thought it was ready for the big time. Its belief in daytime precision bombing, in spite of British experience, was based on a different approach to the problem and the possession of different equipment. The Flying Fortress was much more heavily armed than the British planes were. The most widely used type of Lancaster, the Mark III, carried eight rifle-caliber machine guns, two in the nose, two in a dorsal turret, and four in a tail turret. By contrast, the most numerous Flying Fortress model, the B-17G, featured no fewer than thirteen machine guns, all of heavier caliber than the British guns. The American bomber therefore doubled the defensive armament of the British. There was, of course, a penalty for this: The American plane needed a larger crew and, even more important, carried a smaller bombload. On long raids the normal load of a B-17 was a mere four thousand pounds, where the Lancaster carried fourteen thousand. In fact, the British twin-engined Mosquito, the famous "wooden wonder," with a crew of only two, carried the same bombload as the Fortress.

The other thing the Americans possessed that they believed gave them an edge was the famous Norden bombsight. This was one of the most widely publicized secrets of the war, for everyone knew they had it but no one knew much about it. Publicity photos of B-17 noses almost invariably bore the explanatory caption: "Note the jacket draped over the top secret Norden bombsight." With this, Americans were supposed to be able "to put a bomb in a pickle barrel," in the homely phrase of the day. Therefore, using precision bombing, with their heavily armed planes flying in mutually supporting defensive boxes, the Americans were confident they could fight their way through to a target, hit it accurately, and fight their way back home.

On January 27, 1943, American bombers made the first daylight raid over Germany, hitting Wilhelmshaven. From then on they appeared increasingly in German skies, and the intensity of combat mounted rapidly. The Germans devoted ever greater numbers of fighters and antiaircraft batteries to stopping them, and through the summer there was a steady escalation of the battle. It culminated in August. On August 17, the Eighth Air Force mounted a deep penetration raid into southwestern Germany. The targets were two industrial complexes vital to the war effort. At Regensburg there was a huge factory building Messerschmitt fighters; a hundred miles northwest of Regensburg was the center of the German ball-bearing industry, a lovely town with the inappropriately ugly name of Schweinfurt.

The plan was that the two targets would be bombed more or less simultaneously, swamping the German fighter and antiaircraft systems. As it happened, the 146 aircraft destined for Regensburg, and then routed to fly on to Algeria, took off on time under the lead of an irascible, cigar-chewing air-force reserve colonel named Curtis LeMay; the 230 slated for Schweinfurt and other diversionary targets were delayed three and a half hours by bad weather. Both groups had to fight all the way to the target, for the Germans picked them up soon after they crossed the coast and left their fighter escorts behind. The Fortresses droned stolidly on with the Luftwaffe sending up everything within range—109's, 110's, 410's, Focke-Wulf 190's, even old bombers now used as night fighters. The Americans left a trail of crashed and burned-out bombers behind them, all the way to the target and back. They hit both targets, but they lost 24 Fortresses from the Regensburg strike and 36 from the second group at Schweinfurt. Sixty planes out of 376 was far too many; the damage done to the Germans was simply not proportional to that done to the Americans, and they could not stand the losses.

Yet they tried again, in October. On October 14 they struck at Schweinfurt again. Mission 115 sent 291 Fortresses out against the Luftwaffe, and the Germans shot down another 60 of them. October 14 went down in the Eighth Air Force's history as Black Thursday. Sixty Fortresses down meant the loss of 600 aircrew, without even counting those carried home dead or wounded in their shot-up planes.

However good the planes, and however tough and devoted the men, no force in the world could stand that loss rate for any sustained period. The Schweinfurt raids definitively proved that the Americans could not fly over Germany by day in their unescorted bomber formations. They had been wrong, and thousands of young men were now paying the price for that mistaken theory. The Americans either had to go to night bombing, as the British had done, or give up the whole idea of strategic bombing, as the Germans had done, or find their own answer. By late 1943 the issue still hung in the balance.

XII

WARRIORS FOR
THE WORKADAY WORLD

If the effectiveness of strategic bombing was still unproven as late as the middle of 1943, there had been no doubt whatsoever, right from the first day of the war, that tactical air power was going to be a decisive element. In Poland, Denmark, Norway, the Low Countries, and France, the Germans had demonstrated their ability to develop a war-winning combination of aircraft, armor, and mobility to win overwhelming victories. The panzer and the Stuka provided the modern equivalent of Napoleon's cavalry and fast-marching infantry, and just as the Napoleonic legions had swarmed over their enemies like the advance of an irresistible tide, so the Germans had done the same in this twentieth-century incarnation, lapping around open flanks, attacking from the sky, appearing with devastating effect where least expected.

Tactical employment of air power, however, was a game that all parties could play. The Axis partners might have had an early lead, but they had no monopoly on either the equipment or the techniques, and those Allies who for one reason or another survived the initial onslaught soon showed themselves capable of meeting the Axis on their own ground, and eventually beating them at their own game.

With the end of the Battle of Britain, and Hitler's decline in interest, there came a pause in the land war. The Führer looked eastward, toward his newfound friend and old enemy, Bolshevik Russia. His restless brain began plotting and scheming, and his dutiful sycophants translated his half-developed ideas into concrete operational plans and forecasts. While he and his military men scanned their maps, the scene of action shifted southward, to the Mediterranean. Hitler's henchman, Mussolini, was intent upon fulfilling his own dream, of recreating a Roman Empire, of transforming the Mediterranean back into *Mare Nostrum,* "Our Sea." Thwarted in his desire to take over French North Africa by the rapidity of France's collapse and Germany's willingness to make a quick settlement, Mussolini turned on the British instead, determined to conquer Egypt and the Suez Canal and link up his Libyan territory with his Red Sea colonies.

The British in 1940 might not have been able to handle the German army, but they were more than a match for the Italians. Their weak garrison in the Middle East, outnumbered roughly 4 to 1, beat the Italians back with almost contemptuous ease. In eight weeks at the turn of the year, British forces captured 130,000 Italians for losses of a mere 2,000 of their own. But the real fate of North Africa was to be decided at sea. Who actually had what in the area was less important than who could control access to it. The Italian and later German supply line ran across the central Mediterranean from southern Italy to Tripoli; the British line ran east to west, from Gibraltar to Malta to Alexandria and Suez. The British route was both longer and more vulnerable, but Malta was a bone in the throat of the Axis, and if the British could dominate the sea lanes, they could hold the Middle East.

With Italian forces advancing into Egypt, the Royal Navy prepared its first riposte. The Italian navy was a first-class fleet, possessing modern and powerful battleships and cruisers. It had no carriers, for in the confines of the narrow sea, with Italy enjoying a good geographical location, these did not seem a priority. The air at sea thus belonged to the British, for by the fall of 1940, even though they had had serious carrier losses off Norway, they had two carriers in the Med, the ancient *Eagle* and the brand-new *Illustrious,* name ship of a class of four. As the Italians appeared reluctant to risk their ships at sea, the British decided to go in after them, and on the night of November 11, 1940, the Fleet Air Arm struck the major Italian base at Taranto.

The attacking force was something less than impressive. Originally slated for October 21, Trafalgar Day, the operation was postponed by a fire in *Illustrious*'s hangar deck; by November, *Eagle* was out of action as a result of bomb damage, so some of her planes were flown from the now repaired *Illustrious*. Even so, the attack consisted of a mere twenty planes. The aircraft themselves were Fairey Swordfish torpedo bombers. This antique biplane, universally known to aircrew as "the stringbag," was regarded with enormous affection by all those who had any connection with it. It lasted the entire war and its accomplishments became legendary, including on one occasion flying while missing one lower wing! It was not, however, the most daunting weapon with which to challenge the Italian navy. It had a maximum speed of 140 miles per hour, and to get to Taranto in loaded condition, one of the three-man crew had to be left behind.

Nonetheless, it was more than adequate for the night's work. The first wave of aircraft arrived over Taranto about midnight to find the Italians awake and ready, tipped off by one plane that had gotten lost and proceeded independently, arriving early. Cranking up to full power and diving so low over the water that some planes spun their wheels on the wave tops—a favorite prewar show-off device—the Swordfish bore steadily in. The first planes dropped their torpedoes, and were then followed by others acting as dive bombers. For a loss of two aircraft, the British left the Italian fleet in ruins behind them. Three battleships were hit; *Conte di Cavour* sank, *Caio Dulio* was beached by her crew to prevent her from sinking, and the new battleship *Littorio* took enough torpedoes to put her out of action for the next six months. The whole picture in the Mediterranean was altered in favor of the British by this one dramatic stroke.

The biggest problem with the attack had been getting a torpedo to work in very shallow water, and the British had successfully resolved it. Battleship admirals were quick to point out that, after all, the ships had been in port and at anchor, even though they were awake and firing back. The Fleet Air Arm's greatest-ever victory therefore did not receive as much attention as it might have, except in Japan, where naval aviators were toying with a somewhat similar set of problems and possibilities.

The Royal Navy continued to challenge Italy for control of the central

Mediterranean; its biggest problem, though, was fighting convoys through to Malta and keeping the beleaguered garrison resupplied and fighting. The Italians, and the Germans when they took a hand later, in 1941, had to neutralize Malta if they were to secure their own lines across to North Africa. For that very reason the British had to hold on to it. But to reach it, their convoys had to run the gauntlet of Axis airfields from Sicily and southern Italy. Moreover, distances were such that the convoys were subject to air attack during the daylight hours.

The most famous of these convoy battles was that of Operation Pedestal, in August 1942. The British sent in a convoy of fourteen merchantmen, including one tanker. As a measure of the danger, they provided an escort of two battleships, three carriers, seven cruisers, eight submarines, and thirty-two destroyers. They suffered eleven attacks, from Sardinia, Sicily, and the small island of Pantelleria, with submarines, E-boats, and up to a hundred aircraft at a time. They lost the aircraft carriers *Eagle*, sunk, and *Indomitable*, out of action; two cruisers and a destroyer were also sunk, and only five of the fourteen merchantmen made it through to Malta. One of them was the tanker, and as a result, the planes from Malta's airfields kept on harassing the enemy for the rest of the war.

Malta itself was repeatedly bombed by the Italians and then the Germans. At times it looked as if the island would surely fall, and on the worst occasions, the British had to send material in by submarine. For twenty months the siege went on, and Malta became the single most bombed place in the world. King George VI bestowed the George Cross on the entire island, and Malta, besieged by the Turks in 1565 and the British in 1800, had another page to add to its long and gloriously bloody history.

The brutal efficiency of tactical air power was demonstrated once again in the spring of 1941, when the Wehrmacht rolled over Yugoslavia and Greece. In this much misunderstood campaign, Hitler was securing his Balkan flank for the forthcoming invasion of Russia, and also helping out his ally, Mussolini, who had for some months been bogged down on the Greek frontier. The Italians had seized Albania in 1939, having long considered it a potential client, and in October 1940 they invaded Greece as well, where they encountered far more stubborn resistance than expected. It happened that Greece had an alliance with Britain, and Mussolini's move gave the British an excuse to move Royal Air Force units into the Peloponnese, which put them within bomber range of the Romanian oil fields around Ploesti. Hitler put pressure on Hungary and Romania, which joined the Axis, and Yugoslavia, which balked. British troops were by then in northern Greece, so Hitler ordered his military men to overrun Yugoslavia and go on from there to take Greece as well.

This they did in another blitzkrieg. On April 6 the Luftwaffe bombed Belgrade, totally disrupting the Yugoslav high command and its mobilization plans, and within ten days the country was occupied. In some places the outclassed Yugoslavs fought, but in other places the country's minorities sided with the invaders. Most soldiers took to the hills. Led by their Dorniers and Stukas, the Germans came screaming down the Vardar Valley toward the British and Greeks in the hastily prepared Aliakmon Line.

This they flanked, aided by bad weather, which grounded their own planes but also grounded the British, and in a short time the Greek and British forces were being pursued south, through central Greece and toward Athens. The British planes—relatively small numbers of Blenheim bombers, Gladiator biplanes, and a few newer Hurricanes—were both outclassed and outnumbered. Hustled back to Athens, they were rarely seen by the hard-pressed troops, and British tank officers reported stopping their tanks on hills, hoping that the angle would allow them to elevate their guns enough to use them against the German planes.

One measure of German air superiority was the large number of British aircraft caught and destroyed on the ground. In the entire six months in Greece nearly 200 planes were lost, more than three quarters of them during the last climactic three weeks, and better than half of those were on the ground. The Germans themselves admitted the loss of 164 aircraft.

Even worse was to follow. The British pulled back to the island of Crete, assuming they could hold it just because it was an island. Their possession of it would protect the northern flank of the eastern Mediterranean, and equally allow them to threaten the Italians and Germans in the Balkans and Aegean area. The Germans decided to take it, and, lacking sea control, they did it by air. This required an absolute miracle of improvisation. The five hundred Junkers Ju 52 transports for the operation had all been hard-used in the Greek campaign; now they were flown home en masse, overhauled and in some cases actually reengined, and flown back again.

The British on Crete were not even in condition to improvise. Commanded by General Bernard Freyberg, a New Zealander, they were largely remnants collected from Greece; they had few tanks or artillery, almost no antiaircraft guns, and little transport. Worst of all, they had hardly any air cover. Most of the RAF had been withdrawn back to Egypt, and Crete was beyond the range of fighter aircraft stationed there.

On May 20 the Germans landed by parachute and glider right on the barren airfields of the island. The British fought hard, and for a day and a half held the Germans in a tight perimeter. In desperation the Germans then began landing their transports right on the fire-swept airstrips, especially at Máleme, and this bold stroke, despite heavy losses of men and aircraft, succeeded. Successive waves of German airborne troops got in all right. Units coming by sea were annihilated by the Royal Navy, but once the Germans controlled the airfields on the island itself, the British had to abandon the waters north of Crete. Within a week the weary British were filtering through the mountains to the south coast and evacuating. Suffering a terrible pounding from the Luftwaffe, the navy came in and took them off. Sixteen ships were badly damaged, including a battleship and an aircraft carrier, and three cruisers and six destroyers were sunk.

The feat made the Germans look quite like supermen, and it was their most successful large-scale airborne attack of the war. Göring, whose pet the entire project was, was highly elated. Yet the attack cost them 220 aircraft, about half of them Junkers transports, and virtually crippled the German airborne forces. The 7th Parachute Division was left a shattered wreck, and its commander, General Kurt Student, went off to other tasks. The Germans never tried this sort of stunt again.

Important and disastrous though they were for the British, the Balkans remained essentially a sideshow for the Germans. Hitler was firmly committed to the destruction of Russia, which by a strange choice he code-named Operation Barbarossa, and the preparations were already made. The Germans had deployed huge forces in Poland and eastern Europe, and were ready to move whenever Hitler should give the word. There has been almost endless argument about the effect of the Balkans on his timetable, and Churchill especially, who came under intense criticism for the British intervention there, insisted that the German delay for Greece saved Moscow. Though this contention may perhaps be defended, it was also a very wet spring in Europe, and the soggy ground of Poland and eastern Russia probably would have held the Germans up even without the British sacrifice of their Mediterranean superiority. By June, Hitler had three huge army groups facing the Russians, and the Germans were ready to move.

Given their national reputation for thoroughness and care, the Germans were remarkably ignorant of their enemy. Their operational intelligence was skimpy, and they seemed so convinced of their own superiority that they were not even worried about it. They knew there were a lot of Russians there, but they assumed that however many there were, they would easily be able to handle them. They were very nearly right.

The Russians had of course picked up the German deployment, and had also been warned by the western Allies of the impending move. Stalin chose to ignore all of this, and resolutely believed what he wanted to; in this he and Hitler were much alike. Three Russian fronts, 158 divisions, faced three German army groups, 162 divisions. In spite of these World War I–style masses of men, the Germans expected to fight a blitzkrieg war. Their real strength lay in their 19 panzer divisions and their roughly 2,000 aircraft, which were divided into 4 air fleets. They estimated that the Russians probably possessed 5,500 aircraft, but they thought these were largely obsolete and of poor quality. In this they were right again.

This was a matter of relative insignificance, for most of the Red Air Force was wiped out in the first days of combat, indeed in the first hours. Stalin's refusal to face facts left the Russian planes neatly lined up on their airfields, sitting targets for the German bombers whose arrival heralded the opening of the war. Luftwaffe pilots could hardly believe their eyes as they joyously bombed and machine-gunned row after row after row of Russian fighters and bombers, leaving them burning wrecks on the ground. In the first week of the invasion, the Germans claimed more than 4,000 Red planes destroyed. Their success was equaled only by that of the German army, rampaging forward on the ground and breaking everything that dared to stand in its path. Battered, dazed, betrayed, the Russians floundered before the juggernaut.

The ultimate aim of war, said Clausewitz, is the destruction of the enemy's will to resist. Against that, material is almost—if not quite—inconsequential, as witness the differing French and British reactions to defeat in 1940. The Germans destroyed immense amounts of Russian material, indeed of Russian soldiery as well, but they did not destroy Russia's will to resist. Stalin soon recognized that communism might not be worth dying for, but Holy Mother Russia was, and when the Germans threw away the chance at quick victory by indecisiveness in the late summer, Russia rallied and held. Winter arrived just in time to save her, a winter for which the Germans were not prepared; they had expected their war to be won by now.

In the air, the Luftwaffe functioned as efficiently as always, perhaps even more so, given the initially poor quality of the opposition. Air-force field commanders and staffs were men of vast experience, and their pilots knew all there was to know about tactical air employment. Their eventually fatal errors lay at higher quarters.

The Russo-German War, or Great Patriotic War as the Russians call it, was in the air a tactical war. The Germans had already decided that this supporting role was the true métier of air forces. The Russians essentially agreed with them. Back in the 1920s, Russia, more or less independently, had produced some of the world's biggest and most advanced heavy bombers. The great Soviet engineer Andrei Tupolev was one of the world leaders in experimental all-metal construction. The Soviet Union had also been among the first powers to consider airborne operations. In the Spanish Civil War their aircraft showed that they were close to world-class standards. Development was furthered by the Five Year Plans and by state planning, and equally set back by the Stalinist purges of the late thirties. By that time a new generation of designers was appearing, most notably Alexander Yakovlev, Artem Mikoyan, and Mikhail Gurievitch. The fruit of their labors was to fight much of the war. The German attack thus caught the Red Air Force in the process of changing over from obsolete to new equipment, and the massive attacks on those undefended Russian planes merely hurried along a process already taking place.

Thus, German failure lay not so much in the initial effort, but rather in the long-term assessment, not only in the operational but also in the production sphere. Having missed their chance to wipe out the Russians in those last weeks of summer and fall, they missed it for good. Qualitatively, they never ceased to outperform their opponents; quantitatively, they ended up being swamped by the Russians. They believed the Russians were producing about 5,000 aircraft a year; in fact, in 1939 and 1940 the Reds turned out slightly more than 10,000 a year. And as the Germans aimed at a short-term, tactical type of war, Russian production increased alarmingly: 15,000 in 1941; 25,000 in 1942; 35,000 in 1943; and 40,000 in 1944. In every year from 1941 on, the Russians alone turned out more aircraft than the Germans did, and while the Reds could use these solely against the Germans, the latter had to devote increasing numbers of planes to other theaters, including, eventually and especially, home defense.

Some of the Russian planes, admittedly, were not very good. In many ways their aircraft industry was still learning its business. But the Russians quickly standardized on a couple of major designs, then went on to improve and upgrade them throughout the war. They developed extremely robust ground-attack planes, such as the famous Ilyushin Il-2, the "Stormovik," a mighty tank killer, which was virtually a flying tank itself, with its entire forward section one armor-plated cell.

Figures for the air war in Russia are astounding by comparison with western ones; both Russian and German pilots flew until they were killed, and either side would have scoffed at the western Allies and their tours of duty and rotation of aircrew. There were 203 Russian pilots who shot down more than 20 enemy aircraft, and their ground-attack pilots flew literally thousands of sorties. Their top ace, Major Ivan Kozhedub, shot down 62 Germans. The Germans ran up even more impressive totals. Their highest scoring pilot in the entire war was Major Erich Hartmann, officially credited with 352 enemy aircraft, most of them on the Russian front. Another famous German pilot, Hans Ulrich Rudel, spent almost the whole war flying Stukas, and was busily engaged on the eastern front long after the Stuka had been withdrawn from the west. He made 2,350 operational flights, and was credited not only with killing 500 Russian tanks but also a battleship, the Russian *Marat,* which was bombed and sunk in Kronstadt harbor.

Neither side employed any appreciable amount of strategic bombardment. The Russians developed the concept of the air offensive, reserving and then employing their air forces in masses for a particular purpose. The Germans just wore themselves out in a vain attempt to stem the flood. In one area of operations the Russians were definitely superior; that was in the repair and servicing provided by their ground organization, so that gradually the Germans found themselves trying to do more and more with fewer and fewer aircraft and less and less availability. By 1943 the Russian numerical preponderance was reaching alarming proportions. In their summer offensives of that year they had 10,000 aircraft. The Luftwaffe for its total war effort, not just against Russia, had 3,551. The next year Red strength had grown to 13,500; and by early 1945 there were 15,500 Russian planes to support their offensives. In the final drive on Berlin they had 8,000 planes on that one front alone; the Germans had almost none. Here was an air war of attrition with a vengeance.

As the Germans exercised an early tactical command of the air in Russia, and then slowly lost it to increasing enemy numbers, so too the Japanese went through the same progression. When the Germans were launching Operation Barbarossa, the Japanese were deciding on war with the imperial powers. Bogged down in China, unable to bring that weak but huge nation to its knees, and increasingly frustrated by western pressure, Japan chose to widen her war. Some fatal madness often infects military and political leaders, so that unable to win a war against one country, they conclude that they will be able to win a war against two or three. By a tortuous logic, the Japanese convinced themselves that if they knocked the United States, Britain, and the residual Dutch out of the Far East, they would then be free to create their own Greater East Asia Co-Prosperity Sphere. They possessed one of the best navies in the world, and it was underemployed. When the United States made proposals that meant, all unwittingly, either war or withdrawal of their ambitions for empire, the Japanese chose war. Late in 1941 the moment seemed propitious, for there was relatively little standing in their way.

The Dutch government of the Netherlands East Indies disposed of negligible forces. The British had a substantial land garrison in Malaya and Singapore. Just before the outbreak of hostilities they reinforced it with two heavy ships, the battle cruiser *Repulse* and the new battleship *Prince of Wales;* an intended aircraft carrier was damaged while working up. British air capabilities were laughable. The main opposition to Japan would come from the United States Fleet, a formidable collection of ships then based at Pearl Harbor. The Americans were also building up their strength in the Philippines, and had established there a contingent of B-17's to serve as a strategic bombardment force in the event of war. Still living in a peacetime atmosphere in the midst of a world at war, the Americans thought they were ready for any eventuality.

Against these widely scattered forces the Japanese could pit their fleet, 230 combat vessels, centered around a core of a dozen battleships and ten aircraft carriers. In the air they were well equipped, having a total of 7,500 planes, of which nearly half were first-line combat aircraft. All of them, as it turned out, were better planes than those of their enemies, a most unpleasant surprise for the Allies. The Japanese knew they lacked staying capacity; they could not fight a long-extended, distant war, and they did not expect to have to. Their plan was to drive the enemy rapidly from the western Pacific and east Asia, set up a defensive perimeter, perhaps fight a couple of decisive victories on that perimeter—if indeed that were necessary—and then sit down to enjoy the fruits of their conquest. Thus they chose for war, and on December 7, 1941, they began it with a crushing victory over their major opponent.

Though it would seem every word that can be written about Pearl Harbor *has* been written, argument still continues: Was it a betrayal or merely a colossal bungle? Most serious authorities opt for the latter; the Americans knew the Japanese were on the move—they had lost the Japanese carrier striking force, and they had even put out what was tantamount to a war warning. Yet it was so unthinkable that Japan would attack them that throughout the Pacific they were caught asleep, wrapped in the blanket of their own complacency.

Pearl Harbor was a massive replay of Taranto, which had convinced the Japanese that a torpedo attack in a shallow harbor was in fact feasible. But instead of Britain's twenty Swordfish from one carrier, the Japanese employed six aircraft carriers and 450 planes—Mitsubishi Zero fighters, Aichi dive bombers, and Nakajima torpedo planes. Japanese aircraft nomenclature was sufficiently complicated that the Americans eventually assigned nicknames to enemy planes; they were arbitrarily chosen by an officer who apparently was from a southern state. The three main types used at Pearl became known as Zekes, Vals, and Kates; other names such as Rufe, Nate, Hap, Oscar, Nell, Sally, and Betty were soon in common usage.

Steaming on a circular path through the wastes of the northern Pacific, the Japanese striking force appeared undetected two hundred miles north of Oahu Island on the morning of December 7, launched its planes, and waited with bated breath. The results were spectacular.

Coming in in successive waves, the Japanese found the U.S. Fleet at anchor, and army and navy planes neatly lined up in rows along their airfields. Concerned over possible sabotage, the Americans had put the planes out in the open where they could be guarded. The first wave of attackers was practically unopposed. The second found a hornet's nest and took substantial casualties, but by then the damage had been done. Seven American battleships were disabled, two of them, *Arizona* and *Oklahoma,* total losses. Several other ships were near or total wrecks, almost 200 aircraft were destroyed, and the Americans suffered 4,575 casualties, most of them among the fleet where hundreds of sailors were trapped in their sunken ships. The Japanese missed the American aircraft carriers, which were not at Pearl at the time of the strike, and they did not destroy the dock, storage, and repair facilities of the base. Nonetheless, their war of conquest got off to a smashing start.

Two more victories, equally glorious for the Japanese and unnecessary for the Allies, quickly followed. Across the International Date Line, it was December 8 in the Philippines when the news flashed in that Pearl Harbor was under attack. The commander of the Far East Air Force, General Lewis Brereton, immediately requested permission to send his B-17's off on a strike against Japanese targets in Formosa. General Douglas MacArthur, overall commander in the Philippines, refused. Stunned and appalled by the news, he and his command waffled. American fighter and bomber aircraft patrolled rather aimlessly, then settled back on Clark Field to refuel at lunchtime. There they were caught by the Japanese, who came roaring in to bomb and then strafe. The virtual massacre of American air strength at Clark Field became known as "little Pearl Harbor." In Washington General Arnold was enraged at the loss of his planes, and tore a long-distance strip off the hapless Brereton. All to no avial; the Japanese now had air superiority in the Philippines.

They showed even more graphically what that meant in a third area. The British had regarded the great base at Singapore as the bastion of their Far Eastern empire ever since the Washington Naval Treaty of 1922. They had spent considerable sums on its defense, but they had never resolved the fundamental question of who was actually responsible for it, and the three services had passed the buck to each other in a twenty-year game of musical chairs. When Japanese bombers, flying from bases in southern Indochina, appeared over the city, and

Japanese troops landed on the Malayan peninsula, the British decided on a cast of desperation. Their two heavy ships, *Repulse* and *Prince of Wales,* sortied to break up enemy convoys.

Admiral Tom Phillips, known as "Tom Thumb" because of his short stature, was aware that the RAF could provide only limited air cover for him, with a couple of squadrons of obsolete Brewster Buffaloes, American planes that they had detailed for the purpose. Phillips was not worried; he was a battleship admiral, and he did not even make any liaison efforts with the air-force people. At midmorning on December 10, the two ships were sighted by Japanese reconnaissance planes, and shortly thereafter were attacked by high-level and torpedo bombers. The British were amazed and disconcerted; these were not lumbering Swordfish biplanes, but rather twin-engined modern bombers, Mitsubishi G3M2 Nells and G4M1 Bettys. The ships twisted and turned and fought with everything they had, but the Japanese bravely and skillfully pressed their attack. Both ships were repeatedly hit by torpedoes. *Repulse* lasted but a quarter of an hour, and *Prince of Wales,* with more modern compartmentation and damage control, lasted a little longer, but three hours after the initial sighting, it was all over. Admiral Phillips paid with his life for his belief in the battleship, and 840 sailors paid with him. As *Prince of Wales* slid beneath the shallow waters of the Gulf of Siam, the long argument was over at last—the battleship era was finished for good. For sailors and airmen the subsequent fall of Singapore, in February 1942, was a foregone conclusion, almost an anticlimax.

Singapore and the Philippines invested, the Japanese forces raged on into the Dutch Far East Indies. They leapfrogged from one island to another, seizing ports and airstrips as they went. Everywhere their planes led the way, bombing, strafing, catching Allied ships at sea and pounding them unmercifully. They bombed harbors and dock facilities, and by the end of February it was all over. The East Indies were gone; the Japanese were extending west to Burma and the Indian Ocean, where they raided as far as the British naval base at Trincomalee in Ceylon, and east into the South Pacific, to New Guinea and down toward the Solomon Islands. In less than a hundred days their ocean empire had reached its planned limits.

Billy Mitchell had remarked that ships and army troops would be of use only to capture bases for aircraft, for air power was going to be the dominant element of future wars. He was correct in the sense that much of Allied strategy in the Pacific was dictated by the desire to take or hold airstrips. But he was wrong in two things: He underestimated how big oceans are, and he forgot about aircraft carriers. The war against Japan largely became a war between aircraft carriers, with its aim being the projection of power into and through the Japanese perimeter. To fight its war, the United States built the greatest fleet the world has ever seen, centered not around the battleship but around the fast-carrier task force. From December 7, 1941, to August 15, 1945, the United States Navy launched 5 new battleships and 23 new fleet carriers. American yards also launched 122 smaller aircraft carriers of escort types in the same period, some of them conversions from cruiser, oiler, or general mercantile hulls. The Pearl Harbor strike, and the loss of the older battleships, did for the U.S. Navy the same thing that the German surprise attack on the Russian air bases did for the Soviet Union: It got rid of obsolete equipment. In the process it got rid of obsolete concepts as well. The course of the Pacific battles soon proved that the Americans had been pushed onto the right track, a track they had indeed first mapped out themselves back in the late twenties.

As the western Pacific reached some sort of equilibrium, the Japanese decided to extend their chosen defense perimeter to the southeast, down into the Solomon Islands, threatening the American lifeline to New Zealand and Australia. The Australians were desperately holding on to eastern New Guinea, operating from Port Moresby on the south side of the Owen Stanley Mountains, while the Japanese based at Lae and Salamaua on the north side. In May, thinking to capture Port Moresby, the Japanese sent a carrier task force and a convoy into the Coral Sea. The Americans, reading Japanese codes, moved to intercept them. The Battle of the Coral Sea was another benchmark in naval history. December 10 had settled the ships-versus-aircraft question; the Coral Sea was the first naval action in history in which the opposing ships never sighted each other. It was fought between Japanese aircraft attacking American ships and American aircraft attacking Japanese ships. This was an enormously confused battle, with both sides floundering about literally and figuratively in the dark, striking at isolated units, missing rendezvous, and mistaking identities. Several times Japanese planes approached American carriers thinking they were their own, and one unfortunate pilot was even shot down as he was trying to land on USS *Yorktown*. Several smaller ships were bombed, torpedoed, and sunk, but the big losses were the light Japanese carrier *Shoho*, sunk on her first operation, and, far more important, the big American carrier *Lexington*, hit by two Japanese torpedoes. In terms of losses, the Japanese won, trading a small ship for a big one; strategically, however, the Japanese gave up the initiative when they abandoned their attempt to take Port Moresby. This was not quite the high tide of Japanese Empire, but the flood was slacking.

It was definitely halted the next month, at the Battle of Midway. Here, in an effort to extend their defense line in the central Pacific and bring the Americans to decisive battle before their strength grew any more, the Japanese mobilized virtually their entire resources in one vast, complicated, eccentric plan. The centerpiece of it was the seizure of Midway Island, farthest west of the Hawaiian chain, and the force for this was covered by four aircraft carriers and their attendant escorts. To meet the threat, the Americans mustered three carriers, *Enterprise, Hornet,* and the already battered *Yorktown*, which the Japanese believed they had sunk in the Coral Sea. The Americans' great advantage was that, having broken the enemy codes, they knew their intentions. As the Japanese approached Midway in the first week of June, the Americans stood off to the northeast and ambushed them.

Tardy Japanese scouting efforts missed the American fleet units, so the Japanese concentrated their air bombardment efforts on the base at Midway itself. Their first strike did insufficient damage, and while their carrier planes were refueling and rearming for a second strike, they were caught off guard by the arrival of American planes. The first American effort turned out to be a slaughter; obsolete torpedo planes, the misnamed Douglas Devastators, were shot down with ease by the defending fighters. The most famous unit in this attack, Torpedo Squadron Eight, was wiped out, with only one pilot, Ensign George Gay, surviving to witness the battle from the water. But the Devastators' sacrifice had not been wasted; their attack had pulled the Japanese air patrols down to low level, so that shortly after, when Douglas SBD dive bombers arrived overhead, they found the Japanese open to their attack. Here was the vindication of the dive-bombing school, the naval counterpart to Germany's Stuka: The SBD's, which their crew insisted stood for "Slow But Deadly," came streaking down out of the clear sky. Dropping their thousand-pound bombs from near vertical dives, they hit three of the Japanese carriers within minutes of each other. In the midst of rearming their aircraft, the three ships, *Kaga, Akagi,* and *Soryu,* were turned in moments into blazing hulks. Bomb bursts ignited aviation gas, and that flashed to ammunition. The strike could not have been more perfectly timed, and in the space of four minutes, from 1026 to 1030, June 4, 1942, the American pilots had altered the balance of the war in the Pacific.

One carrier escaped to strike back. *Hiryu* had been slightly distant from the other 3, and therefore had not been spotted by the Americans. She now launched a strike of her own, and her torpedo pilots, pressing their attack with gallantry equal to the Americans', put two fish into *Yorktown.* The carrier, still badly damaged from the Coral Sea attack, slowed, stopped, and took on a severe list. *Hiryu,* in turn, was hit by a second strike from the other American ships. She went down the next day and so did *Yorktown,* hit yet again, this time by torpedoes from a Japanese submarine. In the final tally the Japanese lost 4 carriers, 1 heavy cruiser, and 258 aircraft; the Americans lost 1 carrier, 1 destroyer, 92 fleet aircraft, and another 40 planes from Midway itself.

The Battle of Midway alone might not have been anything more than a signpost, had it not been for all those aircraft carriers being built in American shipyards, and planes rolling off the assembly lines, and pilots learning to fly all over the southern United States. The Japanese, like the Germans, were not prepared for a long war, and they were far less capable than the Germans of producing the men and materials to fight one. They simply did not have the plant capacity, though they made better use of what they had than their European allies did. But there was always a lag in engine production, and in early 1945 Japan had a strength of 4,600 aircraft, while the United States disposed 18,000 against them. Their pilots lost experience and quality as the war went on, and eventually they were training young men to do no more than take off and try to guide the plane into a suicidal crash on an American ship. That was partly because the kamikaze concept accorded with the Japanese ethos, but it was also partly because it was the best they could manage.

As in other things, they gradually fell behind the Americans in aircraft quality. The Zero fighter was a major shock to the Allies; it could fly rings around current American planes. But the Japanese achieved

speed, agility, and long range, at the expense of armor and pilot protection. The Zero's chief enemy for the early stages of the war, the
German F4F Wildcat, was a sturdy little brute that could take far more
punishment than the Zero, and time and again it brought its pilots
home where the Zero broke up in midair. Eventually American pilots
survived to graduate to F6F Hellcats and Vought's bent-wing Corsair;
their Japanese opposite numbers died, to be replaced by younger and
less experienced pilots still flying flimsy planes that gave them little
chance to become veterans. This is of course an oversimplification,
but the main line is accurate enough. Even if the Japanese later produced such excellent planes as the Kawasaki Ki. 61, the "Hien," or
"Tony," they were too little too late. They were outflown, outfought,
and, above all, outproduced by the Americans.

In mid-1942 that was still to come. That summer British troops
racked with malaria and dysentery hung on to the northern frontier
of Burma, Australians held the passes through the Owen Stanley
Mountains of New Guinea, the worst country of the world, and the
Americans, fresh from their crushing but narrow victory at Midway,
began their first offensive against the Japanese perimeter. They landed
on a jungle-covered island in the Solomons, an unknown place called
Guadalcanal.

This island was the extreme southeastern projection of Japanese
power, and on it they were constructing, of course, an airstrip. Planes
based here could threaten the United States-to-Australia route. On
August 7, 1942, U.S. Marines landed on the island and at a seaplane
base on nearby Tulagi. They immediately captured the airstrip from
the unarmed Japanese construction workers, but that first day was
the only easy one for the next six months. Securing the island cost
1,600 killed and 4,200 wounded, plus thousands more down with
tropical diseases. It cost a series of intensely heavy naval and air battles. However important those production lines in Seattle and Wichita
and Waterbury were, it was on the Tenaru River, in The Slot, and in
the humid air over them that desperate old men of nineteen and
twenty-one had to fight the war. To them, production figures meant
less than surviving the next quarter hour.

The battle was eventually done, by February 1943, and the Americans began the laborious task of inching their way up the island
chains. The army, under General MacArthur, worked its way along
the coast of New Guinea, past Buna, Gona, and Salamaua; the navy

and marines clawed up the Solomon chain, from Guadalcanal to New Georgia, to Kolombangara and Vella Lavella, horrible places whose exotic names were synonymous with pain, suffering, and terror. The routine was always the same: air strikes, tactical air command, landings, build an airstrip, secure it, build up a base, move on to the next one. And in the central Pacific, the fast carrier task forces appeared early in 1943, raiding in the Gilberts and the Marshalls, yet another line of operations opening up.

By this time, mid-1943, the air war had reached a crisis. Tactical air power had proven itself absolutely indispensable, the sine qua non, and without achieving command of the air, armies and navies were almost paralyzed. Allied armies and navies, under the umbrella provided by their air forces, were preparing for the final defeat of their enemies by the conventional means of invasion, in Sicily, Italy, and France in Europe, and of the Philippines, Formosa, the Chinese mainland, and eventually the Japanese Home Islands in the Pacific. Strategic bombing was still at the crossroads, still striving to prove the validity of its theories. Yet the Allies now had both the expertise and the capacity to employ a variety of techniques in a variety of theaters. For the Axis powers, still having little idea of the forces they had set in motion, the sky was about to fall.

XIII

SKIES FILLED WITH EAGLES

The tide of the war turned definitively in the summer and fall of 1942. The Battle of Midway in the Pacific, followed by El Alamein and the invasion of French North Africa in November, and Stalingrad over the turn of the year, threw the Axis forces on all fronts into retreat. After those defeats they would never again launch anything but limited tactical offensives. From that time on, though the Allies might move slowly, they moved inexorably forward. By the next summer, 1943, the continent of Europe and the German homeland itself were under threat. In July the Allies invaded Sicily, and a month later landed on the Continent; they invaded Italy on the fourth anniversary of Britain's declaration of war. The Schweinfurt-Regensburg raid, the first deep penetration of Germany by the American Eighth Air Force, occurred that month. A more pressing danger to the Reich was that of the Royal Air Force's Bomber Command. In late July it launched a series of raids known as the Battle of Hamburg.

Near the mouth of the Elbe, Hamburg was Germany's second largest city, a major port and industrial center and a prime target for

Bomber Command. Sir Arthur Harris had indeed wanted to hit it in his first thousand-plane raid back in May 1942. The city had been regularly visited by the British, 137 times before, but never with the intensity they now devoted to it. With a biblical sense of retributive justice, they code-named the battle Operation Gomorrah.

The techniques of area bombing were now pretty well perfected. Diversionary raids confused and scattered the defenders, the Pathfinder force marked the target, the bombing stream of Halifaxes and Lancasters—the Stirling was now being phased out to lesser operations—struck in finely timed intervals. Scientific analysis had achieved the appropriate combination of bombs to drop, in the right sequences: high explosives to create debris, incendiaries to set it afire, more high explosives to deter the fire fighters, more incendiaries to spread the blaze, some phosphorus to add more horror, and some delayed-action bombs to disrupt rescue and recovery efforts. Everything was calculated to a nicety. There were progressive wrinkles as the campaign went along, more effective radar—H2S was in wide use now—and bombing techniques, and, for example, the introduction of Window at Hamburg. This was an extraordinarily simple device, for once. Window consisted of strips of tinfoil, of such a size and shape that when picked up on a radar screen they looked exactly like British bombers, an inexpensive and well-nigh perfect way to confuse the German night-fighter control system and swamp it with apparent targets.

Hamburg was no Cologne. It was even more important, and it was a city used to being bombed. It had probably the best civil defense and air-raid warning system in Germany, but it had nothing capable of reacting to Gomorrah. On the night of July 24, 740 British bombers dropped 2,396 tons of bombs on the city. The enemy defenses, confused by the Window, had fighters milling about mostly over Amsterdam; their flak batteries and searchlights jerking spasmodically here and there in response to their radar controls were completely useless. Of the 740 bombers, a mere 12 were lost. This night was only the beginning. The next day and the day after, small attacks of 68, and then 53, American B-17's aimed at specific targets. On the night of July 27, the British returned. This attack was timed to perfection: 739 bombers dropped 2,917 tons of bombs, and they hit Hamburg's built-up residential areas, crowded with workers and their families. This second major attack was the night of the firestorm. In the still air, flames mounted thousands of feet into the night sky. The fire was fed by the debris from bomb blasts, small fires merged together to become large ones, and the fire began to generate its own air currents as the intense heat sucked air in toward its heart. Soon there was a blazing inferno, and everything movable was being sucked toward the vortex, exactly like a tornado of flame. Temperatures mounted. In the shelters underground people suffocated and then were baked, and finally they burned to ashes. The wind pulling into the fire reached 150 miles per hour, the temperature climbed to 1,400 degrees, and 6 square miles of the center of Hamburg went up in the greatest funeral pyre ever seen, rising 3 miles into the sky.

Finally the fire exhausted itself, but the British were not done yet. On the night of July 29 they returned and dropped another 2,382 tons on areas still relatively untouched. And on August 2 they paid a final visit, in poor weather this time, and dropped another 1,426 tons. With that the battle was over. The British lost 87 aircraft shot down and another 39 written off damaged on landing; Hamburg cost them 606 aircrew. In return they destroyed the city and left behind 6,000 acres of smoking ashes and rubble, 41,800 people killed, and another 37,000 injured, many of whom died soon after or carried their scars to their eventual graves. Herman Göring had boasted, "No enemy plane will fly over the Reich territory," and if any does, "you can call me Meyer." Now a wave of dread swept over Germany. Leaving Hamburg behind, the British turned toward Berlin.

Unlike Cologne more than a year earlier, Hamburg was neither an aberration nor a publicity stunt unlikely to be repeated. Hamburg showed what the British could now do, though, as events were to demonstrate, they could still not achieve that degree of successful destruction at will, not quite yet. But it did mark the beginning of an increasingly offensive phase for the Allies. On other fronts as well as over Germany, they were becoming more and more dominant. Germany simply could not stand the weight of the war. The year 1943 saw the U-boat threat mastered at last. By the end of the year there were only half as many submarines operational in the Atlantic as there had been at the start. U-boat sinkings were up, and between long-range land-based maritime reconnaissance and the increasing numbers of escort carriers available, the Germans found themselves the hunted rather than the hunters. By 1944, though still occasionally deadly, they were but a shadow of their former menace.

North Africa was gone now, the German and Italian forces confined to a shrinking pocket in Tunisia and surrendering in May 1943. In July the British and Americans invaded Sicily, and in five weeks they had overrun the island. The central Mediterranean seaways were freed from the threat of Sicilian airfields at last, with a great bonus for Allied shipping availability; no longer did convoys have to make the long wasteful run around Africa to the Middle East. Allied momentum and enthusiasm carried them on into Italy, and by Christmas, 1943, they were north of Naples, fighting around Cassino. Air power played a key role in all of this, sometimes for good and sometimes less so. Intended parachute drops in the Sicily landing were turned into a shambles by nervous Allied naval gunners, who shot down large numbers of their own transports as they flew over the armada. The Italian landing, at Salerno, was constrained by the short range of Allied fighter aircraft; commanders were anxious to have cover over their beaches, which dictated a landing south of Naples rather than north of it. An excess of caution—the Italians were surrendering, the Germans at the moment had little in Italy—cost weeks of heavy fighting.

One of the prizes of southern Italy was the Italian airfield complex around Foggia. From this base, Allied strategic bombers could strike at targets in the Balkans, especially the Romanian oil fields around Ploesti, hitherto hit by very costly, and only marginally successful, raids from across the Mediterranean. Again the vise tightened on the German war machine. Less successful by far was the tactical employment of heavy bombers in an attempt to get the Allies past the bottleneck at Cassino. Allied soldiers were certain, incorrectly as it happened, that the Germans were using the great Benedictine Abbey, mother house of the order of monks of that name, as an observation point. On February 15 a hundred B-17's bombed the abbey, turning the ancient structure into a mass of rubble. The Germans hastily occupied it and the rubble turned out to be practically impregnable. Heavy bomb attacks employed tactically often turned out to be counterproductive, and ground commanders on both sides remarked in memoirs that they found dive bombers with their pinpoint accuracy useful but preferred artillery to heavy high-level bombers, for the latter made such a mess as to create impassable conditions. There were inverted echoes of the Great War there.

And in Russia too the Germans were coming back. Their last great offensive, at Kursk, in the summer of 1943, had gained them nothing but the destruction of their own armor. By the end of the year the Reds were across the Dnieper; the Germans were isolated in the Crimea, and in the north they were hoping to hold the line of the Vistula. At Kursk the Red Air Force had outnumbered the Germans by at least ten to one, and Russian planes, with the advent of the LaGG 5, the Petlyakov Pe-2, and newer Mig and Yak types, were no longer inferior to the Germans. Everywhere German shortsightedness was beginning to haunt them.

Too little and too late, Germany began mobilizing more fully for war. It was after the Stalingrad debacle that the Germans finally acknowledged they were in trouble in Russia, and that a drastic shift to a wartime economy was necessary. The moving figure in this was Albert Speer, Hitler's architect and organizational genius, who initiated a rationalization of production techniques and schedules. Speer's rapid overhauling of German capacity gave the Allies fits, for they saw the evidence that production was increasing, and this violently contradicted all their predictions of the effects of strategic bombing. It was a dilemma they found difficult to explain, and they did not know until after the war that the explanation lay in the vast underutilization of German capacity until the middle of 1943. However, though Speer could delay the inevitable, he could not alter it. His new programs were introduced too late in the day for the survival of Germany. Increased fighter production in 1943 did not get the aircraft to the squadrons until 1944, and by then the entire infrastructure was collapsing. By then the Allies were at last hitting their panacea, or bottleneck targets, and all the new fighters in the world did no good if there were no gas for them to fly; by 1944 Germany was losing three quarters of its fighters every month, and no matter how many it produced, it could not stand that wastage.

Even Speer could not produce the pilots to fly the planes. Pilot loss escalated rapidly under the Allied attacks, so that the trained reserves dwindled away. In the first years of the war Germany lost about 600 pilots a month, which was an acceptable rate. After the invasion of Russia, this climbed to nearly 1,200 a month, and that was a serious matter. But then, from late 1943 on, with Allied planes challenging the Germans increasingly over Germany itself, and the manpower barrel getting lower, the rate climbed again, to 1,700 a month. Believing themselves superior in training and tactics, the Germans had always preferred quality to quantity. By 1944 they had neither; they were both overwhelmed by Allied numbers and outflown by better Allied planes in the hands of more experienced pilots.

Hitler remained inordinately reluctant to devote any effort to the defense of Germany. He insisted that the aircraft industry keep producing planes that he considered offensive weapons, and when good defensive ones did come out, he then insisted on misusing them. But a defense system had to be created in spite of him. Its active component consisted of the Luftwaffe itself, both its fighter units and their support and control mechanisms, and the antiaircraft batteries that remained under air-force control. West of Berlin, and then in a wide swath on the northwest frontier of Germany, were two searchlight belts, interspersed with flak concentrations around major cities or industrial areas. Forward of them, along the coast and in the occupied countries, were fighter stations, and the night-fighter groups were tied together with radar stations and a control network similar to that employed by the British.

German night fighters were the responsibility of General Joseph Kammhuber, and the defense belt was commonly known as the Kammhuber Line. He fought a constant battle with the Allies on the one hand, and with his own superiors on the other, in attempting to get better and more equipment. The German high command was inordinately opposed to admitting what they needed. For a long time they refused any night-fighter cover for French targets, in spite of the amount of work being done for them by factories in France. They consistently skimped Kammhuber's requests for independent night fighters, long after it was generally recognized that the best and easiest way to shoot down planes was to slip intruders into the landing pattern right over the enemy airfield. The Allies were using substantial numbers of free-ranging night intruders before the Germans employed them at all. Allied scientists had long outpaced the Germans, with the result that by these later years of the war, Allied radar and radar countermeasures were marginally superior.

Yet in spite of the growing disparity, the Germans were able to inflict near crippling losses on their enemies, often with fairly simple means. One such, for example, was the gun fittingly known as *Schräge Musik*. This device consisted simply of fitting two twenty-millimeter cannons in a Messerschmitt Me 110 night fighter in such a way that they fired slightly forward of a vertical line. The fighter would then slip up underneath a Halifax or Lancaster from behind, make his firm identification, and then simply blow it out of the sky with hits in the gas tanks or bomb bays. As the British bombers had no belly turrets, a German so placed could fly there almost indefinitely with no one to see him. In the winter of 1943–44, this attack method was so successful that Royal Air Froce Intelligence was trying to convince its aircrew that the Germans were lighting off fireworks in the night sky to lessen British morale. All those fireworks were in fact exploding bombers, and the aircrew, who could count empty places in the squadron messes better than the intelligence people could, finally convinced rear echelon authority that the Germans did indeed have a new weapon.

But like most of their defensive innovations, the Germans used this one reluctantly, and were their own worst enemies; there were wasteful delays in producing the *Schräge Musik* planes, and ultimately this was another advantage that the Luftwaffe gratuitously threw away. It is entirely possible that if the Germans had concentrated their efforts, and pursued them single-mindedly, they could have defeated the Allied bomber effort. Here, as in everything else, their ultimate decision making lay in the hands of a dilettante. By 1944 there were two million Germans engaged in the air-defense effort, more than in the aircraft industry, but they were not enough.

The issue was not clearly decided at any given moment, as is inevitably the case with battles of attrition. When the British turned from Hamburg to Berlin, they found themselves at full stretch. Sir Arthur Harris officially took the view that his bombers could destroy Berlin by March 1944, and in this way perhaps cause the collapse of Germany before any invasion of France became necessary. He launched the first massive raid on the enemy capital at the end of August 1943, sending six hundred bombers on the raid. But Berlin was a fairly difficult target; it was much farther than the North Sea or Rhineland cities, and as it was inland it offered few good features on which to obtain navigational and radar fixes. The raid resulted in substantial damage and considerable evacuation of women and children to rural areas, but it was not really a concentrated success. Bomber Command reverted to western German targets and did not return until the middle of November. From then until March 1944 there were sixteen heavy raids of from six to eight hundred bombers. Losses were heavy, to both flak and night fighters, bombing accuracy was relatively poor, and the German defenses were depressingly resilient. In Bomber Command the aircrew calculated that the odds were definitely against them; they had to complete thirty missions for a tour, and at a general loss rate of 4 percent per mission, the odds were six to five against surviving to be rotated to a safer posting. Of course, blind chance intruded, and many aircrew flew two or more tours, while many were shot down on their first or second flight. It was still no comfort to know that mathematics was against you.

Occasional miscalculation increased those odds tremendously, as on the famous occasion of the Nuremberg raid of March 30, 1944. This proved to be Bomber Command's worst night of the entire war. Deep in southeastern Germany, Nuremberg was both the site of the Nazi Party rallies and a substantial industrial target. On this night the RAF sent out a main force of 782 Halifaxes and Lancasters. Almost everything went wrong. The sky cleared, so that most of the route, supposed to be flown with cloud cover, was in bright moonlight; the wind was fluky, and took the bomber stream right over night-fighter assembly points. Also because of this, target marking was poor, so most of the effort was wasted. The effort included 108 aircraft lost and 545 crew killed; German night fighters got 79 of the shot-down planes. A casualty rate of more than 13 percent in one night was more than any air force in the world could stand, and those who survived it retained very bitter memories of this raid.

While the British were persevering in their night-bombing campaign, the Americans were still enduring their own calvary. The air-force chronology provides dry listings of terrible effort: October 4, Hamburg; October 8, Bremen; October 9, Danzig; October 10, Münster; October 14, Schweinfurt, where 60 or 230 aircraft were lost. That was the one that almost made them give it up as a bad job. The problem was that the bombers were all right while they could be escorted by American and British fighters, but once they passed beyond the operational range of their own escorts, they were fair game. The Germans knew exactly how far into Germany a P-47 Thunderbolt or a Spitfire could go; as the Allied escorts turned for home, the Germans picked the bombers up and shot them down all the way to their targets and back to their own umbrella again. It was supremely ironic that Douhet's alternative to the endless endurance of warfare on the ground had now become the same sort of endurance in the air.

The obvious answer was to extend the range of the Allied fighters, and in late 1943 this was done. The standard American escort fighter of 1943 was the Thunderbolt, the biggest and heaviest single-engined fighter of the war. Compared to the rapierlike delicacy of the Spitfire, the Thunderbolt, the "Jug," was just a huge brute, and British pilots joked that Americans could take evasive action by running around inside their aircraft. By putting long-range drop tanks on the P-47, the Americans could get it into western German airspace, but that was not far enough.

Deliverance of another sort was at hand, however, in the appearance of the North American P-51 Mustang, a happy marriage of an American airframe designed for a British purchasing mission and the great Merlin engine. The Mustang's conception went all the way back to 1940, but the first American combat group to fly them did not get to Britain until November 1943, which gives some idea of the lead time necessary to create the whole air-force system. On December 1, Mustangs flew their first long-range escort mission, nearly 500 miles to Kiel and back. That was just the beginning. By March 1944, the Mustangs, the bombers' "little friends," escorted Flying Fortresses and Liberators all the way to Berlin, 1,100 miles. No longer were German fighters free to make their killing passes at the hard-pressed formations of plodding heavy bombers. Allied fighters over Berlin meant air supremacy, fulfilling Trenchard's old dictum that command of the air begins at the enemy's aerodromes. The few Germans knowledgeable about air war knew they had lost when they saw Mustangs over the heart of the Reich. The corner was turned at last.

At precisely that point the bombers were diverted once again, as the war resumed its annoying habit of catching up with them, or in this case, getting ahead of them. As late as the end of 1943, Sir Arthur Harris was still predicting the imminent collapse of Germany as a result of intensive area bombing. His superiors had finally lost faith in that, however, and his claims were specifically refuted, complete with facts and figures. The air staff was particularly alarmed at the failure, up to that point, of the American daylight offensive, on which they had pinned great hopes, and at what appeared to be the concurrent revival of the Luftwaffe, which in fact was Speer's rationalization of production coupled with an at last realistic allocation of German air strength. When all these things were put in the context of the forthcoming invasion, firmly scheduled now for the spring of 1944, the air offensive was destined to change course once more. From a general-ized attack on German industry, indeed on German society, it was ordered to aim specifically at the destruction of the German aircraft industry, that is, at the Luftwaffe, from start to finish. A student of war might well argue that this is what should have been the Allies' target right from the beginning, on the old thesis that if you destroy the enemy's armed forces, everything else will follow. That, however, was precisely the thesis that strategic bombing was intended to re-fute in the first place, and Sir Arthur Harris now responded to his new orders in characteristic fashion: He did not agree with them so he ignored them. The Royal Air Force's Bomber Command, making occasional nods in the direction of specificity, went right on with its area bombing campaign, and did so until the end of the war.

Nonetheless, in February 1944, Operation Pointblank got under way, and the Combined Bomber Offensive was off and running at last. The Americans and the British now had the material, the techniques, and the targets. The British could fly by night and bomb with radar; the Americans could fly by day, employ precision formations and bomb-ing, and provide fighter escorts. Big Week started on February 20, when the Eighth Air Force sent over 1,000 B-17's and B-24's against the German aircraft factories; next day 764 heavies hit factories around Brunswick; on February 22 they hit Halberstadt, while the Fifteenth Air Force heavy bombers came up from the Mediterranean and struck at Regensburg. On February 24, 266 bombers from the Eighth Air Force hit Schweinfurt, aiming at the crucial ball-bearing industry again; that night 734 British bombers went for the same target. The same day the Fifteenth hit factories at Steyr and the oil refineries at Fiume. On February 25 it was Regensburg, Augsburg, and Stuttgart, and the British at Schweinfurt again.

Of course they took their losses: 35 bombers on February 22, 44 on February 24, 31 on February 25 from the Eighth Air Force plus an-other 30 from the Fifteenth. There would still be disasters ahead, such as the Nuremberg raid six weeks later, but Big Week brought the sense of the turning tide. German fighter production fell sharply for the next few months, and the Allies now turned their attention to three new items: the forthcoming invasion, the German rocket threat, and the strange new phenomenon of the jet aircraft.

* * *

Given the predominance of strategic bombing theory in both the Royal Air Force and the U.S. Army Air Force, it was often difficult for ground commanders to get air force people to acknowledge that they were both fighting the same war against the same enemy. But there were of course other commands and forces besides those devoted primarily to strategic operations. If British Bomber Command, and the U.S. Eighth Air Force's Bomber Command, got most of the attention, it was because they were the ones trying hardest to vindicate the prewar air theories. The British had all their other commands—Training, Transport, Fighter, Coastal—doing their far from mundane duties, and the Americans by now had four air forces operating around Europe— the Twelfth and the Fifteenth in the Mediterranean, and the Ninth as well as the Eighth in Great Britain. The efforts of virtually all of these were now devoted, with lesser or greater immediacy, to the invasion of France.

From Big Week until spring, American and British fighters and tactical bombers continued to go after the Germans. There were constant fighter sweeps over northern France and the Low Countries, and attacks by fast and low-flying medium bombers on airfields and control stations. Some of the great planes of the war made their marks in these vital but essentially little-known operations. There was the British de Haviland Mosquito, the "wooden wonder," which carried the bomb load of a Fortress; the North American B-25, named after Billy Mitchell; and the sleek Martin B-26. Officially known as the Marauder, it was first sworn at, and then by, its crew. It demanded such a degree of flying skill and attention that it was once known as "the Widowmaker"; because of its very small wing area, crews joked bitterly that it was "a flying whore—no visible means of support." But, once mastered, it was a beautiful aircraft, and it eventually had the lowest operational loss rate of any comparable type in the war. With these and Spitfires, Thunderbolts, Mustangs, and the new British Typhoon, a heavy ground-attack fighter, the Allies went after the Luftwaffe to blast them out of the skies. Air combat reached a crescendo over the Low Countries and northern France in the spring of 1944.

The war by now was so big that personalities were largely unimportant. It was not that they were submerged in a sea of mud, as in World War I, so that aces such as the Red Baron became household names; it was rather that the war was so wide-ranging, so all-encompassing, that the role of the aces was seen in perhaps a more correct perspective than it was in the first war. Some of their scores were well-nigh incredible, and 35 German pilots were officially credited with more than 150 victims each; the highest scorer of all, Major Erich Hartmann, destroyed 352 enemy planes. Even though a great number of such scores were made on the Russian front, often of planes wrecked on the ground, no one on the Allied side came close to that, or to the premier Japanese ace, Hiroyishi Nishizawa, with 87 kills. The vagaries of war indeed played strange tricks, and the highest scorer of the western Allied aces, a South African squadron leader, M. T. Pattle, achieved many of his 41 victories while flying the Gloster Gladiator biplane fighter in the Mediterranean. The Russians had seven men who shot down 50 or more enemies, as well as the only two women aces of the war, Lily Litvak and Katya Budanova. For the British, Group Captain J. E. Johnson was the top scorer, with 38 planes, and for the Americans in Europe, Colonel Francis Gabreski was credited with 31. Two Americans in the Pacific got more, Majors Richard Bong with 40 and Thomas McGuire with 38. But except for a very few of the Germans, not always the top scorers at that, and such highly decorated Russians as Ivan Kozhedub, their top ace with 62, few of these men became known anywhere beyond their own countries. Perhaps the war was now too serious for the knights-of-the-air syndrome to survive.

While the fighter pilots and the medium-bomber crews battled across the Channel, the heavy bombers were also pulled into the preliminaries for Operation Overlord. In March they began a series of raids directed against road and rail communications in northern France and western Germany. Communications was one of the priority targets for the bomber offensive already, but it had received only sporadic attention, especially in the occupied countries, where there was obvious danger to friendly civilians. In April, Air Chief Marshal Sir Arthur Tedder was named Deputy Supreme Allied Commander under General Dwight Eisenhower, and he drew up the Transportation Plan, under which the air forces would isolate the invasion area. The invasion forces had their own air component, the Allied Expeditionary Air Force, commanded by Air Chief Marshal Sir Trafford Leigh-Mallory, one of the group commanders back in the Battle of Britain, but Tedder wanted all the air forces in Britain involved, and he got his way.

From mid-April to D-Day, the RAF hit more than 30 transportation targets in France, Belgium, and the Netherlands, dropping 42,000 tons of bombs. The Americans dropped 12,000 tons on 23 targets. Meanwhile, in May, the tactical air forces hit bridges over all the rivers as far east as the Meuse and the Moselle; they bombed and strafed airfields and radar stations from Brittany up to the mouth of the Rhine, carefully leaving the Germans enough radar in the Pas de Calais area to convince them by feints that this was where the attack would come. By early June the Luftwaffe was destroyed over the invasion area, and Allied air power covered northern France like a blanket. Nothing that moved and looked German was safe. On D-Day itself, Allied planes flew 14,674 sorties; the Germans flew 140, so there were 100 Allied planes in the air for every 1 German. The Germans had practically destroyed their 1 airborne division in the assault of Crete; the Allies dropped 3 divisions over Normandy. Within one day there was an airstrip on the beachhead, by June 10 British Spitfires were flying close air support from behind the front, and in three weeks the RAF had 31 squadrons based on French soil. The air forces' contribution to the invasion was marked less by anything spectacular than by the total absence of anything spectacular.

One of the most innovative of German aircraft firms was that of Gerhard Fieseler. Its most famous product was a light reconnaissance plane known as the "Storch," or "Stork," which would practically hover in midair and had an incredibly short takeoff and landing run. Because of this the plane was used to rescue the captive Mussolini from the Gran Sasso; sprung from his prison, the Italian dictator was hustled aboard a Storch which then flew straight off a cliff with him, climbing away to safety. Another Fieseler product, the Fi 167, was a biplane designed for Germany's only aircraft carrier. It was so ugly it was beautiful, and it possessed the strange capability of being able to sink vertically through the air without any loss of control. In 1939 Fieseler also initiated design studies on something new altogether, a pilotless flying bomb.

This was to be launched from a mother plane, and by December 1942 Fieseler successfully released one from a Focke-Wulf Condor. Meanwhile, the Germans had decided that the bomb should be ground-launched, and they started building ramps in France and along the Dutch coast while development work continued at Peenemünde on the Baltic. The experiments were picked up by RAF photo-reconnaissance flights, and in August 1943 the British hit Peenemünde with a heavy bomb raid. This was a distant target, and the raid cost the British forty bombers, but it killed several key German personnel and did considerable damage to the plant. The Americans hit similar installations thought to be building components for this flying bomb, or rocket, or whatever it was. Through late 1943 and early 1944 the Germans built more and more launching sites in northern France, from Dunkirk to Cherbourg, and both the British and the Americans kept bombing them, the latter from high level and the former with low-level Mosquitoes. As the Allies got most of the sites, the Germans then built portable, prefabricated ones. On June 12, 1944, the first V-1 was fired against England.

The V-1 was really a small, fast airplane, and it could therefore be stopped by more or less conventional methods. The Germans launched about twenty thousand of them before the sites were overrun; about a tenth of these were hit by antiaircraft fire and another tenth caught and shot down by fighter aircraft. The "buzz bomb," as it was called, was too fast for most contemporary fighters, but the newly introduced Hawker Tempest was capable of intercepting it. It was especially unpleasant for Britain to be tormented at this stage of the war, after bearing with hardship for so long. And worse was to come.

On September 8, 1944, when the V-1 appeared largely mastered, the first V-2 hit England. The British had some knowledge of this, from Polish underground workers and from a rocket that went off course during tests and landed in Sweden, to the embarrassment of the Germans. But even though they knew about it, there was nothing they could do, for this was the first of the true rockets—a long-range ballistic missile fired up into the stratosphere, traveling at then-incredible speeds and dropping out of the sky on its target. The Allies had absolutely nothing to stop this, and all they could do throughout the V-2 campaign was frantically attempt to find and bomb the launching sites. Between September and March of 1945 the Germans launched 1,115 of these rockets; they and the V-1's together killed nearly 9,000 people and injured 23,000 more. These were true terror weapons striking indiscriminately and blindly; in this they symbolized the death agonies of the Hitlerian beast, as well as being a harbinger of things to come.

All these new systems were too late to do Germany much good. Her real chances of holding her own in the air war had long ago been frittered away, and given the necessary lead and development time for new types of weapons, mistakes made in 1939 or 1941 were now haunting the Reich. In the late thirties, engineers and designers became interested in the possibility of developing a new kind of engine, the turbojet. The propeller of the conventional aircraft engine pulled the plane through the air; the turbojet operated on the action-equals-reaction theory, sucking the air into the plane and thrusting it out the rear with such force that the plane was rapidly pushed forward.

The real father of the jet engine in Britain was Frank Whittle, and late in 1939 he teamed up with the Gloster Aircraft Company to work out an experimental aircraft using the new propulsion. Together they eventually developed a plane, the Gloster Pioneer, that looked rather like a flying guppy. This evolved, after several stages, into the Meteor, a twin-engined fighter that was the only Allied jet to see operational service during the war. Concurrently, in Germany, Heinkel began the same sort of development independently. Heinkel's He-280 flew for the first time on April 2, 1941, the first-ever jet flight, and the Pioneer made its maiden flight on May 15. As it happened, Heinkel's jet never got past the test stage, largely because the German authorities would not take it seriously; the firm later did build a jet fighter, the He 162 Salamander, of mostly nonstrategic material. It was known as the "Volksjäger," or "People's Fighter," and slightly more than a hundred were completed. It was to be to aircraft what the Volkswagen was to cars, but Germany collapsed too soon for the whole project.

The Americans were also experimenting, though rather slower than the Europeans, and Bell Aircraft built the XP-59 Airacomet, but it did not fly until October 1942 and never reached squadron service. That left one other contender, for in 1938 Messerschmitt began work on an airframe to take the engines being designed by Junkers and BMW, the Bavarian Motor Works. This plane became the Me 262; its progress was inordinately slow, for the engines got low priorities, then airframes were damaged in the raids on Regensburg, and one thing after another set the scheme back. Nonetheless, the two-engine jet flew in July 1942, and from then on there was substantial speeding up. By May 1944 the plane, named "Schwalbe" or "Swallow," was ready for service. It should have been called Shark, for that was exactly what it looked like, a flying shark, and it was intended to be a pure killer in the air, a cannon-armed interceptor.

Then Hitler intervened. Obsessed with revenge for the Allied bombings that were at last really hurting Germany, he decreed that the new airplane should be used not as it was intended but rather as a weapon of revenge. Transformed into a fast bomber, the plane was sent on hit-and-run raids over England, a role for which it was totally unsuited. Many of the new planes were lost in accidents, many more were destroyed on the ground, and of the 1,430 built, only about a quarter saw service, a classic example of the ability of a dictatorship to make wrong decisions unchallenged. The Me 262 enjoyed a 50-mph speed advantage over the Gloster Meteor, 125 mph over the Tempest, which was the fastest thing the British had, used to chase buzz bombs, 150 mph over the later Spitfires, and about the same over the Mustang. Some people believe that used properly it could have altered the course of the war.

One final, interesting straw at which the Germans grasped was an odd-looking little creature, the Messerschmitt 163 Komet. This was actually a rocket fighter; armed with two cannons, it could only stay aloft for a few minutes, time for one diving pass at enemy bombers, but as it came swooping down at more than six hundred miles an hour, it was very hard to stop. Again it was the old story: too little too late. For all Hitler's preoccupation with the reliance on "wonder weapons," he had thrown the thing away, and had largely done it himself.

Notwithstanding the appearance of these strange new manifestations of the future, the war went on its conventional way. By the fall of 1944 the Allies were on the Continent to stay; they had broken the back of German resistance in the west, liberated Paris, and were exploiting to the north and east while the Wehrmacht desperately tried to fend them off. By September the Allies had succeeded beyond their most favorable estimates, and as they extended their lines of operation, the Germans at last began to stiffen and pull together. There was very real controversy among the British and American army group commanders as to what was the most rewarding direction of attack and who was to enjoy priority of supply. The overall commander, General Eisenhower, finally succumbed to the importunities of the British General Montgomery; he agreed that the Allies would gamble on a narrow thrust at the crossings of the Lower Rhine and an attempt to reach the heart of Germany before winter came on. This was Operation Market Garden. "Market" was to drop three airborne divisions at key points, seizing bridges across the various rivers of Holland; "Garden" was then to drive an armored spearhead up the roads to link up with the airborne troops.

This was the most ambitious airborne operation of the war, and in the event it proved just a little too ambitious. The farthest drop, that of the British 1st Airborne Division at Arnhem, had to be made in waves because there was not enough transport to do it all at once. The second wave and subsequent resupply were delayed by bad weather back in Britain. The troops also came down on a German unit newly moved into the area, and though they stubbornly held on to one end of their target bridge, they could not sustain the effort. The survivors were evacuated with heavy losses. As usual, the Allies had underestimated the resilience and rapid reaction time of the Germans; the phrase *a bridge too far* became one of the catchwords of the war.

With the Allies firmly ashore on the Continent, and unarguably winning the war on all fronts, the strategic air people could go back to their cherished task of destroying Germany. Their strength was by now absolutely overwhelming. In June 1944 the Eighth Air Force had forty-four bombardment groups in England, as well as another eighteen fighter groups. It was the single biggest force deployed against the Germans, but it was only one of several American organizations, and they in turn were but one of the Allies. The RAF's Bomber Command and its extensive tactical air forces were all busily at work against anything and everything still held by the enemy, and on the eastern front the Russians possessed equally superior strength. From east, south, and west, the Germans were continuously pounded.

In spite of that, factories in the Reich still churned out equipment, life went on somehow, and the Germans still managed the occasional, very unpleasant surprise. On June 21, for example, the Eighth Air Force flew a shuttle mission, bombing an oil refinery south of Berlin and then continuing on to bases behind the Russian lines. The Germans followed them, then slipped a bomber force through the Russian defense system, catching the B-17's on the ground. In the whole operation the Americans lost more than a hundred aircraft, once again demonstrating the idea that it was far more efficient to destroy planes on the ground than in the air.

The Allies already knew that, of course, and as the year wore on, they achieved greater and greater success at it. The strategic bombers hit oil refineries and aircraft plants, and the tactical air forces found more and more enemy planes sitting on their airstrips. Just for lack of fuel, Luftwaffe flying time grew less and less, and the skies over Germany belonged more and more to the Allies. There was always flak, there were still fighters lurking about, one could never relax, but the Allies were palpably winning.

As evidence of that, the last major German effort to change the course of the war was launched in a period when bad weather grounded air activity. Collecting an unsuspected reserve of some twenty divisions, eight of them armored, Hitler opened a drive on December 16 in the Ardennes sector of Belgium. The Germans caught the American's thinly stretched in a "quiet" area, and broke through. Before they were contained they had made a sixty-mile-deep penetration that was about fifty miles wide on its shoulders, the famous "Bulge." But the Americans held hard to keep the breach narrow. Hitler, still thinking he was in 1940, had hoped to go all the way to Antwerp. His generals were more realistic about their chances, and they were right; the Germans never even got to the Meuse River, less than halfway. By Christmas Day the tide had turned, and the Americans were attacking on both sides of the Bulge. The sky had begun to clear on December 23, and the next day the Allied air forces flew their biggest single operation of the war. The British put up 500 heavy bombers, and the Eighth Air Force sent up an incredible 2,034. Few Germans were encountered, though there were some losses, and the bombers pounded airfields and communications centers on the German side of the Bulge. Allied fighters and fighter bombers covered the Ardennes as the snow lay on the ground, and by mid-January the Bulge was gone. That was mostly due to hard slogging by the ground troops, who after all had to soldier on whether the sky was cloudy or not, but the very timing of the whole battle demonstrated the extent to which air control had become a factor in everyone's considerations.

The Battle of the Bulge graphically demonstrated how thoroughly the table had turned since Germany's glory days. In 1939 and 1940 it had been the Luftwaffe that had dominated the sky, and Germany's enemies that had moved furtively by night or, as was more often the case, not at all. But from the Normandy invasion on, with a couple of notable exceptions, the sky belonged to the Allies. German divisions trying to reach Normandy in June and July, or to escape from it in the summer, were unceasingly harassed by Allied tactical air power. Countless thousands of vehicles were strafed or bombed by the ubiquitous Thunderbolts, Typhoons, Tempests, and medium bombers.

Trains hid in tunnels, armored columns moved only at night and carefully bivouacked in forests during the day, trying to hide all tracks from the sky. In the Falaise Pocket, and as the Germans fled for the Seine, through the Low Countries and up to the Rhine, the attack planes sowed a swath of destruction. They had so far outclassed the German air effort by now that only weather could stop them, and not until heavy rains came in November did the hard-pressed *feldgrau* got some temporary respite. Even that lasted only until the turn of the year, and then the Allies went at it again, right until the final collapse.

While the campaigns of France and Germany were in progress, the bombing effort reached a crescendo. In the entire war the allies dropped 2,700,000 tons of bombs on Germany, and 72 percent of that, 1,944,000 tons, was dropped between July 1, 1944, and the end of the war. Again and again and again the two western Allies hit targets: the Rhineland, the Ruhr, Berlin, Hamburg, the Ruhr, Danzig, Gydnia, the Ruhr, Berlin. Farther and farther east they reached, and by early 1945 Germany lay almost in ruins.

Ironically, at this point the whole bombing effort came under serious question, especially among the British. Though not exclusively connected with it by any means, this ambiguity has come to center around the bombing of Dresden. The old Saxon city, one of the most picturesque and charming in Germany, had not so far been bombed. Though the British were careful in their target analysis and selection of *types* of targets, the choice of any given city in which those types were found was dependent very much on where Sir Arthur Harris's interest happened to light. In late January 1945, as a result of discussions going all the way up to Winston Churchill himself, Harris's interest lit on Dresden. On the night of February 13, two waves of British bombers, 773 strong, dropped 2,659 tons of bombs on the city center. There was another firestorm, as at Hamburg, and much of the town was completely wiped out. Estimates of deaths vary between a low of 30,000 and a high of 250,000. The most authoritative figure seems to be about 135,000. The Americans hit Dresden the next day, and again on March 2, and on April 17.

Though the bombing campaign went on through March and into April, it was increasingly concentrated on transportation and oil, and on assisting the actual advance of the Allied armies into the heart of Germany itself. Other cities were bombed, but Dresden was really the last of the big, famous area-bombing strikes. It was an outstanding example of what the Allied air forces could now do, and it therefore, tragically, after all these years of effort, raised the question: Did they really want to do it?

That question was debated both in the House of Commons and among senior American cabinet members, but, as usual in such cases, the issue was fobbed off with a number of non sequiturs. Late in March, however, Churchill wrote to the Chief of the Air Staff, saying, "It seems to me that the moment has come when the question of bombing German cities simply for the sake of increasing the terror, though under other pretexts, should be reviewed. . . . I feel the need for more precise concentration upon military objectives, such as oil and communications behind the immediate battle-zone, rather than on mere acts of terror and wanton destruction, however impressive." In view of the prime minister's persistent championing of the bomber offensive, this was hardly fair to the instruments of a policy he had himself advocated. Churchill, tired and distressed as he was at the end of a long war which he had so bravely fought, only to see Britain surpassed in the end by her allies, soon had second thoughts and withdrew his memorandum for rewriting. But the question, once raised, would not go away, and still has not done so. In mid-April a new directive was issued to the air forces, giving them the mission of "direct assistance to the land campaign." The strategic bomber offensive against Germany was over. In the Thousand-Year Reich there was nothing left worth bombing.

XIV

ARMAGEDDON IN JAPAN

The Japanese Empire resembled some modern incarnation of eighteenth-century Prussia: It was an army with a state somewhere behind it. The impressive territorial gains of 1942 derived more from the weakness of Japan's enemies than from her own strengths, from a fanatical militarism rather than from a solid economic base for expansion. As the Prussians had set out to conquer their world, and then build a country upon it, so too with Japan: first Manchuria, then China, then the Southern Resource Area. Once those lands were subdued, then exploited and developed, Japan would be the economic as well as the military colossus of the far Pacific.

But by 1943 the flaws in this logic were becoming apparent. The most important of them was that this required the grudging acquiescence of the United States, and the Americans, instead of accepting the new order, had fought back. They had not given up before the sweep of conquest. At the Coral Sea, at Midway, in the Solomons, and in the wastes of the central Pacific they had parried the Japanese thrusts, throwing their weak forces at the might of empire and,

241

amazingly, thwarting its designs. Now, by 1943, they were weak no longer; the tables were turning, the lines on the graphs crossing, as the smaller-based Japanese economy inevitably fell behing the aroused giant. From the Aleutians clockwise all around to China, the Americans and their allies hammered at the Japanese perimeter, launching a series of converging drives that would eventually meet in the Home Islands of Japan.

Ironically, this was not the war the United States government, with its commitment to Germany first, intended to fight; it was rather the war that General Douglas MacArthur, determined to avenge his expulsion from the Philippines, wanted to fight in the southwest Pacific, and it was the war the U.S. Navy had always planned to fight in the central Pacific. Both of these campaigns, it was now generally acknowledged, depended on control first of the air, then of the sea, and finally of the islands and jungles.

MacArthur's New Guinea campaign, waged in some of the worst terrain in the world, saw masterpieces of aerial improvisation. Strips were hacked from the jungle, troops airlifted and resupplied by the fliers, and Japanese communications interdicted from the air in a mad scramble to make do with available forces and equipment. General George Kenney shook up MacArthur's air forces and turned them into an invaluable tool of war; under his driving leadership his officers and men wrote their own tactical manual. It was in this theater that skip-bombing and parachute-bombing were developed, and it was these airmen who worked out a new wrinkle to provide the needed firepower: They took a standard B-25 Mitchell and packed its nose with eight .50-caliber machine guns. Not satisfied with that, they left two of the guns out and between them mounted a .75-mm. cannon, hitherto a gun for a tank. Armament like that could hack a small ship to pieces. Charles Lindbergh came out to the Pacific and showed airmen how to increase their range by tinkering with fuel mixtures and throttle controls, getting more from planes than they were ever designed for.

Harried from air and sea, fought to a standstill on the ground, the Japanese slowly went back. By the end of 1943 the Solomons were gone and Americans were on New Britain, pointing for the big base at Rabaul. Nine months later, Rabaul bypassed and isolated, all of New Guinea cleared, the Americans were at Morotai, getting ready for the big jump to the Philippines.

Meanwhile, the U.S. Navy made even more spectacular gains in the central Pacific. Through 1942 and much of 1943 the navy and the marines were preoccupied with the Solomons campaign, but in that period they also began to receive material, and to develop the concept of the fast-carrier task forces that became the mainstay of the ocean war. These started from almost nothing. At one point in the spring of 1943, the entire American carrier strength consisted of one ship—the grand old *Saratoga*. But by the fall, new ships and new weapons were at last coming out from the States. There were not only the Essex class of fleet carriers and the Independence class of lighter carriers, there were new, better planes, especially the Grumman F6F Hellcat, there was new radar, new radio, better shells, and better guns. Japanese building and development could not keep up with this, and their own plans for enlarging and modernizing their fleet proved increasingly unrealistic.

Given the navy's determination to fight the war in the Pacific, most of this new material went there, even though Allied Mediterranean operations were curtailed by lack of shipping. By late 1943 the Americans were ready to renew offensive operations in the central Pacific. The islands here led through four groups to the heart of the Japanese Empire: the Gilberts, the Marshalls, the Marianas, and the Carolines. Authorized to strike first at the Marshalls, the navy had to settle for the Gilberts for lack of force, and in November 1943 the marines landed on Tarawa. Almost everything that could go wrong did in that bloody battle, but lessons learned the hard way meant that mistakes need not be repeated. In the new year the Americans jumped to the Marshalls. While they did so, the fast carriers ranged ahead of the amphibious forces, striking at Japanese bases and strangling their communications. In mid-February they hit the major base at Truk in the Carolines. The heavy enemy fleet units were not there, but 275 planes and some 200,000 tons of support shipping were destroyed. Japanese capabilities were hamstrung, and eventually Truk and most of the Carolines were bypassed, just as Rabaul was. The fighting in the Marshalls broke the shell of the Japanese perimeter, and they could not stand that. As the Americans landed on Saipan in the Marianas, they came out to fight.

The resulting Battle of the Philippine Sea, on June 19 and 20, 1944, became famous in aviation history and American mythology as "The Great Marianas Turkey Shoot." The first day of the battle was spent with the longer-range Japanese aircraft trying to break through the American air screen to hit fleet units. American pilots shot down 52 of the first wave of 70, 99 of the second wave of 130. American submarines got the carriers *Taiho* and *Shokaku*, and by the end of the day the Japanese attack plan was a shambles. The next day both sides groped for each other unsuccessfully in the morning, and the Americans found their prey late in the afternoon. They sank another carrier and damaged two more. The final tally was more than 425 planes lost, 3 carriers and 2 tankers sunk, and 4 more carriers badly damaged. The Americans lost about 125 planes, two thirds of them as a result of running out of fuel while returning in the dark from the long chase. At the time it seemed as if the enemy fleet had safely gotten away; in fact, the battle broke the back of Japan's navy. From now on their operations would be casts of desperation. In his battle orders, Admiral Spruance had stated, "Our air will first knock out the enemy carriers. . . ." That was precisely what had been done, and that priority demonstrated once more that the aircraft carrier, with a "main battery" that could range out more than a hundred miles, had surpassed the battleship as queen of the seas.

In the other theaters of the war against Japan, air power was a vital component of the fighting, and even more so of the logistical support for combat. Burma had been lost to the Japanese by May 1942, and that cut off the only remaining land access to China for the Allies. Until northern Burma could be liberated, China had to be supplied by air, a tortuous five-hundred-mile flight across incredibly bad terrain, the notorious "Hump." The mission symbol for such a flight was, appropriately enough, a silhouette of a camel. Arduous as the duty was, it was impossible to fly into China more than a trickle of bare necessities, more a gesture of Allied assistance than what China really needed.

Much of what went across the Hump was used not by the Chinese themselves but by the only substantial American unit in the country, General Claire Chennault's U.S. China Air Task Force, which traced its ancestry back to the American Volunteer Group, the famous "Flying Tigers," and eventually became the Fourteenth Air Force. Chennault was a fanatic on the subject of air power; he had done his best to organize an air force in China, and presided over the growth of first a fighter-defense force, then a medium bomber force, and finally a strategic bomber component. He professed to believe that with a small number of big bombers he could knock Japan out of the war from bases on the mainland. Eventually China did get the biggest bomber of the war, the Boeing B-29, and these did actually bomb southern Japan, though the mid-Pacific island approach soon proved more feasible. Meanwhile, the Japanese demonstrated their overall superiority in the theater by launching offensives that overran the bases of Chennault's planes, leaving American General Stilwell, aptly nicknamed "Vinegar Joe," to grumble about the uselessness of "air cover over nothing." In spite of all the valuable tactical work done by the air forces there, China was just too far out on too thin a limb for anything decisive to be accomplished.

The same was almost true of Burma, which for the men who fought there was the forgotten theater of the war. Communications in the northern part of the country and across the frontier to India were so bad that much logistic support was provided by air, and the air forces also did a great deal of interdictory work, trying to break the tenuous Japanese supply lines. Even more innovative was the idea put forward by British Brigadier Orde Wingate to drop highly mobile columns behind Japanese lines and to supply them by air. Wingate was a latter-day Lawrence of Arabia, and he got his chance early in 1943. Though this first "Chindit" campaign was a failure, that was not because of the air supply, which actually worked well, and the Americans soon imitated the idea with a force of their own, known after its commander as Merrill's Marauders.

The climax of the Burma campaign came early in 1944, when the Japanese opened an attack on Kohima and Imphal, British bases on the Indian frontier. Both were surrounded but held on during intense fighting, and it was the Japanese who broke first. Aerial drops kept the garrisons supplied, and eventually the Japanese, their always fragile support system collapsing, had to give up and retreat. They never regained the initiative. By April 1945 the Burma Road was reopened, and by midsummer Japanese forces, though still capable of their usual fanatical fighting, were in total disarray. The British, helped by air supply and mobility, had beaten them at their own jungle warfare game.

Victory in Burma, or even in China, mattered less by late 1944 than what was happening in the Pacific. By the end of the year, leaving major Japanese forces ever more isolated behind them, the Americans were driving into the waist of the Japanese Empire. The links between the Southern Resources Area and the Home Islands became ever more threatened. American submarines were strangling Japan's merchant marine, tanker losses were disproportionately heavy, and the shortages of fuel affected not only such vital matters as pilot training but even fleet strategy; one of the reasons the remaining units of the Imperial fleet were based in the south was so that they could use the fuel there. That too had its effect, for the fuel available in the south was of a cruder, less efficient variety than that in the north; the loss of the *Taiho* in the Philippine Sea after she was hit by torpedo was largely due to the seepage of fumes from her less refined and more explosive Borneo fuel.

Recent authorities have questioned the wisdom of the United States launching a two-pronged strategy against the Japanese, and argued that either the navy's or MacArthur's drives, probably the former, would have been equally effective and less costly by itself. While that may well be correct, it ignores the personalities and preconceptions that are an essential part of history, an academic preference for what might have been over what was. At the time the two principals, Nimitz for the navy and MacArthur, had at least agreed on an assault into the Philippines. That agreement in itself was something, and culminated in October 1944 in the landing on the island of Leyte in the central Philippines. This in turn brought on the greatest naval battle in history, in numbers of ships, men, and aircraft involved.

The Japanese came out to fight, hoping to catch the American battle forces tied to their soft-skinned transports and amphibious vessels. Japan's Sho-Go, or Victory Operation, pitted 9 battleships, 4 carriers, 17 cruisers, and 31 destroyers against an American force of 32 carriers, 12 battleships, 26 cruisers, and 144 destroyers. The Americans had hundreds more planes than the Japanese, though one of the significant features of the battle was that many American carriers were smaller escort types, and their planes were armed and equipped for supporting the troops ashore. At one point, American planes were trying to stop battleships by peppering them with antipersonnel bombs.

Despite that, the end result of the battle was hardly in doubt, from the moment when American picket submarines picked up and attacked the first approaching enemy units. When the smoke cleared, the Japanese had lost all 4 of their carriers, 3 battleships, 10 cruisers, 9 destroyers, and hundreds of planes, including those flying from airstrips on the Philippines. The Americans lost 3 small carriers, 3 destroyers, and less than 200 planes. Leyte Gulf finished the Imperial

Navy as a fighting force, and, appropriately enough, saw the last battleship versus battleship duel; once again tactical naval air power won a crashing victory.

The Japanese went on to wage a long and bitter campaign on Leyte, and then on Luzon, which lasted until the end of the war. For the Americans, larger strategic questions could no longer be ignored. Planning staffs and committees had for many months struggled with the issue of the final defeat of Japan, and it was now time for some hard decisions.

There were several possible ways to wage the ultimate battle and, predictably, each service had its own view of the best, or the most necessary, of them. The navy thought that blockade, battleship and carrier aerial bombardment, and strangulation by the submarine campaign would cause Japan to wither and die. The army thought Japan must be invaded and defeated on its own territory; it expected this would cost an estimated million casualties, but saw no sign of the enemy breaking by any other means. The air force thought that Japan could be defeated by strategic air power, though up to this point, under the handicap of the great distances of the Pacific, it had had little chance to prove it might be right. It is of course oversimplification to identify so closely these particular views with particular services, but by and large people tend to apply to problems solutions derived from their own experience.

At one point the Americans contemplated landing either on Formosa or on the China coast, as an intermediate move between the Philippines and Japan itself, but this was eventually discarded as the final pace of the war quickened. The Joint Chiefs of Staff then developed an invasion brief that called for a landing on the southernmost of the Home Islands, Kyūshū, about November 1945, to be followed in March 1946 by the climactic blow, a landing on Honshū, near Tokyo itself. Meanwhile, they would continue all three services' lines of operation: The navy would push closer, the army would finish the Philippines and build up for the main invasion, and the air force would develop its strategic-bombardment campaign.

By late 1944 the latter was still little more than a declaration of intent, but with the turn of the year it began to assume major proportions. As in Europe, the campaign illustrated once more the long lead time necessary for transforming an idea into reality as well as the intensity of effort required to make it worthwhile.

The bombing of Japan is inextricably linked with one famous aircraft, the Boeing B-29 Superfortress. These had launched their first missions against the enemy homeland from China, and for many months the Americans negotiated fruitlessly with the Soviet Union for permission to base them in Russia's Maritime Provinces. Only after the capture of the Marianas, though, were the big bombers within real striking distance, and in November 1944 they hit Tokyo for the first time. Even that first raid was the end product of a long and painful development. On the design side, the B-29 went back to the XB-15 of 1937, and on the conception side, to the idea of "hemisphere defense" of the late 1930s and the desire of the Army Air Corps to have a "superbomber." In August 1940 the government contracted for two XB-29 prototypes, and in May 1941, authorized quantity production. Rushing the pace under the pressure of impending war, the air corps committed itself to 1,664 machines before the prototypes had even flown, a huge gamble that fortunately paid off. The fact that several new systems, such as pressurization and remotely controlled armament, all had to be developed concurrently, demonstrated just how huge the gamble was.

Meanwhile, the air corps had to train crews, set up a command structure, and design missions for the new plane. The whole mix came together in the Twentieth Air Force, designated particularly for strategic bombing of Japan with the B-29. The plane itself was the world's state-of-the-art bomber in 1944, so advanced and so sophisticated that in 1947 the Russians produced a direct copy of it—using aircraft force-landed in Vladivostock—as their standard strategic bomber, the Tupolev Tu-4. It weighed 37 tons and could carry a 2-ton bombload 2,650 miles in 8 hours. It was somehow almost too clean and neat, too perfect, to replace the Flying Fortress in popular American affection, but in spite of both Fortresses and Liberators it was the sine qua non of strategic bombardment in the war against Japan.

In the midsummer of 1944 the Americans captured the islands of Saipan, Guam, and Tinian in the Marianas. These were 2,500 air miles from Tokyo, bringing the B-29's at last within operating range of Japan's capital. Engineers went to work on the newly secured islands, building five huge airfields, each capable of operating a wing of 180 bombers and 12,000 men. Command shifts accompanied the growth of the new bases. In September 1944 General Curtis LeMay, fresh from successes in Germany, had taken over the 29th Bomber Command in China, but even this dynamic figure had difficulties in making bricks without straw. It took four planeloads of fuel to fly one B-29 raid from China, and the problems were simply too great to make this a paying proposition. Over the winter of 1944–45 the air force decided to downgrade the China effort, abandon its attempts to woo the Russians into providing bases, and concentrate on the Marianas. LeMay arrived there in January with a simple mandate: Make the campaign work.

That it had not worked by this date was due less to the Japanese than to the approach the Americans were so far taking. Japanese measures were now largely passive. They were still producing aircraft, some of their later designs, such as the Nakajima "Hayate" and Kawasaki "Hein," "Frank" and "Tony" in the American lexicon, being remarkably good ones, but they were starved for raw materials, trained pilots, and above all fuel. They therefore relied increasingly on searchlights and antiaircraft batteries, but these produced little more than reassuring noise; the Americans were flying high above gun range. So the government organized volunteer fire brigades, evacuated children to the countryside, had trenches dug, and distributed sunflowers to make life a little brighter. But the bombers kept coming, and life through the last winter of the war slowly got worse.

The Americans kept tightening the vise. Halfway between the Marianas and Japan lay a small island, Iwo Jima, and it had two airstrips, which the Japanese used for fighter defense. Halfway between the Philippines and Japan lay the Ryukyu chain, with its largest island, Okinawa. The Americans decided to take these two stepping-stones to bring them that much closer to their final goal.

Iwo Jima proved an example both of the uses and the limitations of tactical air power. Less than ten square miles, the island was held by some 21,000 Japanese troops, well dug in and determined to fight to the last man for their emperor. For seventy-four days American aircraft repeatedly and heavily bombed and strafed the island, and for three days it was combed by naval gunfire; nothing was safe, no position unreachable from air or by sea. Yet when the marines landed on February 19, the Japanese came up out of their holes to fight, and it took eight weeks of brutal combat to secure this little speck in the ocean. The entire garrison was killed, a mere 200 surviving to become involuntary prisoners of war rather than dying. The Americans suffered almost 25,000 casualties taking the island, but even before it was secured, crippled B-29's were landing on the airstrips, the first of some 2,250 to do so, and by early March fighter escorts from the island were ranging over Tokyo. Iwo was thus a necessary, but incredibly painful, step on the road to Japan; that pain influenced subsequent decisions.

Periodically, as the war in the Pacific reached a crescendo of violence, Japanese pilots or damaged planes had attempted to crash into American ships, at the Philippines, at Iwo, off the coasts of Japan. At Okinawa this sacrifical valor was raised to the level of a military doctrine. As the island was a mere three hundred miles from Japan itself, it was well within range of medium bombers, and even of fighters, especially if they were flying only one way. When the Americans landed on April 1, they knew they had a hard fight on their hands.

The Japanese plan was to hold the island as long as possible, allowing their air force to inflict maximum damage on the enemy fleet. However much the idea of the suicide plane, or kamikaze, might fly in the face of western ideas, or indeed of what air power was supposedly all about, it fit perfectly with the Japanese military ethic. East met West in a way never anticipated by Kipling, as "the fleet that came to stay" battled it out with the pilots who fought to die. All through April, May, and most of June, as the ground forces fought over the island terrain, the Americans and their British allies, now with them in major force, endured the pounding of the Japanese planes.

During the length of the campaign there were 10 major suicide attacks, ranging from a low of 45 planes to a high of 355, plus countless other small-scale raids of one kind or another. The Japanese lost an estimated 7,800 planes in the whole course of operations. But these were able to inflict real damage; 34 Allied ships were sunk, 26 by suicide planes, and 368 were damaged, just about half by the kamikazes. Most of those sunk were small ships, radar pickets, and escorts on the fringes of the main fleet. But capital ships were hurt too. The carrier *Franklin* was badly struck and lost 700 of her crew in one hellish afternoon; the British carrier *Formidable* was hit on her flight deck, which prompted her captain to signal his flagship, "Little yellow bastard!" The admiral replied "Are you addressing me?" To crash into a carrier was the supreme victory for a young Japanese, and too many achieved it. *Bunker Hill* was hit, and so were *Enterprise, Wasp, Intrepid, Hancock,* and HMS *Indomitable;* some fought on, some buried their dead and limped home across the Pacific. The Japanese fleet, with enough fuel for a one-way trip, sortied and was sunk by

American aircraft; the enemy might be palpably weakening, but the hard-pressed sailors, soldiers, and marines at the sharp end were hardly aware of it. By the time Okinawa was secured, men and equipment both were worn down to a fine line by the strain, young men looked gaunt-eyed and hollow-cheeked, and ships' captains and flag officers in their forties looked like old men in their seventies.

Yet for the navy, the crisis was passed with Okinawa. From late June until the end of the war American fast-carrier units ranged virtually at will off the Home Islands, striking shore targets and keeping the pressure on. The Japanese, awaiting the big invasion, husbanded their resources and largely left the carriers alone. They had other problems.

When General Curtis LeMay took over the direction of the Marianas-based bombing campaign, he decided to shake things up. So far it had not achieved a great deal. The B-29's flew higher than 25,000 feet; they had a great deal of engine trouble, the flights were exhausting, and target accuracy from that height was minimal. For all their effort the bombers were more a nuisance than anything else. LeMay undertook intensive training of the aircrews, based on his own experiences over Germany, and he insisted on better control and tighter discipline in the air. After two months things were worse instead of better. Planes still aborted missions, bombs still missed targets, and the Japanese were producing new fighters that could claw up into the rarefied atmosphere where the big bombers flew and shoot them down. LeMay unhappily concluded that his effort was not hurting Japan's productive capacity. It was Germany all over again; unless some radical breakthrough could be achieved, strategic bombing was not worth the effort.

The answer was necessarily simple. A bomb dropped from thirty thousand feet had, by definition, a free fall of six miles through the air before it hit the ground. The margin for error was so great that it made a mockery of the term *precision bombing*. No matter how good the bombsight, how careful the bombardier, no matter to this point even how destructive the bomb, that six-mile drop undid all the previously fine calculations. So, LeMay reasoned, the easy answer was to shorten the drop: Fly lower. It was an easy answer that was not initially well received; the B-29, after all, had been designed for high altitudes and long distances. Aircrew were understandably leery of what might happen to them if they sacrificed that advantage by flying low, where they were vulnerable to fighters and antiaircraft guns. As always in war, it was a trade-off: fly high, be safe, do little damage, versus fly low, perhaps at great risk, perhaps to do great damage. LeMay added an ace; the Americans would fly night operations, on incendiary raids. To this the Japanese were highly vulnerable. They had little night-defense organization, not having needed it so far. And their cities were terribly open to fire-bombing, with much of them constructed of wood, paper, or other flammable materials.

Late on the afternoon of March 9, 1945, some 334 B-29's groaned into the air from the Marianas. They were loaded with incendiary bombs, about seven tons apiece, and they had left behind all their guns and gunners except for the tail positions. The remaining aircrew were highly apprehensive about what this might mean, but General LeMay was confident that "the greatest gamble of [his] career" would pay off. If he were wrong, several hundred airmen would die for it.

The first Pathfinder aircraft arrived over Tokyo just after midnight, and dropped their markers on the Shitamachi district, a rabbit warren of wooden houses, narrow alleys, and small factories. There was no fighter opposition, and the Japanese seemed completely surprised. The first wave of bombers to arrive found the target well marked; later waves could see the fires burning from well out to sea. A huge cloud of smoke and flame roared up into the night sky, and planes at the end of the raid were tossed frantically about. Through the open bombbay doors the crews were choked by smoke and a horrible smell, and a couple of planes were even flipped over by the fantastic air currents.

On the ground the scenes were reminiscent of those in Hamburg or Dresden, made even worse, if possible, by the nature of the city and the lack of Japanese measures for firefighting and relief. A huge firestorm leveled the Shitamachi district; people fled, or were sucked into the flames, or suffocated, or simply disappeared. The river that ran through the district was clogged with corpses. The sun in the morning rose over a vista of utter devastation; sixteen square miles of the city were burned out, and the official American estimate of casualties, almost certainly too low, was that eighty thousand people were killed in those few short hours. Thus was LeMay's gamble vindicated.

Japanese radio castigated the Americans for waging cowardly war on civilians, but this was the country that had raped Nanking, and staged the Bataan Death March, and driven Canadian prisoners over the cliffs at Hong Kong, and massacred the British sick at Singapore. These were, above all, the people who were fighting to the death on Luzon and mounting kamikaze attacks in the Pacific. Their protests about the usages of war did not lessen the American feeling that finally they had accomplished something with the strategic bombing force.

The Tokyo fire raid was but the beginning. Four other major industrial cities were targeted, and the bombers visited one after another Nagoya, Osaka, Kōbe, and Yokohama. By the end of March they had run out of incendiaries, but they had struck Japan a blow which it seemed no country could survive. Yet they still fought on; they saved their planes for the big invasion, they taught their young suicides how to get off the ground, they held the Shuri Line on Okinawa, and they killed themselves rather than surrender.

During the summer the B-29's were still droning away, at lesser targets now but with increasing mastery of the air. By July the Americans were dropping leaflets saying they were going to bomb such and such a target on such and such a date; the Japanese workers and civilians would read these and dutifully file out into the countryside, from which they watched their homes and factories being destroyed. The morale effect of all this was as tremendous as the physical damage, for if the Americans could send such advance warning and still bomb as they pleased, it was obvious they could do anything else they pleased as well.

The Imperial government was indeed considering surrender to the Allies, but was prey to such divided counsels on the issue that little of a positive nature was done. Like the Germans before them, the Japanese had some lingering hope of splitting the Allied coalition and getting some sort of deal with the Soviet Union that would allow them to avoid total surrender. The army was determined to fight to the end. When the Allies issued the famous Potsdam Declaration on July 26, it was sufficiently ambiguous for the various factions, either Allied or Japanese, to put whatever construction on it they chose. The declaration called for "unconditional surrender," and said the "alternative for Japan is prompt and utter destruction." The Japanese military men interpreted this as invasion, and they still thought they had a chance, albeit a slim one, to withstand that. What the Americans meant by "utter destruction" was something rather different. It was the atomic bomb.

In their effort to bring the war to an end, the Americans were prepared to tear apart the very fabric of matter. The story of the development of the atomic bomb is a long and complicated one, going back at least to the achievement of the first fission reaction in Berlin in 1938, and more notably to the letter that Albert Einstein sent to President Roosevelt in August 1939, pointing out the possibility of developing "extremely powerful bombs of a new type." For the next two years, scientists, many of whom were refugees from Germany, were far more worried about the prospects than the United States government was, but gradually the consultative and administrative organization for building a bomb was established, and this emerged eventually as the Manhattan Project. It was 1942 and the Americans were at war when they decided to proceed all out on the program. But then work went forward with a will; money suddenly was no problem. Huge plants appeared at Oak Ridge, Tennessee; Hanford, Washington; and Los Alamos, New Mexico. In December 1942 Enrico Fermi produced a controlled nuclear chain reaction on a squash court at the University of Chicago. That proved the theory; all that remained was to turn it into a workable bomb, an affair of several years and several billion dollars.

A bomb, of course, has to be transportable, so the men designing this one did so with a specific aim in mind: Build it so it could be carried in a B-29. They reached that stage of design by late 1943. Meanwhile, the air force was already setting up the organization and command system for such a B-29 atomic-bomb carrying unit. The bombs themselves got code names to allay curiosity: "Thin Man" and "Fat Man"; Thin Man later became "Little Boy." Secrecy was indeed one of the main elements of the project; speed was another, for throughout the war the Americans were driven by the fear that the Germans would beat them to it and produce an atomic bomb first. When Germany itself was finally invaded, one of the first units behind the infantry was looking for clues as to whether the Germans had the bomb, or were likely to have it, or had even come close. In the event they had not, though both they and the Japanese were working on it. The German war ended before the race was won, and the new American president, Harry S Truman, was meeting his allies at the Potsdam Conference when he received word that the first bomb had been successfully tested at Alamogordo, New Mexico.

By then two other bombs were already on their way to the Pacific. There had been considerable discussion about their employment, but far less than might have been expected. Bombs, after all, are made to be used, and any suggestion that the bomb, once made, might be displayed or publicized but not *really* used, that is, not actually dropped on real people, be they Germans or Japanese, was lukewarm. Men do not devote their careers and billions of dollars to producing a weapon that they see as saving countless of their countrymen's lives and then say, "Let's not use it." President Truman, on whose desk the buck stopped, authorized dropping of the atomic bomb anytime after August 1.

Another of the many ironies of the prevailing situation was that the whole atomic-bomb sequence was done in a planning limbo. So great had been the desire for secrecy that those outside the circle of knowledge knew nothing at all. The navy continued to bombard the Japanese coast, and the army, to plan for invasion. The fighting in the Philippines went on; the regular B-29 force was enlarged in the Marianas, and engineers were starting to build bases for the big planes on Okinawa. As far as the rest of the world was concerned, the war might well go on indefinitely.

An air of secrecy, of there being something different about it, thus surrounded the 393rd Bombardment Squadron on Tinian, but no one knew why, and when Colonel Paul Tibbets's plane, named "Enola Gay" after his mother, took off at 0245 on August 6, it seemed another routine mission. Yet tucked away in the bomb bay of the plane was Little Boy, nearly 5 tons of bomb with a 137-pound heart of Uranium 235. Enola Gay headed for Hiroshima; the Americans had considered Kyōto as a first choice, but decided against it because of its religious and cultural significance. They chose Hiroshima instead because it was an embarkation point and an industrial city, and because it had not previously been bombed. They wanted a clear demonstration of what this bomb alone would do.

The plane reached its target at 0915; on the ground the Japanese paid little attention, as by now they were used to small flights of B-29's making reconnaissance runs. Dropped from an altitude of 31,600 feet, the bomb detonated at 800 feet. Its force was that of 29,000 tons of TNT; it swept almost five square miles of the city and killed almost

70,000 people. As the mushroom cloud rose into the sky, the airmen above stared in awe, and on the ground there was utter chaos. It was as if the world were ending.

Three days later, to prove that the first bomb was not a fluke, the Americans did it again. They bombed Nagasaki, this time through cloud by radar. The primary target, Kokura, had also been obscured, causing diversion to the secondary one. Damage was not as bad as at Hiroshima, contained partly by surrounding hills, but the general effects were the same, and about 35,000 people were killed. That same day, 1,500 miles to the northwest, Russian troops were pouring into Manchuria.

The Japanese were finished. The emperor himself, in his polite and convoluted way, indicated that it was all over, and that the government must surrender. Some die-hard army officers attempted a confused coup, but little came of it. The time for manly struggle was past; the time for endurance was at hand. On August 14 the Japanese surrendered. There were then nearly 1,000 B-29's flying missions, but the bombing now stopped, and when the formal papers were signed on September 22, 462 of the great aircraft flew over the USS *Missouri* in perhaps the greatest single flypast in history. The war was over at last.

XV

PAPER WARS
AND PAPER TIGERS

At the end of World War I, American aviation authorities had stacked together hundreds of stripped-down D.H. 4's in France and touched off what journalists and opposition politicians castigated as "the billion-dollar bonfire." It was cheaper to burn the planes than to bring them back to the United States, where they would have been useless anyway. Was that not, after all, the war to end all wars? Compared to what happened after World War II, the great burning of 1919 was no more than a marshmallow roast. In the jungles of the Pacific islands, or the deserts of North Africa, or the airplane graveyards of the American Southwest, planes, tanks, and trucks by the thousands were left to rot. Many went into storage, many were stripped for spare parts or melted down to make tin cans and new cars, and many more were just left behind as the tide of war washed over them. Forty years later, enthusiastic young entrepreneurs were still hacking P-38's out of the New Guinea fields, or fishing Harvards and Hurricanes out of lakes in Nova Scotia. Though the loss is less tragic, war is as wasteful of property as it is of lives, and not the least wasteful aspect of it is the end, when whole national war machines are thrown into reverse, or simply stopped and forgotten.

In the euphoria of peace, some governments momentarily forgot the age-old dictum that war is waged for political ends. The United States government brought the boys home and went through the most rapid and massive demobilization in history. The blue and olive-drab hordes poured through San Francisco and Hampton Roads and New York, setting aside their uniforms with sighs of heartfelt relief—it was still too early for nostalgia—and resumed interrupted lives as civilians. From a peak strength of nearly twelve and a half million during the war, the American armed forces shrunk to just over a million two years later. In Great Britain a new Labor government, pushed to the wall by the costs of the war and the cutting off of American aid, hastened almost indecently to get rid of an empire that Britons had died by the thousands to preserve. Much of the rest of the world sat hollow-eyed, wondering what might be rescued from the general wreckage.

In Eastern Europe, the Russians clamped down an iron control on their hard-won and newly acquired glacis. Military men inevitably think in terms of defensible frontiers, and if Russia is safe with a frontier on the Vistula, it is even safer with a frontier on the Elbe. Germany in Europe and Japan in the Far East were both occupied, the former by a consortium of the victors who all agreed to act in concert but soon ceased to do so, the latter by a United States that was, in the person of Douglas MacArthur as reigning proconsul, not eager to share its victory with lesser contributors.

Inherent contradictions in these immediate postwar developments soon emerged, especially for the United States. As has so often happened in American history, national commitments and the forces available to meet them were out of proportion, and just as the nation was busily dismantling the greatest armed force in the world, it was assuming vast new strategic responsibilities. For who was going to take care of the occupied areas of central Europe and the Pacific rim if not the occupiers? The United States rebuilt Germany and Japan to be peace-loving—no more goose-stepping for the Germans, no more Bushido for the Japanese—and then found to its chagrin that it was required to defend its clients. America's eastern frontier was now at Berlin rather than the Atlantic seaboard, its western at the China coast rather than Hawaii; and right across those two frontiers loomed the other surviving great power—the Soviet Union and its friends, allies, or satellites.

It was soon apparent that the world was not going to live in uninterrupted peace and harmony after this greatest of all wars. By early 1946, Winston Churchill, at Fulton, Missouri, coined the phrase *Iron Curtain* and urged the United States to take the lead in standing up to a Soviet Union that refused to acknowledge that the war was over. One year and one week later, President Truman announced his doctrine of aid to states threatened by advancing communism, and American assistance went to Greece and Turkey. This was shortly followed by the Marshall Plan, offering aid to virtually anyone, Communists included, to bring the world back to something approaching normality. With the Soviet refusal to participate, and the Communist coup in Czechoslovakia early in 1948, the cold war began.

One of the early results of this was a quite bizarre test for air power of a sort, for in July the Russians cut off access by road and rail to the Western enclave in Berlin. To have reopened the routes forcibly would perhaps have meant the beginning of World War III; rather than chance it, the Western Allies decided upon an air supply, and thus launched the famous Berlin Airlift. Begun as a temporary expedient, largely with C-47 twin-engined transport planes already in Europe, it soon expanded into a major effort. The Americans brought in the larger four-engined C-54, and the air force stripped transport planes from as far away as Hawaii. Civilian planes were also chartered, providing a shot in the arm for the fledgling air-freight business, and a steady stream of planes from the occupation zones, one every few seconds, flew into West Berlin's airports. Just enough supplies reached the city to enable life to go on, and the Russians found themselves seriously embarrassed; having publicly boasted that they would force the British, French, and Americans out of Berlin, they found it impossible to explain why they had not done so. The longer it went on, the sillier they looked. Finally, after fourteen months, they quietly lifted their restrictions, and both the blockade and the airlift came to an end.

It was not only in the external world that the Americans were faced with problems. Internally too, all sorts of difficulties arose that defied simple solution in this strange new world. Against the backdrop of military demobilization and a frustrating civilian economy—116 million working days lost to strikes in 1946—the armed services fell into their usual habit of bickering over who was to get what and who was to do what with it. There had long been one school of opinion within the forces in favor of general unification of the services with an over-all military commander. Opposition to this was usually voiced as a fear of "Prussianizing" the services. The experience of joint area commands in the war had strengthened the arguments for unification, though, and eventually, after several committees and boards of investigation, the government decided on a federal military system, with all services still independent but presided over by a Joint Chiefs of Staff, under the civilian direction of a secretary of defense. As part of the package, embodied in the National Security Act of 1947, the United States Army Air Force was transformed into an independent United States Air Force, at last achieving the status the Royal Air Force had attained in 1918. This was all accompanied by a great deal of good-natured banter about uniforms of "bus-driver blue," but at the higher levels, the bantering was not good-natured at all. The army retained its own aviation branch, so it was not too overtly dissatisfied. This was to handle close support and liaison, observation, and even to give the army its own air-transport battalions for rapid mobility. Most of these tasks were fulfilled by fixed-wing aircraft, though at the time the helicopter was just beginning to appear on the scene.

The real trouble came between the new air force and the navy, and went back to Billy Mitchell's old assertion of the indivisibility of the air. The navy had adjusted during the war to the primacy of the aircraft carrier, and the entire battle-fleet concept was now built around the carrier groups. The navy therefore wanted the air force confined to tactical use of air power over land, and strategic bombing. The air-force, of course, wanted the latter, but not the limitation implied in the former. And as the air force wanted a wider sphere for tactical air, the navy wanted as well to impinge on the strategic side. None of these spheres could be clearly delimited, and therein lay the rub. The whole issue culminated in the great B-36 versus supercarrier battle, better known as "the revolt of the admirals."

The B-36, built by Consolidated-Vultee, shortened to Convair, was a monster hybrid that bridged the gap between the last of the conventionally powered bombers and the first of the real jets. It was powered by six twenty-eight cylinder pusher radial engines and four turbojets, and it had a wingspan almost a hundred feet longer than the B-29; its maximum speed was only 411 mph, but it had a range of nearly 7,000 miles. The air force readily acknowledged that it was an interim type, and that better jet bombers were in the pipeline, notably the B-47 and the great Boeing B-52. But Convair's bomber was available at the time, and the first deliveries began in 1947. At the same time, the navy was busily campaigning for the building of new aircraft carriers, and in particular for "supercarriers," which would be big enough to launch aircraft capable of carrying an atomic bomb, that is, of trespassing on the air force's monopoly of strategic air power. The whole issue was complicated by the fact that the United States was then so weak militarily, it was dependent upon the bomb as a last-resort weapon, but at the same time, within the depths of service discussion, it was skeptical about how useful the bomb would actually be. There was bitter debate over the allocation of the reduced military budgets of 1947, 1948, and 1949, with each service angling for its own views. The navy laid the keel of an 80,000-ton supercarrier, to be named *United States,* on April 18, 1949. Five days later a new secretary of defense, Louis Johnson, ordered its cancellation.

At that the navy exploded. Documents were leaked to the press calling the B-36 a "billion dollar blunder" and hinting broadly that Johnson was in Convair's pocket. Admirals went on the stump to say that strategic bombing had been a failure in World War II, that the air force was all propaganda, that its policies and procurement practices were wasteful, and on and on in an outpouring of vituperation rarely seen before, if often seen since, in public. There were congressional hearings and press conferences, and the Chairman of the Joint Chiefs, General Omar Bradley, hitherto perceived as "the nicest guy in Washington," raked the navy over the coals ruthlessly. As all this was absorbing Washington's attention, the Soviets exploded their first nuclear bomb and the Communists took over China. Faced with the message of these two events, the United States revised its military ideas to accord more with reality. The Truman budget limitations were abruptly set aside, the money began to flow once more, and all three services began to get some of what they wanted. Given the enormous inertia of large institutions when told to do what they do not want to do, and their uncanny ability to do what they *do* want to do, even if ordered not to do it, army, navy, and air force each went its own separate way, happily duplicating and undercutting the others.

A good part of the problem, then and in the ensuing forty years, was that the cost of defense was constantly increasing. This derived not just from inflation and the loss of purchasing power for the dollar—that came only in the sixties when the government tried to fight a war without paying for it—but more from the fact that weapons systems grew more and more complex and sophisticated, and therefore the unit costs soared alarmingly. The P-51 Mustang cost $54,000 to produce in 1942, while the F-86 Sabre, the standard jet fighter of the Korean War, cost $299,000 in 1950. The F-4 Phantom II, the most widely known "fighter"—it was hardly just that—of the Vietnam War cost $2.2 million, and the F-14, one of the sophisticated new fighters of the seventies, carried a price tag of $16 million. Those figures were all at the time of purchasing, but the dollars that bought the P-51 bought almost as much as four of the dollars that bought the F-14, and even the dollars that bought the F-4 were worth twice as much as the F-14 dollars. The answer to that was that when it came to buying military equipment, men's lives were on the line and the country needed the best it could get. However great a fighter it was in its day, no one would want to take a 400 mph P-51 over a 1,200 mph Mig-21. As was to be demonstrated in Korea, American aircraft were only marginally superior in some areas to those flown by the opposition, so that throughout the entire period since World War II, competition has been the greatest spur to development, to sophistication, and therefore to costs as well.

The United States did not have a monopoly as the world entered the jet era. Indeed, in some respects it did not even have a lead. The Germans had come out first with the Me 262, but they were now out of the race. The British were next, with the Gloster Meteor, which entered squadron service late in 1944 and saw only the briefest of action at the very end of the war. By contrast, the first American jet, the Bell P-59 Airacomet, had a disappointing performance and was never used in combat, serving largely as a vehicle to provide jet training. Meanwhile, the Russians got a little help from their friends. Initially using captured German jet engines, then employed Rolls-Royce Nenes, the best available, sold by the British government in 1946, they rapidly developed a jet capability. The Yak-15 and Mig-9 both flew in April 1946. The first truly combat-worthy Russian jet, the Mig-15, was designed and built while the Russians were setting up a plant to build the Nene, which they did under license, and it flew on December 30, 1947. It entered squadron service through 1948, and American pilots would soon discover just how combat-worthy it was. The jet aircraft was rather like the gun, at first no better than and maybe not as good as the weapons it was designed to replace, but introduced anyway because its potential was undeniably so much greater.

As the jets were coming in, the last generations of the piston-engined fighters were going out, and some of them were truly marvelous machines, still beloved by airplane fanciers and sought after by those rich enough to collect and fly "antique" airplanes. In the United States, Grumman capitalized on its long experience in building fighters for the navy to produce the F-8F Bearcat; a pure interceptor fighter, it was designed as the smallest plane that could be built around a 2,100-horsepower, 18-cylinder Pratt and Whitney Wasp engine. There is a perhaps apocryphal but nonetheless persistent story that two pilots once matched a Bearcat and a Mustang from a standing start, and that the Bearcat got off the ground and made two firing passes at the Mustang before the latter had its wheels up. The only combat the Bearcat ever saw was as a ground-support plane for the French in Indochina, for which it was sadly unsuited. In Britain, the Hawker Sea Fury still attracts the same kind of nostalgic devotion the Bearcat does in the United States. A variation on the Hawker Typhoon-Tempest line, it served with the Royal Navy from 1947 to 1954, flying operationally in Korea, where one even managed to shoot down a Mig-15 jet.

In other spheres, of course, the propeller-driven aircraft survived, for transport, for maritime reconnaissance, for artillery observation, for those uses where endurance was more important than speed. But for first-line operations, the prop fighters and bombers went to smaller, less active air forces, where they soldiered on for many years. American-built B-25 Mitchells, Thunderbolts, and Mustangs, British Seafires, Tempests, Mosquitoes, and Lancasters, Russian Migs and Tupolevs, all entered the services of lesser powers, and some of them are still there in the age of 1,500-mph fighters.

A noticeable and perhaps distressing side aspect of the developmental pace was that the aircraft industry was concentrated excessively among the great powers. It became in fact largely the preserve of the United States and the Soviet Union, with Britain and France having sunk sadly from the preeminence they once enjoyed, and the other industrial states building for specialized purposes but not trying to compete across the spectrum of aircraft manufacturing. There were peculiar exceptions to this trend, but they were usually caused more by political or prestige reasons than by the fundamentals of economics.

Israel, for example, has always been dependent upon foreign aircraft suppliers; one of the first Israeli aircraft was, in fact, a late model of the original German Messerschmitt Me 109, built in Czechoslovakia and exported to the struggling state by a variety of subterfuge means. In 1967, after the Six-Day War, the Israelis found themselves the victims of a variety of restrictions and embargoes, so they mated a French Mirage airframe with an American jet engine to produce their own fighter, the Kfir. Both Communist China and India also produced military aircraft which, while not up to world-class standards, presumably satisfied both national pride and the fear of not always being able to purchase what they wanted in the world market.

Rather more peculiar cases are those of Sweden and France. Sweden has been determinedly neutral since the end of the Napoleonic Wars, and has seen one way of preserving that neutrality in having its own indigenous arms industry. Beginning in the late forties, the Saab firm started building jet aircraft, from the tubby little J29 Tunnen through the J35 Drakken and the current J37 Viggen. These aircraft were well up to world standards for their day, but Sweden suffered the same difficulty with them as with small manufacturers in other fields. The break-even point on developmental and production costs usually comes with export orders, and potential buyers are reluctant to buy from producers such as Saab when the market is dominated by the giants.

The French aircraft industry was devastated by the war. Factories were kept in production by the Germans, and firms often ended up producing German designs, such as the Feiseler Storch, which was built in quantity in France at Puteaux by Morane-Saulnier. Even numbers of such first-line aircraft as the Focke-Wulf FW 190, the Luftwaffe's great fighter, were manufactured there, and subsequently served first with the Germans and then with the reconstituted Armée de l'Air. In this case, however, the French, as unwilling helpers of their occupiers, tended to sabotage the aircraft by overtempering steel components, and such planes had a relatively short service life. The postwar fighter-aircraft industry was virtually the single-handed creation of Marcel Bloch, who had designed French aircraft before the war and then been in a German prison camp through it. When he returned home he started out all over again, and built a succession of aircraft that put France in the forefront of world aviation. His first jet was the Dassault MD 450 Ouragan, developed in the late forties and serving through the fifties. This was succeeded by the Mystere, the world's first swept-wing fighter, then by the Super Mystere. In addition to supplying the renascent French air force, enough in itself to keep the company afloat, Dassault also managed to sell to India and Israel, and later to South Africa and Australia.

British evolution was infinitely more painful, a process of watching world leadership gradually slip from their hands and be assumed by the United States. A great deal of space in editorial columns was devoted to damning shortsighted government policies toward the aircraft industry, and there was the constant suspicion that Britain's great technological lead and expertise were being squandered by ideologically antipathetic Labor governments, or by lackadaisical marketing policies, or by inept management, or by any one of several other possible villains. There was enough truth in all these charges to make them hurt, but beyond the accidents of the situation, what was happening to the British aircraft industry was remarkably similar to what had happened to British heavy industry fifty to a hundred years earlier: Britain was simply being outpaced by other countries that had better resource bases, sounder financial backing, and perhaps more aggressive attitudes.

Britain remained in the developmental race, with excellent airliners and various technical wrinkles that other countries were happy to adopt. On aircraft carriers, the angled flight deck, the hurricane bow—enclosed to prevent the flight deck from being peeled back as had happened to American ships during typhoons in the war—the newer catapults, mirrored landing systems, all were initiated by the British. One of the most versatile strike aircraft, the Hawker Harrier, capable of vertical takeoffs, was developed in the late fifties and eventually became one of the few foreign-designed aircraft to be accepted by the United States, serving with the marines. By and large, however, the British simply could not keep up, and growing numbers of American planes appeared in British markings, to the intense chagrin of what had once been the greatest aircraft industry in the world.

These developments were no more than glimmerings on the horizon when a shooting war erupted in the Far East in June 1950. The Korean peninsula had been occupied by Japan in the 1890s, formally annexed in 1910, and ruthlessly exploited since then. At the end of World War II the Russians took over the northern portion of the area, and the Americans the southern. Agreements to unify the country and hold elections were never fulfilled, and the southern part became the Republic of Korea while the northern took the name People's Democratic Republic. Claiming the entire country, the North invaded the South on June 25, 1950. The poorly equipped South Koreans and their relatively few American advisers were swept south in a wave of on-rushing North Koreans, and ended up confined to a tiny perimeter around the southeastern port of Pusan.

Meanwhile, the United States went to the United Nations and, thanks to the fortuitous absence of Russia from the Security Council, had North Korea declared an aggressor, whereupon a small trickle of U.N. aid began to flow in. The main brunt of helping the South Koreans fell to the United States, and President Truman decided that this was a place where the non-Communist powers had to stand firm. This was easier said than done, when the United States had as few disposable forces as it then possessed; there was a rapid commitment, first of available troops from occupation duty in Japan, and then a buildup from the United States. In September the United Nations forces, basically Americans and South Koreans, all commanded by General MacArthur, launched a riposte. The troops around Pusan broke out after heavy fighting, and American forces landed at Inchŏn up the west coast, in one of the most risky and daring amphibious operations in history. The North Koreans, out on a long limb, collapsed and were pursued northward.

Against what proved to be sound advice, MacArthur then succumbed to the temptation to cross into North Korea, in an ill-conceived wish to unify the whole country by force of arms, just as the North Koreans had tried. With a backdrop of ominous rumblings from China, U.N. forces closed up to the border of Manchuria. This in turn brought about massive Chinese intervention, and MacArthur's troops, in the midst of an elated pursuit into the void, were caught flat-footed and hustled back south in some bitter fighting. A line finally stabilized roughly along the original partition line, the 38th parallel, and there it stayed from the spring of 1951 until a truce was signed in July 1953.

American air power played a crucial role, both positive and negative, in the war, because of its peculiar quality. This was a war reminiscent of those waged by the Byzantine Empire of old, when a rich society, weak in manpower but highly superior technologically, fought against overwhelming numbers of relatively primitive hordes. Politically and ideologically, the Americans were reluctant to fight a war of attrition with the masses of Communist China, while the Chinese, lacking much modern technology but possessing any number of bodies, were quite willing to trade men for time, or for useless bits of Korean countryside.

To American infantrymen huddled in lines that resembled the trench system on the western front in 1917, facing mass human-wave attacks by the Chinese and North Koreans, it hardly appeared a sophisticated kind of war, but where the Chinese threw men into the balance, the Americans, as much as they could, threw artillery and air power, and, near the coasts, naval-gunfire support. Interesting questions were raised by the war at four different levels of operations: air support, fighter command of the air, strategic bombing, and, finally, the use of the atomic bomb.

Air support of land or naval operations was initially something of a sore point with the ground troops, for an infantryman's horizons are necessarily limited, and in the middle of a fire fight he is not likely to appreciate that an air attack on a railroad tunnel fifty miles away may be of some assistance to him. That, however, was what was happening, and naval, marine, and air force interdictory strikes on Korean, and later Chinese, supply lines were a key factor in reducing their power. As in a later war, however, the air force found that no matter how heavily or how often they bombed primitive supply routes, some supplies still got through. A man or a file of porters may carry far less than trucks or trains, but they are far harder to stop at night or in rough country.

Close support of troops, by propeller-driven Mustangs, Corsairs, and medium bombers such as the B-26—a confusing renumbering of a different plane from the World War II Marauder—was highly useful, though there were dangers in such operations, and occasionally tragic mistakes. One of these came on September 20, 1950, near Naktong, when British soldiers of the Argyll and Sutherland Highlanders put out panels to guide a strike against a neighboring hill. The Communists put out panels too, and a flight of Mustangs hit the wrong hill in the confusion, killing or wounding about sixty of their own allies. But such strikes, with bombs, cannon fire, and the horrible jellied gasoline, napalm, were generally highly effective, and Chinese after-action assessments repeatedly stressed the adverse effect of tactical air power on their troop movements and morale.

For almost the entire war, the United Nations forces dominated the skies, but there were some nasty shocks in this. First-line American fighters at the time were the Lockheed F-80 Shooting Star and the Republic F-84 Thunderjet. Both were straight-wing aircraft, and both were sound, capable machines. The former, redesigned into a trainer configuration as the T-33, went on for years and trained jet pilots all over the non-Communist world, and is still happily doing so. The latter became a somewhat unsung workhorse of many air arms, evolving into a swept-wing fighter bomber that soldiered on for more than twenty years. However, the top speed of the F-80 was just below, and of the F-84 just over, 600 mph. The U.S. Navy at the time was flying Grumman F9F Panthers, and their top speed, as is usual with aircraft stressed for carrier operations, was even lower, about 526 mph. Therefore, when these planes encountered Russian-built Mig-15's, flying at 660 mph, they were rudely surprised. Fortunately, the Americans had newer models on the way, and with the arrival of the North American F-86 Sabre, they soon regained aerial supremacy. The Shooting Stars and Thunderjets were adapted for tactical support work, while the Sabre quickly drove the Migs from the sky; indeed, it went on to become perhaps the first truly "classic" jet fighter, built in large numbers and serving for a generation with many air forces. As in World War I and again in World War II, the Korean War demonstrated how quickly aerial ascendancy can be changed, won, or lost by the pace of the development. And again, since the Sabre design studies began as far back as 1944, it also showed how long a lead time modern war machinery needs to reach fruition.

Problems of a different order of magnitude surrounded the matter of strategic bombing, for the Communists made no real challenge to the United Nations in this sphere. The question was rather one of what to bomb to what effect. North Korea had enjoyed some industrial buildup under the Russians, but after the end of 1950, the war was more Chinese than Korean. There was of course a great deal of Chinese industry within striking range in Manchuria, but political constraints forbade the Americans hitting it. Early on President Truman and his advisers and government made the policy decision not to widen the war in response to Chinese intervention. In effect, they agreed to fight the war by the enemy's rules. Manchurian sanctuaries remained safe, to the frustration and anger of pilots in combat. U.N. airmen would engage enemy aircraft, or hit targets close to the Yalu River; the Communists would come up from their bases on the northern side of the river, fight, then flee for home, knowing that once over the river they could thumb their noses with impunity at their opponents. At one point, the Chinese did try to build air bases south of the river, with the intent of supporting a major offensive, and these were promptly and gleefully plastered by American bombers. There was little attempt, however, to wage a strategic bombing campaign in the same sense as the ones that had been waged against Germany and Japan.

If the Chinese Communists and their allies were not to be subjected to such blows, they were certainly not going to be hit with an atomic bomb. President Truman hinted at the possible use of nuclear weapons, or at least refused to rule them out categorically, and Air Force General Thomas S. Power, who was vice-commander of the Strategic Air Command at the time, suggested that there was active consideration of using the atomic bomb to relieve the pressure on the Pusan perimeter early in the war. But most advice was against it, for reasons ranging from lack of any really suitable target to the moral issue, which was raised by Dwight D. Eisenhower. In 1950 Eisenhower was the president of Columbia University, and soon to become president of the United States. If you were trying to show yourself as an example for the world, his view was that you could not simply blow up everyone who chose to disagree with you.

The frustrations of playing the enemy's game, of fighting for less than total victory, of seeing men die while forebearing to use weapons that might prevent their deaths, boiled up in the famous Truman-MacArthur controversy. Frustrated by Chinese intervention, and by his inability to win the war in the face of it, MacArthur wanted to use American air power, and anything else available, against the Chinese mainland. He wanted to do anything to win the war, but the Truman administration did not want to do anything that might widen it; all they wanted was to end it, as decently as possible. When MacArthur publicly took issue with his own superiors' policy, he had to go. He was peremptorily relieved of command; indeed, he read of his own relief in the newspapers. It was a sad end to a distinguished career, but it illustrated that Harry Truman, ex-artillery captain from Missouri, understood the new world and the uses and limitations of power differently from the famous General of the Army. The United States no longer possessed a monopoly on nuclear power, and Korea was not the place to start World War III. It was, as acknowledged by all but MacArthur, "the wrong war in the wrong place at the wrong time."

* * *

Korea was far from the only danger spot in the postwar world, as international tensions increased and trouble broke out in one area after another. The colonial powers of Europe, great no longer, attempted to reimpose their shattered rule over their subjects, with almost invariable failure. The Dutch were pushed out of Indonesia, the French lost first Indochina and then Algeria, Britain presided over the transformation of Empire into Commonwealth, and then watched as former holdings drifted away into other orbits. The Middle East was split by the establishment of a new state of Israel, initiating a series of seemingly endless wars.

Over all this hung the threat of superpower antagonism, the Soviet Union and the United States sparring with each other, fighting through surrogates, circling warily and bristling like two angry dogs, neither wanting to fight but both pushing for their respective interests as they perceived them. The ideology of their rivalry was injected into the colonial upheavals, so that men who might have been bandits in the nineteenth century were now patriots or freedom fighters; if the Mad Mullah had lived thirty years later, he would have played Moscow off against Washington and emerged as a successful dictator.

Air power played but a limited role in these conflicts, though on a few occasions its presence or absence was a vital factor. It was extremely difficult to bomb guerrillas out of existence in a desert, and almost impossible in a jungle. The British found that out in Malaya, where an emergency was declared in 1948. The Communist forces they attempted to defeat were simply too elusive, too diffuse, for air power to be able to fix and destroy them, though the Royal Air Force units were absolutely invaluable for reconnaissance, occasional air strikes, and logistics missions of one kind or another. And after the advent of the helicopter and the increased mobility it provided, air power became even more important. But the emergency remained a small-unit action, of jungle patrols, hides, and ambushes, more like fighting the dacoity in Burma in the 1880s than modern war.

There was, however, a rapid evolution of tactics and equipment during this period. When a "confrontation" with Indonesia over North Borneo erupted in 1962, just a few years after the end of the Malayan emergency, the British were able to employ air supply and support, and especially to operate in conjunction with helicopter forces, to such effect that the conflict soon fizzled out. Ground units set up and maintained blocking positions on the frontiers and stalled the Indonesians before they could get going. In effect, the helicopter gave the modern soldier the edge in mobility that the jungle had previously given to his adversary.

While the British were fighting their fire-brigade wars, the French were trying to pretend that World War II had not happened. In 1946 they returned to French Indochina and stumbled into a war against anticolonial and Communist indigenous forces led by Ho Chi Minh and a local military genius named Vo Nguyen Giap, a former school-teacher. In the end they suffered the greatest colonial military disaster of the century. The Battle of Dien Bien Phu was a classic example of the misuse of, or misplaced reliance on, air power.

By 1954 the French government and people had had just about enough of the war in Indochina. They were now seeking no more than some decent victory to improve their bargaining position before they got out. The military men on the spot decided to seize an important road junction, force the enemy to come to them, and then defeat him in a set-piece battle. The chosen spot, Dien Bien Phu, was near the Laotian frontier, on one of the supply routes down from Communist China. It was about 170 miles from the French bases around Hanoi, situated in a long valley under the eyes of surrounding hills. There were two airstrips in the valley, and as the French were sure the Viet Minh could not produce artillery capable of dominating them, they saw no difficulty in supplying their garrison by air.

They were wrong. Even under optimum conditions, the French air supply system would have been hard-pressed to supply Dien Bien Phu; it lacked the material, equipment, and maintenance staff. Indeed, it was just not up to the task. But then the Viet Minh did get artillery into the hills around the valley, so much so that they were soon pounding the French positions in a style reminiscent of World War I. French tactical aircraft, B-26's and Grumman F8F Bearcats, were totally incapable of suppressing the well-concealed guns; the Bearcats could just make it to Dien Bien Phu and back, with little reserve left for action. The airstrips became inoperable and the French had to resort to aerial drops, which meant that much of what they did get there was lost to the enemy. After forty-five days the garrison, fighting heroically against equally heroic attacks, finally went down. Dien Bien Phu is regarded as one of the epic battles of the century, for though it was small in numbers compared to what happened in the world wars, it can be seen as the death knell of colonialism; the Indochinese faced the French on the latter's terms, and beat them completely. It was, ultimately, a victory of human supply power over air supply power.

If in Indochina "the odds were on the cheaper man," in the Middle East Israel maintained a precarious independence and existence by a qualitative and technological superiority over its rivals that has only recently begun to erode. When Israel declared its independence in 1948 it was immediately attacked by all its neighbors, and the Israelis found themselves in a full-scale war for their survival. Their first air force consisted of a few light planes and some pilots who had served during the world wars with various air forces. They soon acquired four Messerschmitt 109's, and their very presence, unexpected as it was, imposed caution on their enemies at crucial junctures. Later they got a few B-17 Flying Fortresses, officially illegally, and with one of them they bombed Cairo in July; this did no real damage, but again the threat made the Egyptians cautious in their own bombing of Israeli targets. By the end of 1948 the Hel Avir, or Israeli Air Corps, had grown to more than 200 planes and was dominating the air. Ironically, though it was a makeshift force with little doctrine or tactics, and though it was part of the army, it tended to go its own way and seek its own missions, just as larger, better organized air forces did.

After the War of Independence the Israelis put a high priority on an air force; they knew they would always be outnumbered on the ground, and they accepted that they might often have to launch preemptive strikes. Ironically, their wars must in effect be blitzkriegs. They put their main strength in fighter-bomber types as the best compromise for achieving what they needed.

The wisdom of their choice was illustrated in the opening moves of the famous Six-Day War of 1967. In about three hours the Israeli air force of some 250 planes knocked out more than 300 of Egypt's 340 serviceable combat aircraft. The Israelis roared in over the desert as the Egyptians were stood down after their morning alert, and caught them absolutely flat-footed. They then went on to attack Syrian, Jordanian, Iraqui, and Lebanese airfields, and by the end of the second day of the war, they had achieved complete air superiority. It was as classic a victory for air power as Dien Bien Phu had been a defeat.

All these smaller wars were fought out against the backdrop of Soviet-American rivalry, and while the little states won and lost their wars, the Americans and Russians went on building up huge armaments, lurching from crisis to crisis, facing each other down in one area of the world after another. The American monopoly of atomic weaponry was lost, but in the early fifties, with a larger arsenal and greater delivery capability, the United States continued to rely on a doctrine of massive retaliation. If the Russians upset, or even tried to upset, the world balance of power anywhere, the Americans could, and might, reply with a full-scale atomic attack. Of course, they never did, and on the occasion of crises, American leadership periodically considered, and always rejected, the idea of such a strike. However, it believed it vital to possess the capability, and to that end the Strategic Air Command became the air force's standard bearer.

Incredible resources in time, money, and manpower went to maintaining a bomber force at a few moments' readiness, to the extent that some American bombers were always airborne, ready for dispatch to Russian targets. B-36's gave way to B-47's and finally to B-52's, while the Russians on their side followed the same progression. Russian Tupolev Tu-20's and Tu-22's, Boeing B-52's, and British Vulcans and Victors carried the manned strategic bomber concept probably about as far as it could, or was likely to go, and these types, produced in the fifties, have been in service in one role or another ever since. Even with the advent of intercontinental missiles, they remain a potent element of their countries' arsenals, their power enormously increased by the ever-growing lethality of the weapons they carry. Argument continues to rage over whether they have been totally upstaged by missiles, but policy makers as well as ordinary men are reluctant to see humans replaced by machines. Even though the familial link between the pilot of a 200-ton bomber carrying a nuclear bomb and the pilot of a D.H. 4 is very tenuous, it is still there, and the manned bomber in one form or another will undoubtedly be around for a long time yet. Just as in Korea, what it could and could not achieve was demonstrated again in later wars.

XVI

THE FRUSTRATIONS OF POWER

In 1962 the cold war reached an early crescendo. The Soviets, frustrated by their inability through the fifties to alter the status quo in their favor, looked increasingly far afield for troubled waters in which to fish, and they found them in the Caribbean. In 1959 a young man named Fidel Castro had ousted the dictator Fulgencio Batista and taken power in Cuba. He soon fell afoul of the United States, which had initially welcomed him but became alienated by his leftist policies, especially when they involved the expropriation of American property. On the principle that the enemy of my enemy is my friend, Castro was welcomed with open arms by the Russians. By 1961 the United States was backing overt but unsuccessful attempts to overthrow the Cuban government, and the Soviets were loudly proclaiming their support of their new ally. In September they agreed to supply arms and technical specialists to Cuba, and in October American reconnaissance flights discovered that the Russians were installing missiles capable of reaching most of the eastern and central United States. Such an altering of the strategic balance was intolerable, and the new

American president, John F. Kennedy, responded by declaring Cuba to be under "quarantine." That was a euphemism for a blockade, which would have been illegal in time of ostensible peace. For a while the world held its breath as Russian freighters continued to steam toward Cuba, to be intercepted by American aircraft and then surface units. Finally, on what was perceived as the knife-edge of a worldwide atomic war, the Soviets backed down. The ships turned about and headed home, and Premier Nikita Khrushchev announced that all missiles would be removed if the United States pledged not to invade Cuba. This President Kennedy did, tacitly abandoning the Monroe Doctrine while insisting it was still valid, and the crisis was over.

Indeed, it looked at the time as if the entire cold war were over, both sides for some years after that learning to live with each other, and a period of relative calm ensued. That, however, did not stop the arms buildup of the two powers, which continued unabated, exacerbated by the frustrations of the previous decade. Long and vitriolic arguments waged over what the most appropriate response was to moves made by the other side. It was, and remains, a situation fraught with grave danger. To illustrate it, European observers created a "nuclear clock," on which they assessed how close the world was at any given moment to "midnight," a full-scale nuclear war.

Both the Americans and the Russians continued to exhibit the messianic tendencies that had led them into confrontation in the first place, and both continued an arms-building program that was quantitatively and qualitatively unprecedented in human history. The fundamental problem was, and is, that they distrusted each other, and therefore found it extraordinarily difficult to reach any agreements on arms limitations. Were they able to get rid of the distrust, the arms would be unnecessary; but as long as the distrust persists, so do the arms.

One of the peculiar problems of the whole matter was, as it was in 1938, the difficulty of figuring out just who had what. This spawned a whole new profession in the defense intelligence community, but it was a profession tainted by the suspicion that it was serving special interests and producing the figures those interests found best suited to their own needs. Analysts connected to the air force consistently estimated that the Soviets had a great number first of bombers and then of missiles building; these were the men who produced the "bomber gap" of the late fifties and the "missile gap" of the early sixties, and these were the people whose figures air force advocates and opposition politicians quoted at budget time. The Central Intelligence Agency was only slightly less pessimistic than air force intelligence. On the other hand, the army and navy intelligence groups produced figures for Soviet bombers and missiles that were generally considered to be ludicrously low—for a long time after 1949 the navy refused even to admit that the Russians had exploded an atomic bomb. Yet when high-flying U-2's, and then subsequently satellite reconnaissance, became available, it was found that even the laughably low figures produced by naval intelligence were far higher than the Russians actually had. But by then, of course, the United States had embarked on a building program of both bombers and missiles designed to preserve its superiority.

Every year the defense advocates pleaded for more funds, because they had to play catch-up with the Russians, who of course were doing exactly the same thing themselves—playing catch-up with the Americans. It was a vicious circle; it was indeed reminiscent of the bad old days of the Renaissance, when condottiere from rival Italian cities would meet between the lines on the eve of a battle or campaign and work out a private deal with each other: If you ask for this from your employer, then I can ask for that from mine. Not that American or Russian generals would even dream of such collusion, but the effect was the same as if they had dreamed of it. The results were a nihilistic balance, Mutual Assured Destruction: You won't wipe me out because if you do, I shall wipe you out too, and we shall all be dead together. By 1972 the United States had 1,054 intercontinental ballistic missiles, 656 sea-launched ballistic missiles, and 522 long-range bombers in the Strategic Air Command; equivalent Russian figures were approximately 1,530 ICBM's, 560 SLBM's, and about 140 long-range aircraft. Twelve years later, American ICBM's were down to 1,037, but warheads were up to 2,129; SLBM's were down to 592, but warheads up to 5,344; bombers were down to about 230, but warheads up to about 2,700. The Soviet Union had about 1,400 ICBM's, 981 SLBM's, and about 600 long- and medium-range bombers, all of these three with appropriately larger warhead numbers. Neither side thought it had enough for its security, since each was convinced the other was intent upon its destruction, with advocates on either side trying to convince themselves and their constituencies that a nuclear war really would be "winnable" in some meaningful sense.

One could argue, and many did, that the prospect of national or racial suicide had indeed managed to preserve a fragile equilibrium and therefore a fragile peace; as Dr. Johnson said in the eighteenth century, "Nothing concentrates the mind like the imminent prospect of being hanged." For the United States, however, the mind was distracted by other difficulties—the long, traumatic, wasting war in Vietnam.

The Vietnam War began and ended in frustration. In 1954, when the French were defeated at Dien Bien Phu and got out of the country, it was partitioned at the 17th parallel; the Viet Minh got the North, and the South became a separate state under the former emperor and French puppet, Bao Dai. The Geneva conference that made this settlement called for eventual elections, but of course they were never held. South Vietnam denounced the agreements and the United States refused to recognize them, though it said it would not disturb the status quo as long as no one else did. It offered money and military aid to the southern government, and the U.S. Navy assisted in the resettlement of thousands of refugees, most of them Catholic, fleeing from the North.

A year later the premier in the South, Ngo Dinh Diem, ousted Bao Dai and proclaimed the Republic of Vietnam. The United States, seeing him as its best bulwark against communism in Southeast Asia, backed him with money and small technical training and advisory missions. A year after that, war began again, with a decision by the North to open guerrilla operations in the South. From these little beginnings the war simply grew and grew and grew. Americans trained Vietnamese for their army and their minuscule air force, and then gradually, by 1961, drifted into reconnaissance, defoliation, and other more active roles. The North kept increasing the pressure; there was Communist and covert American activity in Laos as well as in South Vietnam. The United States was firmly wedded to the domino theory of the day, which saw communism as a creeping amoeba that would inevitably spread from one country to the next.

At the end of 1961, two of Kennedy's staunchest advisers, General Maxwell Taylor and Walt Rostow, visited Vietnam and came home recommending the injection of American combat troops disguised as flood-control workers. The idea was rejected, but the American commitment grew nonetheless, and by the end of 1963 there were 15,000

Americans "in country." The U.S. Air Force's first casualties had come early in 1962, with the crashes of aircraft flying defoliation and leaflet-dropping missions. The fine line between advising and operations became increasingly blurred, and the initial rules of engagement—don't shoot first—grew to be pages and pages of instructions on what might and might not be done in a combat situation. Throughout the entire war, American leadership in Washington was obsessed with trying to control the escalation, trying not to alienate American opinion too far, and trying to "send signals" to North Vietnam. Kennedy's successor, President Lyndon B. Johnson, liked to remark that the air force "couldn't hit a shithouse" without his permission. If indeed the war ever was winnable, in itself a highly dubious proposition, the way the United States government chose to wage it almost guaranteed that it would be lost.

The war kept defying American attempts to limit and control it. Diem was deposed with American connivance late in 1963, just before President Kennedy himself was assassinated. In August 1964 American naval vessels in the Gulf of Tonkin came under attack, and Congress subsequently passed a resolution giving the president power to commit American forces to more active roles, a blank check subsequently regretted by the legislature.

The air war over South Vietnam went on right until the end of the conflict, and air power, largely American, combined with an escalation that made the ground war largely American as well, gradually turned the military tide. Vietnam became a proving ground for new tactics and new weapons, new techniques of airmobility and gun support with helicopters, and new liaison, observation, and tactical airstrike methods. The Americans employed everything from supposedly obsolete propeller-driven strike aircraft, such as the famous Douglas Skyraider, the "Spad" or "Able Dog," to helicopter gunships, to advanced jet fighter-bombers such as the F-105. With these, and with several hundred thousand ground-combat troops, they slowly turned the tide of combat. Possessing mobility and firepower the French never had available, they pushed the indigenous Viet Cong and the soldiers of North Vietnam farther and farther back. The Chinese Mao Tse Tung, the archetype of guerrillas, had written that the country is the water and the guerrilla is the fish. In Vietnam, the Americans first held the cities and the highways, but the guerrillas held the villages and the paths. When the Americans took those, the guerrillas held the jungle. Eventually the Americans took the jungle too, and the guerrillas literally went underground, building immense tunnel complexes. At the risk of oversimplification, the fundamental difference between the Americans and the French was air power, and with the advantages it conferred, the Americans won control of the battlefield.

Yet, they could not win the war. The government of South Vietnam never managed to convince its own citizens of its legitimacy, and the more obviously successful the Americans were, the more the local government looked like their puppets. The leaders of the North kept on fighting; they knew that in the long run South Vietnam was more important to them than it was to the United States. They knew that a substantial and vocal segment of American opinion wanted to get out of this nasty war, and they knew that one of their best weapons was the ubiquitous American television camera. With it they turned even such massive military defeats as their 1968 Tet offensive into moral victories. So the American government's problem was not how to win the war in the South, but how to make North Vietnam admit that it could not win the war in the South. To do that they applied, in effect, General Guilio Douhet's favorite weapon, strategic air power.

If the North Vietnamese leadership would not keep its forces out of the South, the war must be brought home, and done, the Americans believed, in carefully calculated stages so that at any point, when they had finally received the right signal, the North Vietnamese would end the war. It is unfortunately the nature of signals, even more than of words, that they are subject to misinterpretation; what to one is a signal of resolve but forbearance may to the recipient be a signal of impatience and weakness. This is especially the case if the signaler is a stereotypically "impatient Westerner" and the receiver is an equally stereotypical "inscrutable Oriental."

The United States began bombing North Vietnam in August 1964, soon after the Tonkin Gulf incident, with both carrier-based naval and U.S. Air Force planes from southern bases. In February 1965 the first operation began, under the code name "Flaming Dart"; this was followed by a short pause, to see if North Vietnam had got the message. Apparently it had not, for the war continued; so later in the month the United States launched a major air campaign, known this time as "Rolling Thunder" (perhaps because the aim of all this was to make the Communists talk, there was a certain embarrassing obsession with sonorous names for operations). The operation began with strikes at targets close to the 17th parallel, the Americans hitting bridges, assembly points, road crossings, and highways.

Stringent rules were laid down, in an attempt to avoid large-scale civilian casualties, and though through the course of the war more bombs were dropped on North Vietnam than on Germany or Japan in World War II, casualties were indeed kept relatively low. That meant, of course, that much of the bombing was wasteful, for in an attempt to avoid hitting people, the fliers also often had to avoid hitting targets. So anxious was Washington leadership not to give offense that at one point Americans were denied permission to strike at surface-to-air missile, or SAM, sites, until the missiles had actually been installed and the Americans shot at, a delicacy of feeling that could hardly be appreciated by the aircrew on the receiving end of the missiles. As Hanson Baldwin wrote, paraphrasing Winston Churchill, "Never in the history of human conflict have so many hampered, limited, and miscontrolled so few as in the air campaign against North Vietnam."

Slowly the bombing campaign crept northward, from the original strikes near the border toward Hanoi and Haiphong, the major cities of the North. The strikes were largely by fighter-bomber types, especially the F-105 Thunderchief, or "Thud," as its crews called it. The famous F-4 Phantom II was initially employed in combat air patrols, and earlier American types, such as the F-100 Supersabre and the F-104 Starfighter, the "bullet with blades," were gradually pulled out as unsuitable for these kinds of operations. It was not until 1966 that the air force's major strategic bomber, the B-52, was committed, and it was used mostly in the southern part of North Vietnam, where it would not be opposed by the enemy's missile system.

The North Vietnamese were not merely passive recipients of the bombing, and they quickly responded with antiaircraft defenses that became extremely tough. From the Russians and Chinese as well as other Communist countries, they received large numbers of guns and missiles and a small number of fighter aircraft, mostly Mig-17's and Mig-21's. The antiaircraft and missiles became most formidable, though, and planes flying low to avoid the latter too often became victims to the former. Both sides employed highly sophisticated electronic measures and countermeasures, and the picture of the Communist with his old Bren gun from the French war versus the American in his supersonic jet aircraft is a highly colored one. In fact, they had the best-developed antiaircraft defenses in history.

The campaign was broken by a series of "bombing pauses," one in

May and a second at Christmas, 1965. There were by then 200,000 American troops in Vietnam, and they had already defeated the Viet Cong in a major clash in the Ia Drang Valley. The pauses were to give the North Vietnamese time to think things over and come to their senses; instead they spent them strengthening their defenses. Through 1966 the Americans crept ever closer to Hanoi itself, but still gave immunity to such important targets as enemy airbases around the capital. They destroyed thousands of trucks, barges, small boats, bridges, and made heavy hits on oil facilities. Still the North Vietnamese would not give up. Losses were relatively low for the level of the fighting, but gradually the number of downed planes and captured pilots grew to be a major concern in its own right, especially as the treatment accorded American prisoners was disgusting. It was far more a tribute to themselves than to the government that asked them to fight such a war as this that most prisoners preserved their sanity and their sense of duty. Throughout the entire year, both in the North and the South, the U.S. Air Force lost 2,257 aircraft on operations; several hundred naval aircraft were downed as well, and captured Americans were treated by the North Vietnamese as war criminals, rather than as prisoners of war.

The bombing went on through 1967, with both sides again at an impasse. President Johnson regarded the campaign as his big stick to bring the Communists to the negotiating table, and he repeatedly said that if they would agree to talk, he would halt the bombing. They repeatedly replied that he must halt the bombing first, then they would agree to talk. It was a Mexican standoff, one stage short of the endlessly stalled truce talks in Korea in the previous war, and no one could find a way out of it that was satisfactory to both sides. The Americans and the North Vietnamese kept fighting, and the South Vietnamese kept suffering. The Americans finally hit targets within the hitherto spared Hanoi-Haiphong area, including major bridges and the airfields from which the Migs flew. Losses continued to mount, but neither side would concede anything to the other.

A crisis came early in 1968. By that time there were close to half a million American troops in Vietnam, and the air force was flying about 12,000 sorties a month. In the United States public opposition to the war was increasingly shrill, and major political advisers were slowly losing faith in the whole affair. The military commanders had always been pessimistic in their private assessments, but dutifully enthusiastic in their public ones. In early January the Communists launched a two-division assault against marine positions at Khe Sanh, and for three weeks this absorbed the attention of almost everyone. There was good reason to believe that the enemy was trying for another Dien Bien Phu, but the Americans successfully stood the siege, particularly with the help of intense tactical air support and resupply.

Then, at the end of the month, the Viet Cong staged the famous Tet offensive, coinciding with the national holiday. They infiltrated many cities, killed government officials, and seized and held the imperial city of Hué. They even managed to penetrate the American Embassy compound in Saigon. About 84,000 troops took part in the series of attacks, and the Americans and South Vietnamese killed some 37,000 of them and wounded or captured another 6,000 for losses of only 3,000 of their own. It was a resounding defeat for the Communist forces on the purely military plane.

Politically, however, it was a great victory. It gave the lie to all the American statements about "light at the end of the tunnel" and "turning the corner." The American news media downplayed the Communist losses and stressed the fact of their capability for mounting the attack. Very shortly after this, at the end of March, President Johnson ordered a bombing halt north of the 20th parallel, offered to talk to the North Vietnamese, and announced he would not run for reelection. By the end of August he ordered another rollback, and American activities were confined to the area immediately above the original 17th parallel. North Vietnamese and American emissaries were negotiating in Paris now, and on November 1, 1968, Operation Rolling Thunder officially came to an end. In the nearly four years it had lasted, the Americans had flown more than 300,000 missions and dropped 643,000 tons of bombs on North Vietnam. They had inhibited but not destroyed, obviously, the enemy's war-making capacity, and they had certainly not broken his will to fight. Nor, as events showed, had they done much to end the war.

In November Richard M. Nixon was elected president to replace the outgoing Johnson. He announced a policy of Vietnamization of the war, but that could mean little to the highly sophisticated air force units involved. For the next three years, though, there were relatively few strikes at the North, while negotiators backed and filled and argued over, among other things, the shape of the table at which they might talk. As the Communists' terms were essentially total victory, and the American terms were something less than total defeat, there was still no meeting of minds. The new American government retained air power as its biggest stick and bombed Cambodia, supply areas in Laos, and occasionally the North in retaliatory strikes for attacks on reconnaissance planes. Men continued to fight and die, but the war was definitely on hold for some time.

In 1972 it flared up once again, when the North Vietnamese opened a major drive into South Vietnam. The Americans responded with a strong tactical air attack in support of largely South Vietnamese ground forces, and finally, in May, President Nixon suspended the talks in Paris and authorized major air strikes in the area of Hanoi itself. By now the North Vietnamese had both rebuilt their air forces and overhauled their missile and antiaircraft artillery defense systems. Nevertheless, the U.S. Air Force sallied forth with blood in its eye and the notorious rules of engagement seriously relaxed. In and around Hanoi they hit bridges, power plants, petroleum farms, missile sites, Mig airfields, and anything else they could spot. They had a new wrinkle in the form of "smart" bombs, laser or optically guided, recently developed, and infinitely more cost-effective than the old type. It was the most telling use of air power yet, and the Paris talks soon resumed.

And soon stalled. Whereupon the Americans launched the last big bombing assault, named Linebacker II. For eleven days in the fall they pounded targets around Hanoi, many of them previously restricted; losses were fairly heavy at first, especially among the big B-52's, fifteen of which were brought down by Communist missiles. But within a little over a week, the North Vietnamese defenses were totally swamped, and for the last couple of days the Americans flew as they pleased with impunity. By this time, unlike the situation thirty years before, it actually was possible to bomb with precision, and civilian casualties were relatively low, considering the intensity of the campaign. Though a lot of this depended on the new bombs, Linebacker II still served as an illustration of what might have been achieved earlier had not the Americans agreed to hamstring themselves with their own self-imposed rules.

By January 1973 the negotiators were talking again, there was yet another halt to air operations, and this time an agreement was finally signed. By the end of March the Americans had gone home. Two years and one month later, the Communists had "unified" all of Vietnam, and, except for the victims, the war was indeed over.

The Vietnam War was for Americans the most traumatic event since the Civil War. Its possible or potential lessons were legion, but hardly anybody agreed what they were, except that, as in Korea before, the political constraints upon the use of force were such as to make wars both difficult to win and frustrating to wage. Such, of course, has always been the case—we are not nearly as unique as we think we are—and the only real difference is that the available force is now so much greater than it formerly was, and therefore the frustrations and restraints are greater too.

The United States was not the only major power frustrated by its inability to make the world accord to some perceived reality. Ironically, practically all of the world's major modern military establishments have suffered the same kinds of tribulations. The Russians got involved in a little contretemps in Afghanistan, which bogged down and threatened to go on endlessly in spite of absolute air superiority over tribesmen with homemade guns. And the Israelis and the British had their troubles too.

On October 6, 1973, the Jewish High Holy Day of Yom Kippur, the Egyptians and Syrians launched a joint drive against Israel. It was a revenge they had been preparing ever since their crushing defeat in the Six-Day War of 1967, and they had worked long and diligently, and with unusual care, to achieve it. They had modernized their armed forces with the aid of the Russians, they had absorbed the lessons taught them by Israeli air power, and this time they were determined to do the job right.

The Israelis for their part knew that something was in the wind, but they did not know what. They were at the moment preoccupied with the terrorist campaign put on by the Palestine Liberation Organization, and they expected, as much as anything, an intensification of that type of activity. They seriously underestimated the extent to which their enemies had overhauled and modernized their military forces in the last six years. As the crisis developed, they also decided for political reasons to forfeit the advantages of a preemptive strike.

One reason for that decision was the knowledge that the Egyptians and Syrians both had revised their thinking about air power. In 1967 the Israeli attacks had been absolutely crippling in the first hours of the war, and their air power had been dominant for the rest of it. This time it was to be different, and the Arab states had made diligent and effective efforts to boost their air defenses, including better, newer

Russian types of aircraft, better training for the men who would fly them, and, even more significantly, a surface-to-air missile capability, built again around new Russian models, that far surpassed anything in earlier experience. Not only would Israel forfeit world sympathy by attacking first, but it might do so to little avail in the face of the enemy defenses.

It was therefore air power in a negative sense that gave the Arabs the initiative when they attacked across the Suez Canal and along the Golan Heights on October 6. For a couple of days, by ingenious new devices and very daring tactics, they held that initiative, and they very nearly swamped the Israeli defenders, who were thin, overconfident, and somewhat slow to receive support. The most significant new element on the battlefield was its incredible rate of attrition. Both sides were employing tactical guided missiles against tanks and aircraft, and in spite of the fact that both were also employing electronic or other countermeasures and jamming devices, these new gadgets proved distressingly effective. Aircraft and tanks, the great restorers of mobility since World War I, were knocked out by the hundreds, and the lowly infantryman, provided he had a guided missile and enough courage to stay in position and use it—and the men on either side had both—came into his own again.

Within a couple of days the front had stabilized, with alarming losses to both sides, and the Israelis went over to the offensive. They eventually pushed to within twenty miles of Damascus, on the Syrian front. In both areas there were the heaviest tank battles since World War II. They also undertook a lightning-bombing campaign against Syria. The Syrians launched a number of Russian-made Frog missiles against Israeli targets. The Frog has a range of about forty miles, which is a lot in a country the size of Israel, and the Israelis replied with attacks on vulnerable Syrian targets that were not defended, as their combat units were, by heavy concentrations of SAM batteries. So Israeli fighter-bombers, Skyhawks and Phantoms, hit power plants, port facilities, and even the Syrian Defense Ministry in Damascus. This caused some dispersal of the missile batteries for defense, and it also brought the war home dramatically to Syria's leaders. Intervention late in the day by the Jordanians and the Iraquis was largely ineffective, just providing the Israelis with more targets.

A feature of the war that surprised everyone was the fantastic rate of expenditure of ammunition, rockets, missiles, tanks, and aircraft.

Both sides almost immediately sent pleading messages to their respective backers, the Soviet Union for the Arabs and the United States for the Israelis, and both backers replied, the Russians rather more quickly than the Americans. But a shuttle was soon flowing, with Russian transports flying material to Syria and Egypt, and Americans doing the same to Israel. The two superpowers had to engage in a minuet to stay out of each other's way while their surrogates fought, and at one point American forces worldwide were put on a standby alert.

Fortunately, the war quickly burned itself out. A reluctant cease-fire was accepted on October 24, just two and a half weeks after the first attack. In that short time the Arabs lost about 2,000 of their 4,200 tanks, and the Israelis about half of their 1,700. Israeli air superiority was more marked, the Arabs losing about 500 of 800, to only 115 of 500 for Israel. About 2,500 Israelis were killed for 16,000 Arabs, but the latter could afford the losses, proportionately, better than the former, and many of the Israeli losses were in junior-officer categories, always a sign of real trouble. The most significant loss for Israel was of the myth of her invincibility; she emerged from the war sadder, though not necessarily wiser, than she had gone into it.

As the first full-scale combat between more or less equally matched modern and mobile forces since World War II, the Yom Kippur War was avidly analyzed. Its most startling lesson was probably the tremendous destructive power of the new smart weaponry, and therefore the enormous material loss rate. Commanders suddenly discovered that their inventories would have to be trebled or quadrupled if they anticipated any kind of sustained combat operations. As an almost entirely land war, Yom Kippur did not offer much to sailors, but in the next small war of any significance, they learned the same lesson—of the paradoxical destructive power and fragility of modern systems.

In 1982 a long-standing but low-level dispute over the ownership of the Falkland Islands came to a head. The group, some four hundred miles east of southern Argentina, was settled by the British but always claimed by the Spanish, and the Argentinians inherited the claim along with independence from Spain. Periodically they had moved to assert it, and always were rebuffed by Britain, which found the islands a bit of a nuisance but accepted its obligation to the fiercely loyal islanders. At the time of the crisis, the islands were garrisoned by little more than a platoon of Royal Marines and a weather ship, HMS *Endurance*. On April 2 the Argentinians invaded, quickly overpowered the little garrison, and announced they were taking possession of their territory, the cherished "Islas Malvinas."

The British government reacted strongly, but the Falklands are a long way from Britain, and the conflict revealed the dangerously low levels to which British forces had been reduced by successive budget-paring ministries. With very commendable rapidity, a task force sailed from Britain a mere three days after the islands were seized. Its composition revealed the nature of British strength, or lack of it. The main force consisted of two aircraft carriers, but one was the aging *Hermes,* twenty-three years old and due for the breakers, and the other was the small *Invincible,* about to be sold to Australia. Neither ship was big enough to handle F-4 Phantoms, once a mainstay of the Fleet Air Arm, and they had to settle for Harriers, short- or vertical-takeoff jets. Then there was a variety of guided-missile destroyers and frigates. Some troops went on the carriers, some on naval assault ships, and much of the equipment, backup forces, and even extra planes had to be carried on hastily requisitioned merchantmen.

No one worried about the Argentine navy, which was even more ancient and rickety than the British, or the army either, but the Falklands, and therefore the British fleet, would be well within range of strike aircraft flying from Argentina itself. The Argentine inventory consisted of rather dated but dependable American Skyhawk fighter-bombers, about seventy strong, about forty French Mirages, also a proven design, and some ten French Dassault Super Etendards, not thought to be much as planes but armed with French-built Exocet missiles, an unknown and as it turned out dangerous element. The real problem was that the nearest British base was Ascension Island, one of the world's better forgotten spots, a speck in the mid-Atlantic just below the equator, about three thousand miles from the Falklands.

By May the British fleet was within striking distance. On May 1 Vulcan bombers tried to put the airstrip at Port Stanley out of operation with a high-level attack; most of the bombs missed the strip itself. Argentina's only cruiser, the ancient *General Belgrano,* was sunk by a submarine, and then the battle was joined in earnest. It very quickly turned into a struggle, reminiscent of the American Pacific amphibious operations, between the fleet and its aircraft and the land-based Argentine strike planes. The Harriers soon proved their worth, but ship losses were almost unbearably heavy. On May 4 the destroyer *Sheffield* was hit from long range by an Exocet missile; modern destroyers have lots of weight-saving but flammable superstructure, and *Sheffield* had to be abandoned. There was a lull while the British made their approach and picked up some isolated real estate; then, in the third week of May, they descended on the main islands and made a firm landing. But on May 21 the frigate *Ardent* was sunk in Falklands Sound by Mirages that got through the Sea Harriers and the antiaircraft missiles and gunfire of the British ships. Two days later, *Antelope,* another frigate, was hit, and she sank the next day, and the day after that, May 25, was even worse. The destroyer *Coventry* went down, victim of the Skyhawks, and the transport ship *Atlantic Conveyor,* carrying helicopters, parts for the Harriers, and much needed equipment for the troops ashore, was hit by an Exocet and abandoned, burning and in sinking condition. She was latter reboarded, but was of no more use to the fleet.

May 25 represented the naval crisis, though. The troops were successfully ashore, the Harriers bombarded Stanley airport and began to assert local control, and the Argentinian attacks subsided in the face of their own heavy losses. The ground forces went on to capture the garrison at Port Stanley, and the fighting soon came to an end. Once again, this had proven to be an extremely costly little war, in which tactical air power, and the ability to control the air space over the battle, be it on land or water, were absolutely decisive. The equation was the same as it had always been, but jet aircraft, rockets, standoff missiles, and radar-controlled missiles and gunfire, had provided a speeded-up effect. It was like looking at an old movie when the film runs at the wrong speed and things happen faster than they are supposed to. About the only thing that stayed exactly the same was that people died.

In one long lifetime then, in a mere blink of history's eye, air power has changed the dimensions, if not the nature, of warfare. It has not quite lived up to its greatest prophets' claims, but what new invention or new system ever does? It has not rendered war obsolete, it has not even rendered wars of attrition obsolete, and indeed, in some cases, such as the strategic-bombing campaign of World War II, or the bombing of North Vietnam, it has become an instrument of attrition itself. But at all levels of conflict and in all ways, air power is an element no military force dares ignore. For intelligence, logistics, and tactical support, it is an imperative no modern force can do without. Those low-level or primitive forces not possessing air power must adjust accordingly, must fight by night or live underground, must always beware of the sky.

Indeed, in the current world we must all beware of the sky, primitive or not, in the age of the missile, the great bomber, the nuclear standoff. One of the giants of the aircraft industry, Boeing, the company of the B-17 Flying Fortress, the B-29 Superfortress, and the B-52 Stratofortress, ran a commercial on television some years ago that showed its beautiful passenger planes soaring through the sunlit heavens while an announcer crooned that no one had ever brought as many people together as Boeing had. United Airlines asks people to "fly the friendly skies." But for much of the time airplanes, and air power, have been in existence, the skies have not been friendly, and air power has not always been a means of bringing people together. It is an unfortunate truism that man's greatest accomplishments in science and technology have often been for the creation of instruments of defense or destruction; the modern bomber or missile, even the simplest of modern fighters, possesses a complexity and capacity that staggers the imagination. But until our political and social accomplishments catch up with our technological ones, aviation and air power must be regarded with as much fear as wonder.

SUGGESTIONS
FOR FURTHER READING

The literature available on aviation, aircraft, and air-power history is extensive but rather imbalanced; it ranges from serious academic and official histories to illustrated books on given planes or wars for aviation buffs to books of the boys'-own-wonders type. Coverage of different events is equally spotty; there is a large list of books available on such famous affairs as the Battle of Britain, while relatively little has been written on air operations in the southwest Pacific in World War II. Similarly, there is any number of books or articles on the Spitfire, while the fancier of the Douglas A-20 will have to look a good deal harder to find material on his favorite plane. The same is true for biographies of leading figures.

The following list of suggestions is in no way comprehensive. It contains, as one author puts it, "books I used, should have used, or should like to use." Many of the books listed have extensive bibliographies of their own; a reading list should be like a spider plant. Finally, books are mentioned where they first become useful; many have a more general applicability.

SUGGESTIONS FOR FURTHER READING

Some useful overall studies are Robin Higham, *Air Power: A Concise History* (New York: St. Martin's Press, 1972); Basil Collier, *A History of Air Power* (New York: Macmillan, 1974); and Charles H. Gibbs-Smith, *Flight Through the Ages* (New York: Crowell, 1974). A general survey of naval aviation is Brian Johnson, *Fly Navy: A History of Naval Aviation* (New York: William Morrow, 1981). J.D.R. Rawlings, *The History of the Royal Air Force* (Feltham, England: Temple, 1984) is a sumptuous and well-illustrated book. An earlier American general history is Alfred Goldberg, ed., *A History of the United States Air Force, 1907–1957* (Princeton, N.J.: Van Nostrand, 1957), officially produced for the U.S. Air Service/Air Force's golden anniversary. There are more or less equivalent histories of other air services, such as General Pierre Lissarague and General Charles Christienne, *Histoire de l'Aviation Militaire Française* (Paris: Lavauzelle, 1980) for France, and Larry Mulberry, *Sixty Years* (Toronto: Canav Books, 1984) for Canada.

Books on specific aircraft, or certain types, or the aircraft of a given war, are legion. One of the more general ones is Enzo Angelucci, ed., *The Rand McNally Encyclopedia of Military Aircraft, 1914–1980* (English edition, Chicago: Rand McNally, 1981), a large book for general material, but one in which specific facts need to be checked with care. In the 1950s and early 1960s, the Harleyford House, Letchworth, England, published a whole series of aircraft books, such as Bruce Robertson, ed., *Aircraft Camouflage and Markings, 1907–1954,* and others to be mentioned specifically later. Shortly thereafter, Putnam and Company, London, began issuing the Putnam Aeronautical Books, covering all the aircraft of services such as the Royal Air Force and the U.S. Navy, and all the products of certain manufacturers such as Hawker and Boeing. As naval aircraft, at least, are inseparable from aircraft carriers, this is a good place to mention the excellent Norman Friedman, *U.S. Aircraft Carriers: An Illustrated Design History* (Annapolis, Maryland: Naval Institute Press, 1983).

There is a considerable number of books on the early years of aviation and the Great War, though not as many as on World War II. Two good books on pre- and early air history are David W. Wragg, *Flight Before Flying* (Reading, England: Osprey, 1974); and Charles H. Gibbs-Smith, *The Invention of the Aeroplane, 1799–1909* (London: Faber and Faber, 1965). Harry Combs, *Kill Devil Hill: Discovering the Se-*

cret of the Wright Brothers (Boston: Houghton Mifflin, 1979) is probably the best of several studies, and for the fledgling period there is Sherwood Harris, *The First to Fly: Aviation's Pioneer Days* (New York: Simon & Schuster, 1970). General histories of the air war are Norman Aaron, *The Great Air War* (New York: Macmillan, 1968); and the even more popularly written Quentin Reynolds, *They Fought for the Sky* (New York: Rinehart, 1957). Three of the Harleyford series of books are Bruce Robertson, ed., *Air Aces of the 1914–18 War* (1959); H. J. Nowarra and K. S. Brown, *Von Richthofen and the Flying Circus* (1958); and O. G. Thetford, *Aircraft of the 1914–1918 War* (1954). Topical histories that begin with the first war are J. E. Johnson, *Full Circle: The Tactics of Air Fighting, 1914–1964* (New York: Ballantine, 1964); Edward H. Sims, *Fighter Tactics and Strategy, 1914–1970* (New York: Harper & Row, 1972); and the more recent Richard P. Hallion, *Rise of the Fighter Aircraft, 1914–18* (Baltimore, Maryland: Nautical and Aviation Publishing Company, 1984). The official British history is Walter Raleigh and H. A. Jones, *The War in the Air* (London: Oxford University Press, 6 vols., 1922–37). Other studies are Douglas Robinson, *The Zeppelin in Combat: A History of the German Naval Airship Division, 1912–1918* (Seattle: Univ. of Washington, 1980); Kenneth Poolman, *Zeppelins over England* (New York: John Day, 1961); and J. H. Morrow, *German Airpower in World War I* (Lincoln: Univ. of Nebraska, 1982). An indispensable biography is Andrew Boyle, *Trenchard: Man of Vision* (London: Collins, 1962), and there are numerous memoirs, autobiographies, and biographies of participants, of which a few examples must serve for many: William Mitchell, *Memoirs of World War I* (New York: Random House, 1960); Eddie Rickenbacker, *Fighting the Flying Circus* (Garden City, N.Y.: Doubleday, 1965); Duncan Grinnell-Milne, *Wind in the Wires* (New York: Ace, 1968); and the classic novel by V. M. Yeates, *Winged Victory* (London: Johnathan Cape, 1934).

Naturally enough, the years between the wars are the middle ages, if no longer the dark ages, of air-power history. Any look at the period must begin with the Clausewitz of air power, Giulio Douhet, *The Command of the Air* (reprint, Washington: Office of Air Force History, 1983). Civilian aviation was the dominant theme of the twenties: Harold Mansfield, *Vision: A Saga of the Sky* (New York: Duell, Sloan, and Pearce, 1956), tells Boeing's story; and Marilyn Bender and Selig Altschul, *The Chosen Instrument* (New York: Simon & Schuster, 1982), tells Pan Am's. Walter S. Ross, *The Last Hero: Charles A. Lindbergh* (New York: Harper & Row, 1968) is a judicious biography. General treatments of the era are Frank Courtney, *The Eighth Sea* (Garden City, N.Y.: Doubleday, 1972); and Alan Wheeler, *Flying Between the Wars* (Oxfordshire: G. T. Foulis, 1972). The stormy petrel of the period is covered in Alfred F. Hurley, *Billy Mitchell* (New York: Franklin Watts, 1964). A contemporary view of new dimensions in war is J. C. Stessor, *Air Power and Armies* (London: Oxford Univ. Press, 1936).

The wars and crises of the thirties have inspired a number of studies, most more general but some specifically on air power. On Spain there is Hugh Thomas, *The Spanish Civil War* (New York: Harper & Row, 1963); Christopher Shores, *Spanish Civil War Air Forces* (New York: Sky Books, 1977); the Duke of Lerma, *Combat over Spain* (London: Nevill Spearman, 1968); and Jesus Larrazabal, *Air War over Spain* (London: Ian Allan, 1974). There is little on Ethiopia or China. Telford Taylor, *Munich: The Price of Peace* (New York: Doubleday, 1979), discusses air power in the context of that event; and a new work by Malcolm Smith examines *British Air Strategy Between the Wars* (Oxford: Oxford Univ. Press, 1984). Hanfried Schliephake covered *The Birth of the Luftwaffe* (Chicago: Henry Regnery, 1971); and Robert Jackson, *The Red Falcons* (London: Tandem, 1972) is a general history of the Soviet air force from its founding in 1919. A specific monograph by John McV. Haight covers *American Aid to France, 1938–1940* (New York: Atheneum, 1970). The colorful aircraft that inspired so much dread in the period are illustrated in Kenneth G. Munson, *Fighters Between the Wars, 1919–1939* and *Bombers Between the Wars, 1919–1939* (both New York: Macmillan, 1970).

World War II has received the greatest amount of attention. First there are the official and the overall air histories. For the United States there is Wesley F. Craven and Frank L. Cate, eds., *The Army Air Forces in World War II* (Chicago: Univ. of Chicago, 7 vols., 1948–58); and the navy is covered in S. E. Morison, *History of United States Naval Operations in World War II* (Boston: Little, Brown, 15 vols., 1947–1962). The British official history is by Denis Richard and H. St. G. Saunders, *The Royal Air Force, 1939–45* (London: H.M.S.O., 3 vols., 1974–75). Almost overshadowing these are the official studies of strategic bombing: Sir Charles Webster and Noble Frankland, *The Strategic Air Offensive Against Germany, 1939–45* (London:

H.M.S.O., 4 vols, 1961); and the massive work edited by David MacIsaac, *United States Strategic Bombing Survey* (New York: Garland, 31 reports in 10 vols., 1976). The translation of the official Russian history was edited by Ray Wagner, *The Soviet Air Force in World War II* (Garden City, N.Y.: Doubleday, 1973). R. J. Overy, *The Air War, 1939–45* (New York: Stein and Day, 1981) is an exceptionally thoughtful appraisal, and my debt to it will be apparent to anyone who has read it. John Terraine's *A Time for Courage: The Royal Air Force in the European War, 1939–1945* (New York: Macmillan, 1985) should become a standard work.

Books on or by specific important figures, or about battles, campaigns, or aircraft, are legion. A few examples must again serve for all. For airplanes there are William Green, *Famous Bombers of the Second World War* (London: MacDonald, 2 vols., 1959–60) and *Famous Fighters of the Second World War* (London: MacDonald, 2 vols., 1947, 1962); also, Green's *War Planes of the Second World War* (London: MacDonald, 10 vols, 1960–68), which got through everyone's fighters (4 vols.), flying boats (1 vol.), float planes (1 vol.), and bombers (4 vols.), ending, unfortuantely, with the German Messerschmitt ME 328B. Some of the major leaders are treated in Allen Andrews, *The Air Marshals: The Air War in Western Europe* (New York: William Morrow, 1970); H. H. Arnold, *Global Mission* (New York: Harper, 1949); Sir Arthur Harris, *Bomber Offensive* (London: Collins, 1947); Curtis LeMay (Garden City, N.Y.: Doubleday, 1965); George C. Kenney (New York: Duell, Sloane, and Pearce, 1949); and Claire Chennault (New York: Putnam, 1949); all wrote their memoirs too. For the British there are lives of *Portal of Hungerford* by Denis Richards (London: Heinemann, 1977); and Robert Wright's *Dowding and the Battle of Britain* (London: MacDonald, 1969); as well as Harris's own work and others about him. For the Germans there is Williamson Murray, *Strategy for Defeat: The Luftwaffe, 1933–1945* (Maxwell, Ala.: Air University Press, 1983); the popularly written and highly defensive Cajus Bekker, *The Luftwaffe War Diaries* (New York: Ballantine, 1969); and Werner Baumbach, *The Life and Death of the Luftwaffe* (New York: Coward-McCann, 1960).

On battles or campaigns the available material is uneven. For Poland overall there is R. M. Kennedy, *The German Campaign in Poland (1939),* (Washington: G.P.O., 1956); and Jerzy Cynk, *History of the Polish Air Force, 1918–1968* (Reading, England: Osprey, 1972).

The Scandinavian campaigns are covered in general histories of the war, such as Kingston Derry, *The Campaign in Norway* (London: H.M.S.O., 1952). On France there is Lionel F. Ellis, *The War in France and Flanders, 1939–40* (London: H.M.S.O., 1953); and a host of campaign studies, most notably Alastair Horne, *To Lose a Battle: France, 1940* (London: Macmillan, 1969) and William L. Shirer, *The Collapse of the Third Republic* (New York: Simon & Schuster, 1965). Given the virtual library available on the Battle of Britain, a few examples, such as Derek Wood and Derek Dempster, *The Narrow Margin* (New York: McGraw-Hill, 1961) and Peter Townsend, *Duel of Eagles* (New York: Simon & Schuster, 1971), must suffice.

For the bombing campaign against the Germans, overall coverage is in Lee Kennett, *A History of Strategic Bombing* (New York: Scribners, 1982); Max Hastings, *Bomber Command: The Myths and Realities of the Strategic Bombing Offensive, 1939–45* (New York: Dial, 1979); Hans Rumpf, *The Bombing of Germany* (New York: Holt, Rinehart, & Winston, 1963); and Roger A. Freeman, *The Mighty Eighth: Units, Men, and Machines* (Garden City, N.Y.: Doubleday, 1970). Individual landmark raids are covered by Ralph Barker, *The Thousand Plan: The Story of the First Thousand Bomber Raid on Cologne* (London: Chatto and Windus, 1965); Martin Middlebrook, *The Battle of Hamburg: Allied Bomber Forces Against a German City in 1943* (London: Allen Lane, 1980) and the same author's *The Nuremberg Raid* (New York: William Morrow, 1974); Thomas M. Coffey, *Decision over Schweinfurt* (New York: David McKay, 1977); and David Irving, *The Destruction of Dresden* (London: William Kimber, 1963). Of a host of individual memoirs, or treatments of special topics, the following are interesting accounts: Ralph Barker, *The Ship-Busters: The Story of the R.A.F. Torpedo Bombers* (London: Chatto and Windus, 1957); C. F. Rawnsley and Robert Wright, *Night Fighter* (New York: Holt, 1957); Charles Lamb, *War in a Stringbag* (London: Cassell, 1979); Pierre Clostermann, *The Big Show* (London: Chatto and Windus, 1951); and Hans Ulrich Rudel, *Stuka Pilot* (New York: Ballantine, 1958).

Naval operations, naturally, range widely. Continuing with the European war theme, there are general naval histories, such as Morison mentioned above; or S. W. Roskill, *White Ensign: The British Navy at War, 1939–45* (Annapolis: Naval Institute Press, 1960); and, more specialized, Kenneth Poolman, *Illustrious* (London: Kimber, 1955) and

Ark Royal (London: Kimber, 1956); and Don Newton and A. C. Hampshire, *Taranto* (London: Kimber, 1959); while William T. Y'Blood has written *Hunter-Killer: U.S. Escort Carriers in the Battle of the Atlantic* (Annapolis: Naval Institute Press, 1983).

The war against Japan is something of a poor relation, though less so as time passes. Excellent overall studies are John Costello, *The Pacific War, 1941–1945* (New York: William Morrow, 1982); and Ronald H. Spector, *Eagle Against the Sun: The American War with Japan* (New York: Free Press, 1985). For the Army Air Forces in the Southwest Pacific, in addition to Kenney's memoirs, there is Walter D. Edmonds, *They Fought with What They Had* (Boston: Little Brown, 1951). The indispensable book on carrier air power is Clark Reynolds, *The Fast Carriers: The Forging of an Air Navy* (New York: McGraw-Hill, 1968). Assorted Japanese views are in Saburo Sabai, Martin Caidin, and Fred Saito, *Samurai!* (New York: Dutton, 1957); Masatake Okumiya, Jiro Horikoshi, and Martin Caidin, *Zero!* (New York: Dutton, 1956); and, on the suicide campaign, Rikihei Inoguchi, Tadashi Nakajima, and Roger Pineau, *The Divine Wind* (London: Hutchinson, 1959), and Jean Larteguy, ed., *The Sun Goes Down: Last Letters from Japanese Suicide Pilots and Soldiers* (London: Kimber, 1956). Thomas G. Miller, *The Cactus Air Force* (New York: Harper & Row, 1969) is on air operations in the Solomons. Key figures are covered in Thomas E. Buell, *Master of Seapower: A Biography of Admiral Ernest J. King* (Boston: Little Brown, 1980) and the same author's *The Quiet Warrior: A Biography of Admiral Raymond Spruance* (Boston: Little Brown, 1974); E. B. Potter, *Nimitz* (Annapolis: Naval Institute Press, 1976); and, for the Chinese imbroglio, Barbara Tuchman, *Stilwell and the American Experience in China* (New York: Macmillan, 1970). Excellent battle studies are in Thaddeus V. Tuleja, *Climax at Midway* (New York: Norton, 1950); William T. Y'Blood, *Red Sun Setting: The Battle of the Philippine Sea* (Annapolis: Naval Institute Press, 1980); Stanley L. Falk, *Decision at Leyte* (New York: W. W. Norton, 1966); and James H. Belote and William M. Belote, *Typhoon of Steel: The Battle for Okinawa* (New York: Harper & Row, 1969).

On the strategic bombing of Japan, there is Wilbur H. Morrison, *Point of No Return: The Story of the 20th Air Force* (New York: Times Books, 1979); Martin Caidin, *A Torch to the Enemy: The Fire Raid on Tokyo* (New York: Ballantine, 1960). And of numerous works on the atomic bomb there is Herbert Feis, *The Atomic Bomb and the End of World War II* (Princeton, N.J.: Princeton Univ. Press, 1966); Walter S. Schoenberger, *Decision of Destiny* (Athens, Ohio Univ. Press, 1969); and Peter Wyden, *Day One: Before Hiroshima and After* (New York: Simon & Schuster, 1984).

Material on the wars and trends since 1945 is necessarily diffuse. General material on development is in Walter J. Boyne and Donald S. Lopez, *The Jet Age: Forty Years of Jet Aviation* (Washington, D.C.: Smithsonian Institution Press, 1981); and, on air power itself, in M. J. Armitage and R. A. Mason, *Air Power in the Nuclear Age* (Urbana, Il.: Univ. of Illinois Press, 1983). There are numerous studies of specific aircraft, such as Edward Shacklady, *The Gloster Meteor* (Garden City, N.Y.: Doubleday, 1963). A general survey of the wars is Michael Carver, *War Since 1945* (New York: Putnam, 1981). The arms race has been an overriding concern, and several organizations try to keep score; useful on this is the International Institute for Strategic Studies, *The Military Balance* (London, Annual); or various of Brassey's publications such as *International Weapons Development: A Survey of Current Developments in Weapons Systems* (Oxford, 1980); or the Brookings Institution in Washington, such as William D. White, *U.S. Tactical Air Power: Missions, Forces, and Costs* (1974). On the nuclear question there are many books, ranging from impassioned polemics to sober and sobering appraisals; two sound ones are Lawrence Freedman, *The Evolution of Nuclear Strategy* (New York: St. Martins Press, 1981) and the new G. H. Clarfield and W. M. Wiecek, *Nuclear America: Military and Civilian Power in the United States, 1940–1980* (New York: Harper & Row, 1984). Two recent critical appraisals of the defense intelligence community are Fred Kaplan, *The Wizards of Armageddon* (New York: Simon & Schuster, 1983) and Gregg Herken, *Counsels of War* (New York: Knopf, 1985).

For the different conflicts of the era there are many specific studies. On Korea, J. Lawton Collins, *War in Peacetime* (Boston: Houghton Mifflin, 1969); Robert Futrell, *The United States Air Force in Korea, 1950–53* (New York: Duell, Sloane, and Pearce, 1961); and for the navy, Malcolm W. Eagle and Frank A. Manson, *The Sea War in Korea* (Annapolis: Naval Institute Press, 1957). The Berlin Airlift is covered in Walter P. Davison, *The Berlin Blockade: A Study in Cold War Politics* (Princeton, N.J.: Princeton Univ. Press, 1958); and the "early" cold war in Louis J. Halle, *The Cold War As History* (New York: Harper & Row, 1967). On Indochina there is Edgar O'Ballance, *The In-*

dochina War (1945–1954) (London: Faber and Faber, 1964); and the best book on Dien Bien Phu remains Bernard Fall, *Hell in a Very Small Place* (Philadelphia: Lippincott, 1967). British experience and problems are treated in C. J. Bartlett, *The Long Retreat: A Short History of British Defence Policy, 1945–70* (London: Macmillan, 1972); and Sir David Lee, *Eastward: A History of the Royal Air Force in the Far East, 1945–1972* (London, H.M.S.O., 1984) and his *Flight from the Middle East* (London, H.M.S.O., 1980). The Israelis and the Suez crisis are covered in Donald Neff, *Warriors at Suez* (New York: Simon & Schuster, 1981); and Edward Luttwak and Dan Horowitz, *The Israeli Army* (New York: Harper & Row, 1975); as well as, episodically, in Drew Middleton, *Crossroads of Modern Warfare* (Garden City, N.Y.: Doubleday, 1983).

There is a growing number of histories of the U.S. Air Force, institutionally as well as operationally, produced by the Office of Air Force History in Washington; there is also the new first volume of the *History of the Office of the Secretary of Defense,* by Steven L. Rearden, *The Formative Years, 1947–1950* (Washington, D.C.: Historical Office, Office of the Secretary of Defense, 1984). A less formal and more vitriolic treatment of the Admiral's Revolt is in Omar Bradley and Clay Blair, *A General's Life* (New York: Simon & Schuster, 1983). The multivolume series, *The United States Air Force in Southeast Asia,* is now appearing, with the first volume by Robert F. Futrell and Martin Blumenson, *The Advisory Years to 1965* (Washington, D.C.: Office of Air Force History, 1981). Stanley Karnow's well-known *Vietnam: A History* (New York: Viking, 1983) provides general coverage, and Carl Berger, ed., *The United States Air Force in Southeast Asia, 1961–1973* (Washington, D.C.: Office of Air Force History, 1977) is an illustrated history. Those who wish to share vicariously in the risking of other men's lives must read Colonel Jack Broughton, *Thud Ridge* (Philadelphia: Lippincott, 1969).

Last of all, many of the journals or magazines on aviation have useful articles on aircraft technology and development, and rather less often on organizational or operational history. Among them are *Air International, Air Pictorial, Aerospace Historian, Air University Review, Airpower Historian,* the *Journal of the Royal United Services Institute,* the *United States Naval Institute Proceedings,* the *Army Quarterly,* and the *Defense Journal.*

INDEX

INDEX